Oracle E-Business Suite Financials R12: A Functionality Guide

Know what Oracle E-Business Suite can do before you implement it

Mohan Iyer

PUBLISHING

BIRMINGHAM - MUMBAI

Oracle E-Business Suite Financials R12: A Functionality Guide

First published: April 2012

Production Reference: 1180412

Published by Packt Publishing Ltd.
Livery Place
35 Livery Street
Birmingham B3 2PB, UK.

ISBN 978-1-84968-062-2

www.packtpub.com

Cover Image by David Gutierrez (bilbaorocker@yahoo.co.uk)

Credits

Author

Mohan Iyer

Reviewers

Brian R. Bouchard

Faun deHenry

Alex Fiteni

Scott Gordon

Jeffery T. Hare

John Peters

Ajay Pradhan

Thomas Simkiss

Ketan J Thanki

Acquisition Editor

Rukshana Khambatta

Lead Technical Editors

Arun Nadar

Meeta Rajani

Technical Editors

Joyslita D'Souza

Veronica Fernandes

Project Coordinator

Shubhanjan Chatterjee

Proofreader

Aaron Nash

Indexers

Monica Ajmera Mehta

Tejal Daruwale

Graphics

Valentina D'Silva

Manu Joseph

Production Coordinators

Aparna Bhagat

Nilesh R. Mohite

Cover Work

Aparna Bhagat

Foreword

I have known Mohan Iyer for many years, first professionally and now personally. Mohan is a tireless advocate for the development of best practices and for making the Oracle E-Business Suite world a better place. He is one of those guys who digs into issues and understands it both technically and functionally before making a recommendation to a client. Mohan is also a great asset to the user community through Oracle Applications Users Group (OAUG), NorCal Users Group, and other forums.

This book is the culmination of many, many years of Mohan's experience and research. Readers of this book will be blessed with great insight and comprehensive analysis of the functionality and best practices related to Oracle's R12 E-Business Suite release. I am pleased to be able to recommend this book.

This book focuses primarily on issues related to functionality. If you have questions on internal controls or security relating to this content, feel free to e-mail me at `jhare@erpra.net`.

Jeffrey T. Hare, CPA CISA CIA

CEO, ERP Risk Advisors

About the Author

Mohan Iyer has more than 20 years' experience in system implementations with the last 15 years implementing Oracle Financials. He has a strong background in Finance and Accounting, having had these as his major subjects in college. He has an Accounting degree from the University of Bombay (Mumbai), India.

His skill set includes a full range of financial applications in Oracle Applications and related modules where there is a financial impact. His broad range of skills have helped him with his implementation of, Record to Report, Procure to Pay, and Quote to Cash processes, with reengineering and crystallizing processes during implementations. His tenure as a Consultant and a Manager of financial applications in corporate America, brings to the table a wide range of experience with financial processes that include inter-company, multi-currency, statutory needs, and process flows to manage operational changes that will lead to efficiency and appropriate accounting results. He has been a board member of the NorCal OAUG and Multi-National SIG. He is the coordinator of the GL SIG and has presented various papers at OAUG and related conferences.

He lives in California with his wife and two kids. He can be contacted at mohan@fscpsolutions.com or on 408 859 4484.

Visit www.fscpsolutions.com for a peek at training material (the training material can be found under the "Training Collateral" link) and other content that he has presented at various conferences and public meetings. The presentation collateral can be found under the link "Presentation Collateral".

He has worked on multiple projects where training has been a key deliverable and has developed multiple formats of delivering effective training.

FSCP Solutions Inc. also has generic training material and is building content that will help the finance user get an easy path to effectively use the E-Business Suite. The training collateral on the website is generic training material.

Acknowledgement

I have to acknowledge the support and patience from my wife and her continued support in allowing me the time to research and write this book. It would not have been possible to make this effort a success without her support. I would also like to extend an acknowledgement to people who are my peers and helped me immensely in reviewing the book and giving me valuable feedback regarding content and writing style. My heartfelt gratitude and thanks go to – Alex Fiteni, Ajay Pradhan, Brian R. Bouchard, Faun deHenry, John Peters, Ketan J Thanki, Scott Gordon, and Thomas Simkiss.

I would also like to thank the many others that I have reached out to ask specific questions related to content in some of the chapters where their expertise was far higher than mine.

Last of all and once again, I would like to thank my family, my wife and two kids who bore the brunt of the long hours when I researched and wrote the book.

About the Reviewers

Brian R. Bouchard is a passionate person who enjoys helping others understand the complexities around Oracle Financials applications. He was introduced to Oracle Applications back in the 90s when he served as the Fixed Assets Manager at Motorola. Playing an integral role in the implementation and rollout of the application, he decided to change career paths from Accountant to Consultant. In his consulting career, he has designed, developed, and implemented over 50 full life cycles of Oracle EBS Applications ranging from Release 9 – Release 12.1.3. He has always strived to help others and to find the most efficient ways to perform tasks and to utilize the system. This characteristic led him to develop bolt-on products for Oracle Assets and he opened the doors of his own company in 2006. As President and CEO of Chi-Star Technology SM, he is striving to improve the utilization of Oracle Assets and to streamline manual efforts by automating some of the most tedious processes in Oracle Assets. Due to his passion to educate people on the complexities of Oracle Applications, he has also conducted well over 200 training sessions on various applications and releases. In the summer of 2009, he founded the CST Education Network, which was started to offer low cost education on Oracle Applications via webinars and video training.

He realized the areas of opportunity in Oracle Assets: Asset Transfers and Reconciliation. In April 2006, the introduction of AssetCross® came to the market as a solution to the manual asset transfer procedure. The AssetCross® software will transfer single or multiple assets between corporate depreciation books, transfer full or partial (cost or units) assets, translate transferred amounts to the receiving depreciation book's currency, and maintain an audit trail with the original asset. In June 2008, the introduction of AssetTie® came to the market as a solution to the reconciling Oracle Assets procedure. The AssetTie® software will capture balances from Oracle General Leger and compare them to balances in Oracle Assets and identify variances. The same technology is used to compare the transactions copied from Corporate Books to the Associated Tax Books. Within seconds of posting a journal entry from Oracle Assets, the user can determine if there are any reconciling differences.

The introduction of AssetCross® and AssetTie® to the business world has revolutionized the asset transfer and reconciling processes. Fortune 500 corporations as well as mid-sized family-owned companies can all benefit from this software.

Visit Chi-Star Technology at `http://www.chistartech.com` to learn more about the bolt-on products and education session/training offered.

I would like to acknowledge my family who have been with me every step and who have endured the schedule of a business traveler.

Faun deHenry is President and CEO of FMT Systems of Texas, Inc. Her appreciation for business process excellence and love of teaching have lead her into a very successful career. She has worked more than 15 years operating regional and national consulting organizations before embarking on her own corporation.

She is a recognized speaker and writer on topics including managing and sustaining virtual teams, business process innovation, Oracle's E-Business Suite, and business intelligence. She has co-authored *Business Process and More* (e-book series published by *FMT Systems of Texas, Inc.*) and *Installing, Upgrading and Maintaining Oracle E-Business Suite Applications Release 11.5.10+ with Solution Beacon, LLC;* additionally she is an accomplished contributor with the BPM Institute and her own site at `processconnectionsblog.com`.

I'd like to thank my many friends and family members who have supported me through the lengthy process of reviewing Mohan's book. They have each played their integral part in my success by bringing me Cook Out shakes during the late night editing sessions and by walking Meg during the "wee" hours of the morning. But mostly, I'd like to thank Hope Malone, for just being Hope.

Tosses kisses loftily into the wind.

Jeffery T. Hare, CPA CISA CIA, has an extensive background in public accounting (including Big 4 experience), industry, and Oracle Applications consulting experience. He has been working in the Oracle Applications space since 1998 with implementation, upgrade, and support experience. He is a Certified Public Accountant (CPA), a Certified Information Systems Auditor (CISA), and a Certified Internal Auditor (CIA). He has worked in various countries including Australia, Austria, Canada, Mexico, Brazil, United Kingdom, and Germany. He is a graduate from Arizona State University and lives in northern Colorado with his wife and three daughters. You can reach him at `jhare@erpra.net` or (970) 324-1450.

His first solo book project *Oracle E-Business Suite Controls: Application Security Best Practices* was released in 2009. He has written various white papers and other articles, some of which have been published by organizations such as ISACA, the ACFE, and the OAUG. You can request for these white papers from `http://www.oubpb.com/`. Jeffrey is a contributing author for the book *Best Practices in Financial Risk Management* published in 2009.

His LinkedIn profile is `http://www.linkedin.com/in/jeffreythare` and his Twitter profile is `http:www.twitter.com/jeffreythare`.

John Peters is an independent Consultant specializing in the Oracle E-Business Suite, Oracle Database, and Oracle Application Server products. He has worked with Oracle products for over 20 years on a variety of projects in a variety of roles. He has presented on a variety of topics at multiple OAUG, IOUG, and OpenWorld conferences. Copies of his papers can be found at `http://www.jrpjr.com`. He is one of the founding board members of the Northern California OAUG GEO. He is also the coordinator for the OAUG Workflow SIG. He has worked on *The ABCs of Workflow for E-Business Suite Release 11i and Release 12 Shining a Light on Oracle Workflow*, published by *Reed-Matthews, Inc.*

Ajay Pradhan has 25 years of industry experience with 15 years in the ERP area. Currently, he is the Global Applications Director at a Silicon Valley startup responsible for managing Oracle ERP, SalesForce, Workday, and other business applications.

Thomas Simkiss is the Chief Operating Officer and Applications Practice Director at Biztech, a mid-Atlantic Oracle Certified Advantage Partner based in King of Prussia, Pennsylvania. He has 14 years' Oracle Applications E-Business Suite experience both as an end user and implementer across many industries, including Telecom, Membership Organizations, Healthcare, Government, and Social Services. He has had a wide range of roles both utilizing and implementing Oracle Financials, Supply Chain, Discoverer and Business Intelligence as a business analyst, team lead, and project manager. He is a member of the New Jersey State Society of Certified Public Accountants, and a member of the Pennsylvania and New Jersey Bar Association.

Ketan J Thanki is a Senior IT Professional with more than 15 years of combined expertise in Finance, Accounting, Application Implementation, Application Support, and Project Management. He is skilled at understanding business requirements and mapping business processes with application functionality. He is experienced in recommending leading practices using standard application functionality for Finance, Accounting, Internal Audit and Internal Controls, and Human Resources processes. He has successfully and effectively worked with onshore, nearshore, and offshore resources and vendors. He has a proven track record of managing project and departmental budgets. He has several years of international work experience.

Currently, he is serving as a Chairperson of Procurement Special Interest Group at the Oracle Applications Users Group (OAUG). He is also a member of the Oracle Usability Advisory Board.

www.PacktPub.com

Support files, eBooks, discount offers and more

You might want to visit www.PacktPub.com for support files and downloads related to your book.

Did you know that Packt offers eBook versions of every book published, with PDF and ePub files available? You can upgrade to the eBook version at www.PacktPub.com and as a print book customer, you are entitled to a discount on the eBook copy. Get in touch with us at service@packtpub.com for more details.

At www.PacktPub.com, you can also read a collection of free technical articles, sign up for a range of free newsletters and receive exclusive discounts and offers on Packt books and eBooks.

http://PacktLib.PacktPub.com

Do you need instant solutions to your IT questions? PacktLib is Packt's online digital book library. Here, you can access, read and search across Packt's entire library of books.

Why Subscribe?

- Fully searchable across every book published by Packt
- Copy and paste, print and bookmark content
- On demand and accessible via web browser

Free Access for Packt account holders

If you have an account with Packt at www.PacktPub.com, you can use this to access PacktLib today and view nine entirely free books. Simply use your login credentials for immediate access.

Instant Updates on New Packt Books

Get notified! Find out when new books are published by following @PacktEnterprise on Twitter, or the *Packt Enterprise* Facebook page.

Table of Contents

Preface   **1**

Chapter 1: Overview of Oracle E-Business Suite   **7**

  ERP and Oracle E-Business Suite   **8**

  Integration and process flows   **10**

    Order to Cash modules and processes   11

    Procure to Pay Modules and Processes   12

  Shared entities   **13**

  Fundamentals of flexfields   **14**

    Additional flexfield information   19

      Segment qualifiers   19

      Allow dynamic inserts   20

      Cross-validation rules   21

      Aliases   21

      Security rules   21

  Fundamentals of organizations   **21**

    Multiple Organization Access Control   24

  Application security   **24**

    Core Security   25

    Administrative security   26

  Navigation   **26**

  Summary   **30**

Chapter 2: General Ledger   **31**

  Primary and secondary ledgers   **32**

  Accounting Setup Manager   **33**

    Translation versus reporting currencies   38

  Ledger and Data Access Sets   **38**

    Ledger sets   39

    Data Access Sets   39

Journal entries   **40**
  Mass Allocations   44
  Posting   45
  Account Inquiry   45
Parents, Rollup Groups, and Summary Accounts   **46**
Budgeting   **50**
Multi-currency   **51**
Consolidations   **53**
Intercompany   **56**
  Advanced Global Intercompany System (AGIS)   57
Financial reporting   **59**
  Row definition   60
  Columns   61
  Content Sets   62
  Row Order   63
  Report Manager   63
Oracle Web ADI   **64**
  Settings in Excel and Internet Explorer for Web ADI   64
Summary   **65**
Chapter 3: Subledger Accounting (SLA)   **67**
Controls   **69**
  Online Accounting   69
  Preview Accounting   70
  Control accounts   71
  Streamlined Accounting   71
Accounting Policy Management   **71**
  Comprehensive Accounting   71
  Accurate Accounting   72
  Configuration options for SLA processes   72
Additional functions   **74**
  Configuration   75
  Open Balances Listing   76
  Supporting References   76
  Accounting Reports   77
  Subledger journal entries   78
  Account Inquiry   79
  Reporting Sequence   80
Important SLA profile options   **80**
Summary   **81**

Chapter 4: Inventory — 83

Organizations — 84
Items — 89
  Item categories — 89
  Status controls — 90
  Item attributes — 91
Transactions — 94
  Transaction configuration — 94
  Transaction managers — 96
  Transaction processing — 97
Cost management — 101
Summary — 101

Chapter 5: Purchasing — 103

Supplier management — 103
  Additional supplier management functionality — 105
Approvals — 105
  Workflow notifications — 107
Requisitions — 108
  iProcurement — 109
  Core requisitions — 110
  Expense category accounts — 111
RFQ and quotations — 112
Purchase orders — 113
  Configuring purchasing options — 114
  Transactions — 116
Receiving — 119
  Configuring receiving options — 120
  Transactions — 121
Accruals — 123
Summary — 124

Chapter 6: Payables — 125

Suppliers—Payables specific — 125
  Configuration — 127
Transactions — 128
  iExpenses — 129
    Approvals — 131
  Invoicing — 131
    Expense report — 131
    Automatic debit memo — 132
    Pay on Receipt — 132
    Standard invoices — 133

Procurement card transactions   135
Hold management   135
Approvals   136
Payments   **137**
Configuration   138
Payment Process Profiles   139
Payment transactions   141
Payment batches   142
Quick and manual payments   144
Refunds   144
AP-AR netting   144
Summary   **146**
Chapter 7: Assets   **147**
Configuration   **148**
Flexfields   149
Asset key flexfield   149
Category flexfield   149
Location flexfield   150
System controls   150
Calendars   151
Books   151
Asset categories   152
Transactions   **153**
Mass additions   153
Merge   154
Split   155
Adding to an asset   155
Future dated transactions   156
Post Mass Additions   156
Manual entry   157
Short tax years   159
Transferring assets   159
Construction-in-Process (CIP)   159
Asset impairments   160
Retirements   161
Mass transactions   162
Other transactions   162
Tax Books   **163**
Depreciation   **164**
Group depreciation   166
Capital budgeting   **166**
Accounting   **167**
Summary   **168**

Chapter 8: Cash Management   169
Configuration   170
Bank setup   170
Cash Management integration   172
Receivables integration   172
Payables integration   172
Payroll integration   173
Treasury integration   173
Bank Reconciliation   173
Bank transaction codes   174
Open interface   174
Cash forecasting   174
Managing bank account balances   176
Cash positioning   176
Cash transactions   177
Transfers   177
Cash flows   178
Summary   179

Chapter 9: Treasury   181
Configuration   181
Transactions   184
Foreign exchange deals   184
Money market deals   184
Inter-company funding   184
Equities   186
Hedging   187
Bank balance management   187
Settlements   188
Transaction validation   188
Accounting actions   189
Summary   191

Chapter 10: Order Management   193
Items   194
Trading Community Architecture   195
Customers   196
Customer profiles   196
Customer addresses (sites)   198
Salespersons   199
Price lists   199

Order capture/entry **200**
    Back to Back orders 202
    Drop-ship orders 203
    Sales agreements 204
    Order Import 204
    Return Material Authorization (RMA) 205
    Item Orderability 206
    Configuration 206
    Configure to Order (CTO) 207
Order actions **207**
Shipping execution **208**
Accounting **210**
Summary **211**

Chapter 11: Receivables **213**
  iReceivables **214**
  E-Business Tax **214**
  Trading Community Architecture **216**
  Receivables configuration **217**
    System options 217
    Descriptive Flexfields 217
    Remit-to address 218
    AutoInvoice (AutoAccounting) 219
    Approvals 220
  Customers **221**
  Transactions **221**
    Invoices and debit memos 222
    Credit memos 223
    Adjustment transactions 224
    Commitment transactions 224
    Revenue management 224
    Bills Receivable 226
  Receipts **227**
    Receipt classes 227
    Receipt reversals 228
    Miscellaneous receipts 229
    Automatic receipts 229
    Notes receivable 231
    Credit card payments and refunds 231
    Chargebacks 232
    Prepayment 232

QuickCash	233
Lockbox processing	233
Discounts	233
Receipt write-offs	234
Collections	**234**
Document printing	**235**
Accounting	**236**
AP/AR Netting	236
Summary	**237**
Chapter 12: Credit Management	**239**
Payment terms	**240**
Credit check rules	**241**
Pre-Calculated Exposure	243
Credit checking	**244**
Credit Management	**246**
Managing customer data	247
Scoring model and checklists	248
Data points	250
Automation	251
Summary	**254**
Chapter 13: E-Business Tax (EBTax)	**255**
Overview	**255**
Configuration	**258**
Legal entity	260
Self-assessment (use tax)	261
Tax profiles	261
Operating unit	262
TCA classifications	263
Managing migrated data	**264**
Tax content service providers	**265**
Using E-Business Tax	**266**
Third-party tax profiles	266
Tax exemptions	266
Tax Rates and Rules	268
Summary	**269**
Chapter 14: Oracle Workflow	**271**
Major features and definitions	**272**
Oracle Workflow Builder	272
Workflow engine	272
Business event system	272

Workflow definitions loader	273
Complete programmatic extensibility	273
Electronic notifications and mail integration	273
Monitoring and administration	273
Workflow usage	**274**
Processes and functions	274
Approval workflows	276
Notifications	**277**
Workflow Builder	**282**
Business events	**284**
Summary	**285**
Chapter 15: Approval Management Engine (AME)	**287**
Transaction types	**289**
Item classes	**290**
Attributes	**290**
Approval rules	**291**
Conditions	292
Actions	294
Action types	295
Business Analyst Dashboard	**296**
Summary	**298**
Index	**299**

Preface

Implementing a packaged ERP is a major task. It takes months of planning, running test cycles, resolving issues, and testing again. In many cases, asking the right questions when the project starts will reduce the stress of the project lifecycle. Implementation partners know the software; only you know your business!

Oracle E-Business Suite Financials R12: A Functionality Guide, helps in bringing the two skill sets together, knowledge of the software and the business knowledge of the user. Implementation projects are a learning experience. If you knew the ERP system capabilities at the outset, your questions would be different. This book helps you ask those "right" questions.

This book will lead a user who is going in for an implementation to the capabilities of E-Business Suite R12 at a high-level as an overview. It will help the user understand what the E-Business Suite can do and what questions should be asked of an implementation partner. It will also help you understand which functionalities will meet which business requirements in your enterprise.

What this book covers

Chapter 1, Overview of Oracle E-Business Suite, provides a brief overview of the framework of the structure of Oracle E-Business Suite. The chapter sets a baseline for the rest of the chapters that follow and helps with the knowledge of some of the key words and data points that are used in the book.

Chapter 2, General Ledger, covers the book is based upon. General Ledger is the cornerstone of the suite and manages to bind together all the data for financial purposes within a single ledger for tracking and reporting purposes.

Chapter 3, Subledger Accounting (SLA), introduces a new and fundamentally dynamic aspect of accounting, the accounting engine. This is new in Release 12 and helps intrinsically manage all accounting entry creation from transactions in all the E-Business Suite products. The engine is a user manageable rules repository that can be modified to engage the transactions in creating accounting as needed by your business.

Chapter 4, Inventory, introduces a warehouse management tool that allows enterprises to manage stocking, storage, and tracking of products, parts, and assemblies. Most enterprises use this product in their day-to-day business and manufacturing processes.

Chapter 5, Purchasing, covers procurement and its related processes, including the definition of suppliers and how to manage the activity of procuring goods for the enterprise. You will note that the book covers only MRO purchases and effective accounting for these activities.

Chapter 6, Payables, introduces the reader to an end point of the Procure to Pay business flow. Oracle Payables tethers the end point for the Procure to Pay process. The chapter also covers the payment processes.

Chapter 7, Assets, introduces the reader to the integrated view of how Oracle Assets works to enable the enterprise to manage assets. This chapter will also briefly address Construction-in-Process (CIP) assets and processing assets for tax reporting purposes.

Chapter 8, Cash Management, walks the user through how Oracle Cash Management helps the organization manage banks and financial institutions from within a singular and central portal in an integrated manner. This chapter will also introduce the new and formal bank management central repository for all dealings with banks including their definition, upkeep, and maintenance.

Chapter 9, Treasury, is a superset of the Cash Management product that allows the enterprise to manage legal entity relationships with ease and allows transfer of funds in an automated manner. This also gives the user additional functionality of other financial institution related transactions such as hedging, interest, and so on.

Chapter 10, Order Management, initiates the second leg of the process flows covered in this book. The chapter introduces the reader to the Order to Cash flow and introduces order capture, management, and fulfillment capabilities for managing your sales cycle.

Chapter 11, Receivables, manages invoicing and cash receipts that allows the enterprise to manage their cash flow. It is also the last leg in the Order to Cash process flow covered in this book.

Chapter 12, Credit Management, covers a new product introduced in the later releases of Version 11. The chapter also includes the existing credit check functionality that has been the major control perspective for the sales cycle. There have been multiple discussions about whether the business function of managing credit is incomplete without additional products, namely, Oracle Trade Management and Oracle Deduction Management.

Chapter 13, E-Business Tax (EBTax), is a product that was introduced in Release 12 to manage all the tax requirements such as, content, calculation, rules engine, and reporting from a centralized repository that is fully integrated with all E-Business Suite business flows and products. E-Business Tax is configurable and scalable for adding and maintaining country-specific tax content.

Chapter 14, Oracle Workflow, delivers a complete workflow management system that supports business process based integration with approvals for transactions. In some cases, workflow also enables generation of account code combinations as part of specific processes. Its technology enables modeling, automation, and routing information according to user-defined business rules.

Chapter 15, Approvals Management Engine (AME), is a product that was introduced in E-Business Suite 11*i*. This was after the persistent requests of many users to provide a more flexible rules engine to manage approvals of transactions in the E-Business Suite software.

What you need for this book

You do not need any specific software to read or understand this book. However, the book is based on the E-Business Suite (version R12) software—an Enterprise Resource Planning (ERP) software sold by Oracle.

Who this book is for

This book is for first time users and users who want to get a quick review on the capabilities of Oracle E-Business Suite; possibly helping improve the use of the systems functionality. The book covers all the Financial modules and highlights a few modules that relate to Order Fulfillment. The book provides information about what can be done in Oracle E-Business Suite and, in some cases, how to get the correct configuration. The book does not walk through all the configuration options, just a few to highlight the nuances of the specific impact of several configuration steps.

Conventions

In this book, you will find a number of styles of text that distinguish between different kinds of information. Here are some examples of these styles, and an explanation of their meaning.

Code words in text are shown as follows: "Another implication of this value is that, on failure of Journal Import, the data will be rolled back to SLA tables and will not have any resultant hanging data in `GL_INTERFACE`."

New terms and **important words** are shown in bold. Words that you see on the screen, in menus or dialog boxes for example, appear in the text like this: "The users can click on the **Preferences** link on the web form and manage default preferences and options for their use."

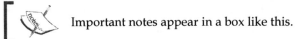 Important notes appear in a box like this.

Reader feedback

Feedback from our readers is always welcome. Let us know what you think about this book—what you liked or may have disliked. Reader feedback is important for us to develop titles that you really get the most out of.

To send us general feedback, simply send an e-mail to feedback@packtpub.com, and mention the book title through the subject of your message.

If there is a topic that you have expertise in and you are interested in either writing or contributing to a book, see our author guide on www.packtpub.com/authors.

Customer support

Now that you are the proud owner of a Packt book, we have a number of things to help you to get the most from your purchase.

Errata

Although we have taken every care to ensure the accuracy of our content, mistakes do happen. If you find a mistake in one of our books—maybe a mistake in the text or the code—we would be grateful if you would report this to us. By doing so, you can save other readers from frustration and help us improve subsequent versions of this book. If you find any errata, please report them by visiting http://www.packtpub.com/support, selecting your book, clicking on the **errata submission form** link, and entering the details of your errata. Once your errata are verified, your submission will be accepted and the errata will be uploaded to our website, or added to any list of existing errata, under the Errata section of that title.

Piracy

Piracy of copyright material on the Internet is an ongoing problem across all media. At Packt, we take the protection of our copyright and licenses very seriously. If you come across any illegal copies of our works, in any form, on the Internet, please provide us with the location address or website name immediately so that we can pursue a remedy.

Please contact us at copyright@packtpub.com with a link to the suspected pirated material.

We appreciate your help in protecting our authors, and our ability to bring you valuable content.

Questions

You can contact us at questions@packtpub.com if you are having a problem with any aspect of the book, and we will do our best to address it.

1
Overview of Oracle E-Business Suite

Oracle E-Business Suite (EBS) is an integrated suite of enterprise software modules for financial management, supply chain management, manufacturing, project management, human capital management, and customer relationship management. Oracle E-Business Suite history dates back to nearly 25 years ago when Oracle started the Oracle Applications division, a group focused on building business management software closely integrated with Oracle database. The first Oracle ERP Application, Oracle General Ledger was launched in August 1988. Since then, Oracle Application releases have continued at regular intervals. May 2000 saw the introduction of Release 11*i* and in January 2007 Release 12 was launched.

This book is intended to serve as a quick guide for Oracle E-Business Suite users and implementers. This handbook discusses two key business process flows—Order to Cash and Procure to Pay.

In this chapter, we will discuss the foundation features and various products that make up Oracle Financials:

- Navigation within Oracle E-Business Suite with focus on Release 12
- Fundamentals of flexfields
- Shared entities
- Multiple Organization (MO) concepts
- Multiple Organization Access Control (MOAC)
- Integrated flows
- Globalization support
- Key aspects of application security

ERP and Oracle E-Business Suite

Oracle E-Business Suite has multiple products that support the capability to manage an enterprise. The term often used with these type of software solutions is ERP, which stands for **Enterprise Resource Planning (ERP)**.

There are various ERP software solutions in the market but this book focuses on the solution from Oracle and the latest version is most often referred to as "EBiz Suite R12" or just simply R12 in this book (and in discussions and forums).

This handbook focuses on Oracle Financial products for **Procure to Pay (P2P)** and **Order to Cash (O2C)** business flows. As we will also be covering Oracle Fixed Assets and some reporting aspects in the following chapters it might seem like we are also covering additional flows or portions thereof, but the focus will remain on these two flows mentioned previously.

It is important to note the fact that these are separate products (and were at some point in time developed as stand-alone products) and there are differences in the way they feel, act, and look. Though they accomplish their goals in an integrated fashion, some of the technological framework is different. This does in many cases lead to interesting scenarios.

Over the following chapters, you will be introduced to key setups and key configurations considerations of Oracle Financial Applications products and transaction processing concepts.

The modules that will be covered are:

- General Ledger
- Subledger Accounting
- Accounts Payables
- Accounts Receivables
- Cash Management
- Treasury
- Fixed Assets
- Inventory
- Purchasing
- Order Management
- Credit Management

The following common products are integrated with the Oracle Financials suite and serve as important building blocks:

- Oracle E-Business Tax
- Oracle Workflow
- Oracle Approvals Management Engine (AME)

Key setups and configurations will be discussed for the common modules.

Oracle E-Business Suite is a complete set of business applications that enables corporations to efficiently track detailed business transaction data to help gather decision-making information. Oracle Financials are a subset of the E-Business Suite and are a family of products designed to capture and analyze your financial data. Oracle Financials applications helps to meet your obligations in key areas such as:

- Compliance
- Financial control
- Regulatory reporting
- Cost containment
- Risk management

Though the following chapters do not necessarily cover all these aspects in detail the controls and reporting capabilities are inherently built into the suite and are available to be implemented and used as needed.

Some products may need additional licensing. One of the data entities we will talk about in this chapter is generically called organizations. The financial suite supports the capability to help represent various business models in its configuration structure and are represented with related data entities. These can be listed in brief as follows:

- Your organization
- The role of your Legal entities
- Representing your organization in the system
- Organizational classifications in Oracle Financials
- Chart of Accounts
- System entities

We will briefly cover the inherent aspects of the organization in this chapter and the details will be covered in subsequent chapters where they are more relevant and configured. In Oracle E-Business Suite Release 12 (R12) the legal entity has been upgraded to an important data entity and now controls the ownership of various transactional and master data within the product suite. This is covered in more detail in *Chapter 2, General Ledger*.

The Chart of Accounts is a key feature in capturing your transactional accounting information to be able to report in a manner that supports and benefits the organizations' various organizational requirements.

Organizations and what they denote and identify will be briefly covered in a later part of this chapter.

Integration and process flows

As mentioned in the earlier part of this chapter, E-Business Suite is an integrated solution that has the capability to manage multiple business processes that support any given enterprise. The supported processes are:

- Financial Control and Reporting
- Corporate Performance Management
- Corporate Governance
- Credit to Cash
- Procure to Pay
- Asset, Real Estate, and Lease Management
- Cash and Treasury Management
- Travel and Expense Management

The business flows depict the close integration between the products as data flows from one to the other and also highlight the shared data sets that they use.

The two main business process flows associated with Oracle E-Business Suite Release 12 financial modules and the ones that we intend to cover in this book are as follows:

- Order to Cash (O2C)
- Procure to Pay (P2P)

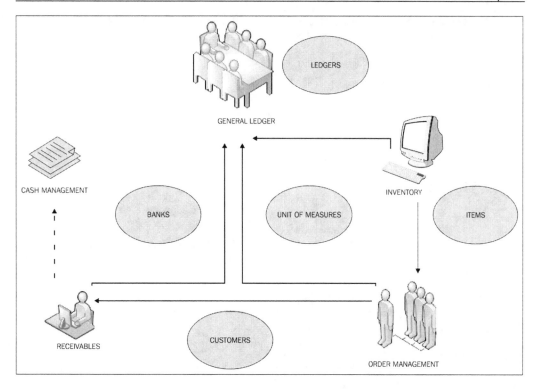

Order to Cash modules and processes

The Order to Cash (O2C) process is the revenue generating business process in the enterprise and is supported by the following E-Business Suite products:

- **Oracle General Ledger**: Accounting journals for Receivables and Inventory activity
- **Oracle Receivables/iReceivables**: Book receivables for goods shipped and services rendered (only if Service Contracts is not installed)
- **Oracle Inventory**: Items, inventory relief
- **Oracle Order Management**: Manage Orders, ship goods, and services

- **Oracle Cash Management**: Banks for collecting Cash Receipts

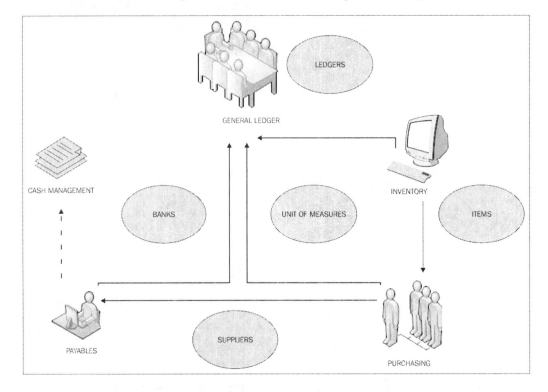

Procure to Pay Modules and Processes

The Procure to Pay (P2P) process is the procurement and related activity in the enterprise, and is supported by the following E-Business Suite products:

- **Oracle General Ledger**: Accounting journals for Accruals, Invoices, Payments, and Inventory receipts
- **Oracle Cash Management**: Reconcile cash payments, adjustments and corrections to cash payments and manage Banks
- **Oracle Payables/iExpenses**: Record invoices and employee expense reports
- **Oracle Inventory**: Set up inventory/expense items, record inventory activity such as receipts of inventory, returns, and corrections.
- **Oracle Purchasing/iProcurement**: Procure goods and services, record periodic and perpetual accruals

Shared entities

The financial application suite of products share a common data model and a set of integrated applications to give the enterprise a holistic view of their data. This enables the enterprise to view their business/financial information in a consolidated view and assist in their making informed decisions.

The products also share—due to the tight integration—data elements across them so that an entity (say an Employee) that has been defined in one product is the same entity that is used across all products that require that entity. This reduces maintenance overhead and leads to accuracy in the data that is used across the products.

Shared entities allow one-time definition of a business object so that it can be used across various modules. The ownership of a shared entity within a business organization may vary but technically the ownership is linked to a single module.

Here is a list of some often used shared entities with corresponding product owners:

Shared entities	Product owner
Unit of Measure	Inventory
Items	Inventory
Suppliers	Purchasing
Customers	Receivable
Salespersons	Sales
Employees	Human Resources
Locations	Human Resources
Currencies	Application Object Library

The last product **Application Object Library (AOL)** is a technological layer that owns a lot of internal data elements and the currencies happen to be part of this product.

Not many other data sets that you will work on at a functional level are owned by this product. We will identify in this chapter one more such important data set owned by this product.

Fundamentals of flexfields

Most enterprises have a multitude of data that they capture as part of their business transactions. To manage transactional capture of these data elements E-Business Suite has gathered most of the requirements and has more than what most enterprises would consider a data element that would need to be captured. However, the most will probably cover only 90 percent of the needs. This is a fact; it's just not a gap that can be completely covered. To compensate Oracle has allowed the facility to capture additional data in most of their transactional and master data entry forms. These are called **Descriptive Flexfields (DFF)**. They help to capture these additional data elements and these additional columns are built into the existing database tables and can be configured to capture whatever data you need.

There are a fixed number of columns depending on the transaction (between 7 to 15).

There is a concept of a driving field that can be used to manage what data is captured in these additional fields if needed. The driving field is called a **Context Field**, and the data capture can be context sensitive to enable an enormous flexibility in what you capture.

In addition to this functionality there is another flexfield component that Oracle E-Business Suite has deemed necessary to provide a flexible data capture environment. These are predefined flexfields that the system will use in its designed framework to capture and manage data. An excellent example of this is the Accounting Flexfield.

These are called **Key Flexfields (KFF)** due to the very reason that they are *the* key in the framework and processes that E-Business Suite will help manage for the user.

The name flexfield has been derived from the fact that these are made up of multiple segments (data columns) that are user defined. Here are a set of comparisons between Key and Descriptive Flexfields:

- Predefined:
    - KFFs are predefined and have a specific use and are required to be set up for proper functioning of the E-Business Suite
    - DFFs are just additional pieces of data that are captured as needed

- Structured:
  - ° Need a structure to be defined in each case (user defined)
  - ° This structure is limited to the number of columns in the database table that exists for each transaction
  - ° Both KFFs and DFFs can support multiple structures based on a data condition in your form or application data
- Segmented:
  - ° Both KFFs and DFFs are segmented (think columns)
  - ° The number of segments is dependent on the transaction table
- Value set:
  - ° KFFs must have value sets, but these are optional for DFFs and are driven by business needs
  - ° You have predefined value sets that can be used
- Values:
  - ° Each DFF and KFF segment can have a set of values, when assigned to a value set

A Key Flexfield appears on a form as a normal text field with an appropriate prompt. A Descriptive Flexfield appears on your form as a two-character-wide text field with square brackets [ ] as its location on the form. When opened for data entry, both types of flexfields appear as a pop-up window that contains a separate field and prompt for each segment in use.

 This is configurable if you do not need to have the pop-up window appear each time. However, if you click on the **List of Values (LoV)** icon or the three-dots at the end of the field it will pop-up a window.

Each segment has a name and can have a set of valid values. The values may also have descriptions.

There is another set of flexfields called Globalization Flexfields that are used for specific localization functionality within E-Business Suite and require additional configuration. The discussion of the specifics is outside the scope of this book.

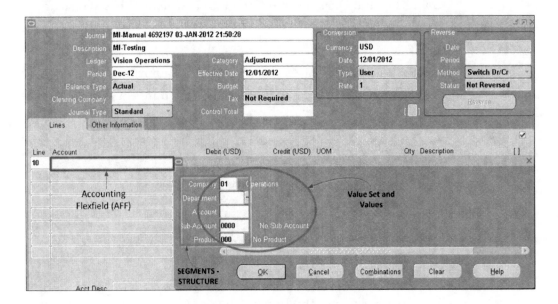

A few examples of Key Flexfields in Oracle E-Business Suite finance modules with corresponding owners are shown in the following table:

Key Flexfields	Owners
Accounting Flexfield	General Ledger
Asset Key, Asset Location, and Category Flexfield	Assets
Territory and Sales Tax Location Flexfield	Receivables
Item Categories, System Items, Item Catalogs	Inventory

We will be using the Accounting Flexfield (AFF) as an example basis to demonstrate much of the details in this chapter. The AFF given later in this chapter is one that is used in the Vision Instance of Oracle E-Business Suite that is delivered with your installation by Oracle with a sample set of data that you can use as a sandbox for review and understanding functionality.

The vision installation has been the basis for most of the screens and examples in this book.

To configure a flexfield, the following four elements need to be set up:

- **Structure**: A flexfield structure is a specific configuration of segments. As an example, different Accounting Flexfield (Chart of Accounts) structures can be defined in Oracle General Ledger for different ledgers if needed. The structure is made up of one or more than one segment.

- **Segment**: A segment is a single subfield within a flexfield structure. You can define the appearance—display size, prompts, and assign a value set. You can also define if it is required and if any security is enabled, when defining the structure. A segment is represented in your database as a single table column.

- **Value set**: A value set is defined to create a definition for the segment, such as the length, format type, including format definitions and validation type.

- **Validation types**:
  - **None**: This value set has no list of approved values associated with it.
  - **Independent**: Independent type value sets perform basic checking but also check a value entered against the list of approved values you define.
  - **Dependent**: A dependent value set is associated with an independent value set. Dependent value sets ensure that all dependent values are associated with a value in the related independent value set.
  - **Table**: Table value sets obtain their lists of approved values from existing application tables. When defining your table value set, you specify a SQL query to retrieve all the approved values from the table.
  - **Special**: This specialized value set provides another flexfield as a value set for a single segment.
  - **Pair**: This specialized value set provides a range flexfield as a value set for a pair of segments.
  - **Translatable independent**: A translatable independent value set is similar to an independent value set in that it provides a predefined list of values for a segment. However, a translatable independent value set can contain display values that are translated into different languages.
  - **Translatable dependent**: A translatable dependent value set is similar to a dependent value set. The available values in the list and the meaning of a given value depend on which independent value was selected in a prior segment of the flexfield structure.

- **Values**: Generally, the flexfield validates each segment against a set of valid values using a value set that defines the type of value, length, and min and max values. You can also have segments that have no predefined values.

 It is advisable to use a predefined set of values for Key Flexfield segments.

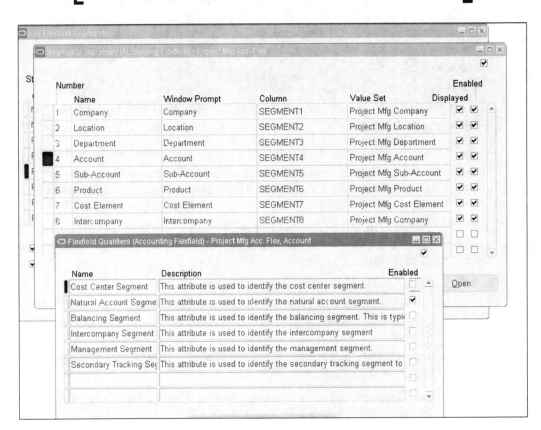

There are additional aspects that are unique to the Key Flexfields that allow them to focus on functionality that is built into the design of the E-Business Suite. These are specifically important for the functionality and the capability to manage the quality of the data for a financial transaction. These aspects also manage to enforce accuracy in data capture and processing.

These help, if configured accurately, in managing to help the enterprise gather the financial data as required by the business and process and report on the resulting data sets with accuracy and adhering to GAAP rules.

Additional flexfield information

Due to the fact that E-Business Suite is a packaged application and is expected to cater to the requirements of multiple businesses, there are some framework elements that enhance the functionality of the generic data capture facility. Some of these are described here in brief.

A qualifier is defined as an element that enhances or identifies a need to specifically note the use of a specific field/data set. In Oracle E-Business Suite segment qualifiers are used extensively to manage functionality within the system.

Segment qualifiers

One of the most important ones is the segment qualifier (for the Accounting Flexfield).

We will discuss the segment qualifiers that are available and used as part of this flexfield.

The AFF has the following segment qualifiers:

- Cost center segment
- Natural account segment
- Balancing segment
- Intercompany segment
- Management segment
- Secondary tracking segment

Each segment qualifier is used by the system to process data in each case for a specific purpose.

The balancing segment is used by the system to ensure that a balanced trial balance report can be generated for a value in that segment.

The natural account segment has to be identified with additional tracking segments to identify — asset, income, expense, liability, and so on. Then the system will also automatically rollover the net balance of income and expense balances to the retained earnings account and zero out the balances when a new fiscal year begins as defined in the system.

These are predefined Key Flexfield qualifiers, and this manages to identify to the application that there is a special need for some activity to be performed based on these values.

 There is no easily supported way to add additional qualifiers to flexfield segments.

Descriptive Flexfields used with the Accounting Flexfield segment qualified as a natural account identify usage for each value as follows:

- Allow budgeting
- Allow posting
- Account type (Asset, Expense, Liability, Ownership/Stockholder's Equity, Income, and Revenue)
- Reconcile
- Third Party Control Account (Yes, No, Customer, Supplier, and Restrict Manual Journals)

The budgeting and posting qualifiers are available for all the AFF segments.

Allow dynamic inserts

The Accounting Flexfield structure is made of multiple segments and each segment has valid values as per your configuration. When these segments are used together they create a combination (accounting flexfield combination). This happens normally when you are entering an accounting transaction such as a journal entry. Dynamic inserts for your Accounting Flexfield allow creating combinations as the transactions are entered. As long as values for each segment are valid the combination will be created.

This is an easy method to create combinations, but also allows inaccurate combinations to be created when a user inadvertently chooses the wrong set of values in each segment. The inaccuracy cannot be controlled by the system and is normally an error due to a business requirement.

To manage creating only accurate combinations you can either choose to not allow dynamic inserts, or use cross-validation rules (CV rules).

 If you do not allow dynamic inserts then your business must create each combination for your transaction to use manually.

Cross-validation rules

Cross-validation rules (CV rules) are another level of functionality that allows you to use the segments and manage the combinations that get created when you use the segment values together in a transaction. The important point to understand is that the CV rules are only effective when the combinations are being created for the first time.

This is the reason that CV rules should be created when beginning an implementation and before creating any transactions that create accounting code combinations.

Aliases

Another way to make sure that users do not create incorrect combinations is to use an alias. An alias is a label that you create for oft-used combinations. This way the users do not need to enter all the segment values (or remember what they should be). Another benefit is that with an alias you can also have specific segments blank so that a user can choose to fill them in as appropriate at the time of transaction entry.

Even if the alias has specific values defined these can be changed at the time of transaction entry.

Security rules

One more functionality to manage transactional accuracy is to manage specific values that can be chosen by a user in a transaction. A security rule is built to allow access to a subset of values within the list of valid values for a specific "responsibility". It is important to note that when defining segment details there is a data element that controls if security rules can be used or not and this should have a value other than "No Security" for security rules to work.

Fundamentals of organizations

There are multiple system entities that are in a generic fashion referred to as **organizations** in the applications suite. These however, have classifications that identify how they will be used and their effect on the configuration and usage.

The Oracle E-Business Suite includes the following important system entities:

- Business Group
- Government Reporting Legal Entity (known as GRE in previous releases)
- Legal Entity

- Ledgers
- Operating Unit
- Inventory Organization
- Human Resources Organization (also commonly identified with Departments)

Each system entity is assigned to a classification that determines its functionality and indicates how you might want to deploy it. These system entities sit at the highest level of the configuration basis in the suite and are shared across all the products within the E-Business Suite.

We will be focusing on the Operating Unit in this chapter. This is due to the fact that the Operating Unit (OU) provides the seemingly unique aspect of being able to segregate data within a ledger, legal entity, and business group.

The functionality that an OU provides, commonly referred to as multi-org, enables multiple business units in an enterprise to use a single installation of E-Business Suite Applications products while keeping transaction data separate and secure. This was first introduced in an earlier release (Release 10.4). Prior to this release this functionality required users to install multiple versions of the software to manage these segregations.

The segregations were managed by assigning a responsibility (or a role) to a user that secured data to an Operating Unit (OU). This allowed users to use a single installation of the applications suite and manage data segregation and transactional capability to specific areas within the enterprise. This has been enhanced to allow access to multiple organizations, called **Multiple Organization Access Control (MOAC)**, from within a single responsibility with Release 12.

Some of the modules that support the multi-org structure are:

- Oracle Cash Management
- Oracle Order Management
- Oracle Shipping Execution
- Oracle Release Management
- Oracle Payables
- Oracle Purchasing
- Oracle Receivables

The functionality secures access to data so that users can access only information that is relevant to them. You can also sell products from one Operating Unit that uses one primary ledger, but ship them from another Operating Unit using a different primary ledger, while automatically recording the appropriate intercompany accounting by posting intercompany accounts payable and accounts receivable transactions.

The multi-org model provides a hierarchy that can dictate how transactions flow through different business units and how those business units interact. In the next illustration, note the different shapes used for each organization type. The shapes are helpful when drawing multiple organization diagrams.

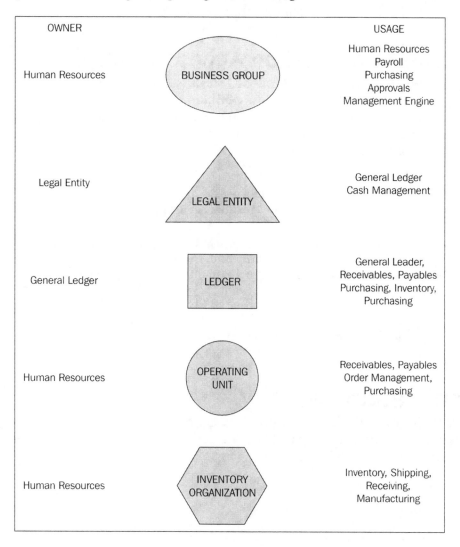

With E-Business Suite Applications accounting, distribution, and materials management functions, you define the relationships between inventory organizations, operating units, and ledgers to create a multi-level company structure. Each organization classified as a legal entity must specify a primary ledger to post accounting transactions. A legal entity points to one and only one primary ledger. An inventory organization is used to define, manage, and store items (products, parts list) and must reference an operating unit for sales and procurement transactions. In R12 an inventory organization can point to only one operating unit. Items are defined in the master inventory organization (master parts list) and added to the appropriate child inventory organizations for transactional purposes. This is explained in a little more detail in the *Chapter 4, Inventory*.

Multiple Organization Access Control

Multiple Organization Access Control (MOAC) is basically the ability to access multiple operating units from a single application responsibility. In prior releases, a single responsibility allowed access to process data only for one operating unit. If a user was managing Payables for Sweden, Norway, and Finland a user needed to have three different responsibilities to do their tasks.

The operating unit is used to manage data in subledger products—as listed earlier—General Ledger does not use operating units to segregate data.

In Release 12 a security profile is used to assign multiple operating units as required. This security profile when assigned to a responsibility will grant access to multiple operating units. Given the example of a user above managing payables for Sweden, Norway, and Finland they could now manage all payables for these three countries from within a single responsibility. MOAC is not enabled and used for the iProcurement and iExpense modules.

Application security

Oracle E-Business Suite Release 12 provides significant enhancements to the Oracle E-Business Suite security system. This model is now called Oracle User Management and a depiction is shown in the following figure:

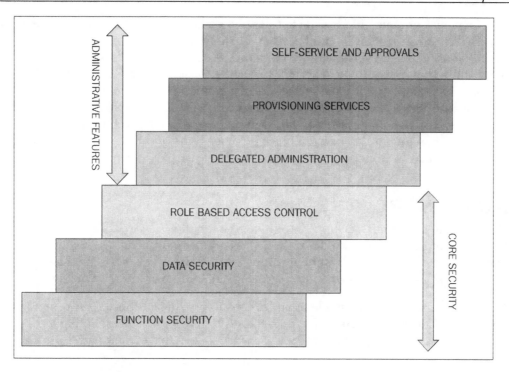

Core Security

The Core Security now includes a **Role Based Access Control (RBAC)** model that builds on the existing function security (menu functions) and data security (OU access across subledgers, security rules in GL, project organization access in Oracle Projects, and so on) model. The function security is the base layer of access control in Oracle E-Business Suite. It restricts user access to individual menus and functions within the system, but does not restrict access to the data contained within those menus.

Data security is the next layer and builds on function security. This layer provides access related to the data that a user can access. Oracle E-Business Suite restricts access to individual data that is displayed on the screen once the user has selected a menu or menu option.

RBAC enables organizations to create roles (also called responsibilities as in previous releases) based on specific job functions and to assign these roles the appropriate permissions (a lower level access model than a responsibility). Access control is defined through roles, and user access to Oracle E-Business Suite is determined by the roles granted to the user. In Cash Management for example the RBAC functionality is used to grant access to a role (also called a responsibility) to a specific legal entity and that allows the bank account to be used for a given legal entity (and its related operating unit). For example, cash management security based on a legal entity uses RBAC for internal bank accounts.

Administrative security

Delegated administration is a privilege model that builds on the RBAC system to provide organizations with the ability to assign the required access rights for managing roles and user accounts. Administration privileges determine the users, roles, and organization information that delegated administrators can manage.

The registration processes enable organizations to provide end-users with a method for requesting various levels of access to the system. Based on their eligibility these access requests can be granted (approvals can also be managed before these grants are made).

Self-service requests and approvals enable end users to request initial access or additional access to the systems. Approvals for these requests can be managed systematically and tracked for audit purposes before the grant is made. Notifications can be generated to the requestor so that there is a seamless process to granting access.

Navigation

Oracle E-Business Suite Release 12 introduces the Swan user interface, which has a browser look and feel.

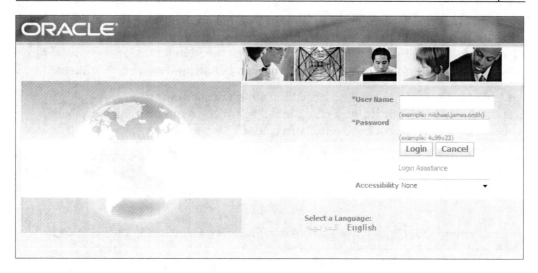

To gain access to use the E-Business Suite the system administrator has to create a username and a password, and assign specific responsibilities to access functions in specific products.

Oracle E-Business Suite Release 12 can support multiple languages and the user can select a language of choice during the login process.

The access to each product is defined by a *responsibility* (also called a role). The following screenshot shows a personal home page with a list of responsibilities. The user clicks on a responsibility to access the available functions. Oracle provides default responsibilities that have access to all the functions and many enterprises may want to change this to manage SOX compliance issues.

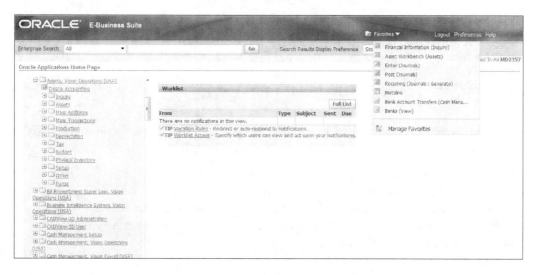

In earlier R12 releases there used to be a three panel launch page. The responsibilities were listed on the left pane, the functions were displayed in the center pane, and favorites were listed in the right pane. This has changed in R12.1.3. You now have a two panel page and **Favorites** has been moved to a drop-down on the title bar.

The other major change in 12.1.3 is that the submenus and functions for a responsibility now show up in a cascade fall below the main responsibility pane. The favorites list now contains a mix of standard forms, web pages, and web links.

If you look at the icons on the favorites list, they tell a story. The icons on the first five **Favorites** link are standard forms explained a little later, called GUI forms. The next **Favorite** is a web link to an external site—Metalink—Oracle support site. The last two are web pages.

The following screenshot is a graphical user interface form also known as a GUI form, and referred to previously as a standard form. This user interface has been available and in use from release 10.7 GUI and is still prevalent in many cases.

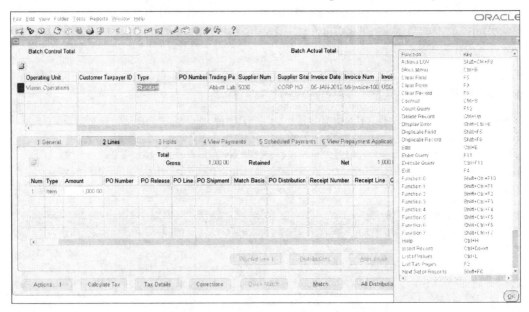

This form is used in most places in the all products and has shortcut keys as shown in the box on the right-hand side of the previous screenshot.

The list of these shortcuts is another document in itself and there are other ease of use icons on the top as well as the menu bar. This is well documented in a paper presented to the OAUG in 2007. The paper is titled *Wow, I Can do That in Oracle Applications!* The paper was presented by me at the conference and is available in the conference papers database.

On the Oracle forms graphical user interface (GUI) form has shortcuts for navigation. These shortcut keys only work in the GUI form. This is invoked by using the *Ctrl+K* command (pressing the *Ctrl* and *K* keys together). These commands are used in general in combination with the *Ctrl* key, and this may be different in different environments, so you need to check at your particular environment.

In these forms you will see multiple ways in which data is presented—tabs that hold additional data sets (for capture and display) in the middle of the image, columns on the top of the form, and the scroll bar just above the tabs shows that there are more columns to the right.

Just above the columns on the left-hand corner you see a folder icon . This is an interesting functionality to allow users to manage how they see their columns laid out for ease of data entry. This is called Folder functionality and is useful to move, add, or remove the columns shown on the screen.

> You cannot add columns that are not inherently exposed by the applications framework. You can only choose columns from a predefined list.

The folder functionality is also described in detail in the paper referred to earlier.

The following is a screenshot of the new web page that is now used for some functions:

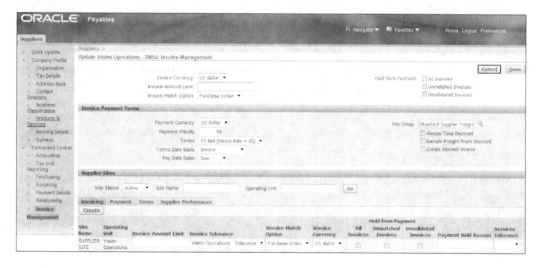

The users can click on the **Preferences** link on the web form and manage default preferences and options for their use. This is only for the user and is not system wide.

Here is a list of items that can be managed from the **Preferences** page:

- **default language**
- **date format**
- **time zone**
- **number format**
- **change password**
- **notification email style**

The **Navigator** link is visible form web forms and is similar to a change responsibility 🔄 icon on the standard form. Clicking on the **Navigator** link will show a drop-down of available responsibilities to a user. You can go back to the home page by clicking on the **Home** link.

A **Help** link is available from various web forms and is similar to the ? icon on the standard form. This will open a new window where help documentation is available about the form and fields on the form or page. This requires some additional configuration and should be done by the person who is installing and administering the E-Business Suite.

Summary

In this chapter, you were introduced to an overview of the E-Business Suite and a little about how it works and some fundamentals to what makes it flexible and usable at multiple enterprises.

You learnt about the flexibility and uniqueness of flexfields, organizations, Multiple Organization Access Control (MOAC), and navigation.

In the following chapters we will introduce you to business process flows, Procure to Pay, and Order to Cash, delving deeper into each of the products that are used within these processes and highlighting unique aspects related to usage, configuration, and transactional areas.

2
General Ledger

The **General Ledger (GL)** is the collector of all data—financial and accounting—that is eventually used to produce financial reports for the enterprise. Transactions are transferred from the subledgers (AP, AR, PO, Inventory, and so on) to the General Ledger typically at month-end or at periodic intervals.

In R12 a new process has been introduced to manage the creation of the accounting entries and the transfer process to the GL. This new process is called **Create Accounting**.

The General Ledger gathers data as transactions from AP and AR are transferred to GL from the subledgers). A new Subledger Accounting layer manages all accounting representations and is the conduit for accounting entries into the GL and the basis for accounting reports in R12.

Here is what we will cover in this chapter:

- Legal Entity
- Ledgers (including primary, secondary, and reporting)
- Accounting Setup Manager (ASM)
- Security and Transactional processes including Budgeting
- Translation and Consolidation
- Intercompany Processing

- Financial Statement Generator (FSG) and Report Manager

Primary and secondary ledgers

A primary ledger is defined as a ledger where all your day-to-day transactions are performed and you would typically have a secondary ledger to reflect these same transactions in one of the following probable scenarios:

- In a different Chart of Accounts
- In a different Accounting Basis
- In a different Currency (also called a Reporting Ledger)

This is an evolving functionality of Multiple Reporting Currencies (MRC) that was first introduced in the Release 11 to help with the transition to the Euro currency.

A secondary ledger is one that would, in most cases, replicate the transactions from the primary ledger so that these transactions can be adjusted and can be reported for specific financial or management purposes. The secondary ledger can also have a different accounting basis or a different Chart of Accounts. This functionality assists in maintaining the true value (at transaction time) of a single transaction in two (or more) scenarios.

There is no systematic upper limit to the number of secondary/reporting currency ledgers you may have, though more than three is expected to cause performance issues for data handling.

The secondary ledger (including a reporting ledger) is configured at the same time when you define the primary ledger or can be added later. By default the first ledger you define is termed as primary and then you can attach secondary/reporting ledgers as needed. If the secondary and reporting ledgers are added at this time there is always a benefit as they will all be in sync from the beginning.

As in most cases the reason for attaching the secondary ledgers (and reporting ledgers) is to assist in maintaining a reporting basis, it is prudent to configure these at the same time. They can however, also be added at a later date.

As an example, if both a statutory and corporate accounting representation is required for a legal entity's transactions, two ledgers for the same legal entity can be used: a primary ledger for the corporate representation and a secondary ledger for the statutory representation. This would mean that you would make adjustments required to report for statutory purposes in the secondary ledger.

These configurations are performed in the Accounting Setup Manager.

There are options that can be managed to ensure that all the relevant transactions are effectively copied to the secondary/reporting ledgers.

All account balances are maintained in the GL_BALANCES table for each currency transacted, converted, or translated. Standard reports, including Financial Statement Generator (FSG) reports can be used to report on these balances. Trial Balance is one of the standard reports that can be used to review these balances easily.

The tasks listed previously are now supposed to be all done from a wizard.

Accounting Setup Manager

The setup for a set of books has now changed dramatically. The set of books has been renamed to Ledgers, and the method to set up a ledger has been now been changed to a setup wizard.

Before we get into details of how we use the Accounting Setup Manager (ASM) we should review a *new* data element that has been around since the implementation of E-Business Suite, but has now gained an importance and prominence in the setup process.

The legal entity is now an integral part in the transactional setup in E-Business Suite and has become important in the ledger creation process.

You have to define a legal entity before you start creating a ledger in the Accounting Setup Manager. The legal entity owns all the transactions in the tables, though the ledger (the legacy set of books) and Operating Unit are still present. The legal entity importantly owns a bank account and can be transacted only for subledgers (AP, AR) that are linked through the ledger to that legal entity. Legal entity in E-Business Suite corresponds closely to *legal entity* or *company* in the legal world. This is not a hard and fast rule and does not need to reflect your legal entity status for each company in your business hierarchy.

 The legal entity concept is now being used predominantly to own data in E-Business Suite and integrations to other systems may not see this in the same manner.

The following screenshot shows a form where you define the legal entity:

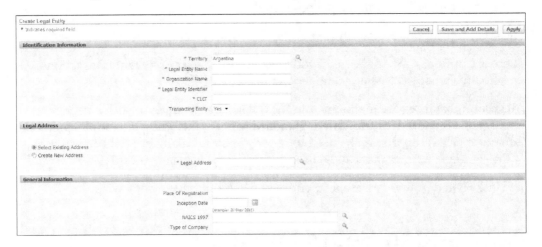

The address for a legal entity can be defined in this form and will be tagged as a **legal address**. Only **legal addresses** show up on the List of Values (LoV) on this screen.

Ideally, it would be easy to understand if it were that each of your ledgers was to be associated with a single legal entity. This is not true in all cases. A legal entity definition is required to start the ledger definition, but you may choose to have multiple legal entities associated with your ledger. Alternatively, you can also have company codes in your Chart of Accounts defined as balancing segments, and not define them as legal entities.

How do I know what is a legal entity for me? You will need a legal entity to address one of these concerns/scenarios:

- Statutory and legal requirements for legal entity accounting, such as document sequencing, tax accounting, and intercompany accounting

- The number of subsidiaries that use different charts of accounts, calendars, currencies, and subledger accounting methods and ledger processing options (maintain average balances, and so on)

- There could be a reason not to assign a legal entity to a ledger, but in this case the assumption is that this will be used to integrate data from an external system and will not be using any subledgers in the E-Business Suite

A more detailed list of the options that would necessitate a separate legal entity and thereby a separate ledger are listed in the Oracle Financials Implementation Guide (Part No. E13425-05).

The Accounting Setup Manager in the following screenshot shows tasks that you can perform for a ledger, the top portion of the screenshot shows the Legal Entities associated with this ledger, and the portion below shows tasks that have to be configured for each ledger.

Not all the tasks are required, but you must complete the first step, which is detailed options for the ledger, shown as a link with the ledger name in the screenshot.

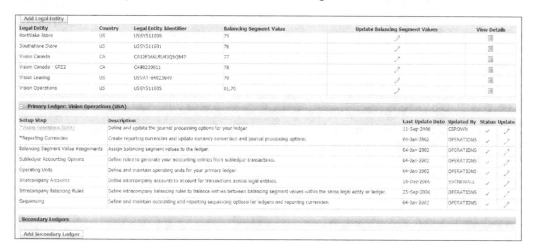

Legal Entity	Country	Legal Entity Identifier	Balancing Segment Value	Update Balancing Segment Values	View Details
Northlake Store	US	USSYS11000	75		
Southshore Store	US	USSYS11001	76		
Vision Canada	CA	CA12F1AKLRU43QSQ647	77		
Vision Canada - GRE2	CA	CA90220011	78		
Vision Leasing	US	USVAT-64623649	79		
Vision Operations	US	USSYS11005	01,70		

Primary Ledger: Vision Operations (USA)

Setup Step	Description	Last Update Date	Updated By	Status	Update
*Vision Operations (USA)	Define and update the journal processing options for your ledger	11-Sep-2006	CBROWN	✓	
*Reporting Currencies	Create reporting currencies and update currency conversion and journal processing options.	04-Jan-2002	OPERATIONS	✓	
Balancing Segment Value Assignments	Assign balancing segment values to the ledger.	04-Jan-2002	OPERATIONS	✓	
Subledger Accounting Options	Define rules to generate your accounting entries from subledger transactions.	04-Jan-2002	OPERATIONS	✓	
Operating Units	Define and maintain operating units for your primary ledger.	04-Jan-2002	OPERATIONS	✓	
Intercompany Accounts	Define intercompany accounts to account for transactions across legal entities.	18-Dec-2006	SSCNEWALL	✓	
Intracompany Balancing Rules	Define intracompany balancing rules to balance entries between balancing segment values within the same legal entity or ledger.	25-Sep-2006	OPERATIONS	✓	
Sequencing	Define and maintain accounting and reporting sequencing options for ledgers and reporting currencies.	04-Jan-2002	OPERATIONS	✓	

Secondary Ledgers

Add Secondary Ledger

Once you have identified and defined the legal entity, you can continue with the configuration of the ledger.

A new functionality in R12 assigns a balancing segment value to your legal entity (and ledger). This identifies the legal entity with a balancing segment value for the ledger. You can have additional balancing segment values to the ledger in the ASM. Transactions in the ledger are restricted to these balancing segment values.

You should have already defined your Chart of Accounts structure and calendar, enabled the currency you wish to use with your ledger, and will most probably use the default Accounting Method (Standard Accrual) for the ledger.

 If you choose to use a secondary ledger with a different accounting method, say Cash, then the step following this is where you would attach that as a secondary ledger.

The following screenshot shows the confirmation screen after you have defined the basic constituents of a ledger definition:

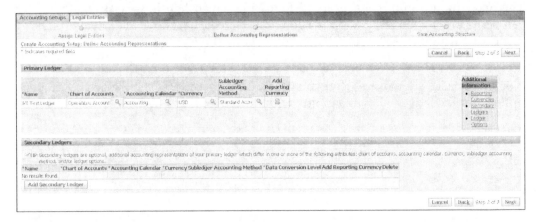

E-Business Suite provides multiple options to manage transactions in the secondary ledger. Transactions can be replicated in the secondary ledger in four ways:

- Balance
- Journal
- Subledger
- Adjustments Only

When **Balance**, **Subledger**, and **Adjustment Only** options are used, the system allows for a self-explanatory method to manage this functionality. Using the **Journal** option requires a set of other considerations to be reviewed.

There are multiple journal sources and categories and instead of using each combination using **–Other** for **source** and **category** will include all values.

A reporting ledger is the same as the secondary ledger except that it is in another currency, and another important difference is that you can assign reporting currencies to both primary and secondary ledgers.

When you perform translations, a new ledger called a reporting ledger is created, and it is similar to (pre-R12) translation balances.

This new ledger cannot be accessed separately as a transactional ledger, thus no open and close periods are needed. It can be accessed through the primary ledger for reporting translated balances.

There are multiple ways by which you can manage and maintain reporting ledgers:

- Maintain a complete currency representation of your subledger journals, General Ledger journals entries, and balances
    - ° Subledger level reporting currencies are maintained using both Subledger Accounting and the General Ledger Posting program to create the necessary subledger journals

 Subledger level reporting currencies can only be assigned to primary ledgers.

- The journal level reporting currency maintains General Ledger journal entries and balances in another currency representation
    - ° Journal level reporting currencies are maintained using the General Ledger Posting program
- The balance level reporting currency only maintains balances in another currency
    - ° Maintains the translated balances of the source ledger, every time the general ledger translation program is run in the source ledger
- The adjustment only secondary ledger is with one of the new functionalities in Subledger Accounting where an adjustment activity can be used to transfer these to a secondary ledger

Translation versus reporting currencies

The General Ledger's translation feature (mostly balance level reporting currency) is used to translate amounts from your ledger currency to another currency at the account balance level.

Reporting ledger can convert amounts from your transaction currency to a reporting currency at the transaction or journal level. Reporting currencies are not intended as a replacement for the General Ledger's Translation feature.

Translation only applies to the General Ledger. It cannot be used to translate transaction amounts in your subledgers.

A benefit of reporting currencies over the General Ledger's Translation feature is that with reporting currencies, you can inquire and report on transaction amounts directly from your subledgers.

 A key point to note is that in a pre-R12 scenario for this to be possible the transactions had to be replicated in the subledger; with R12 and Subledger Accounting, the transactions are not replicated, and only journals in the SLA level are generated for each reporting currency.

Comparing the results of using amounts as a result of your reporting currency conversion rather than translated amounts, you will find there will be rounding differences in your accounts.

These differences arise because:

- Translation converts ledger currency amounts to the designated currency
- Reporting currencies convert amounts from the transaction currency to the designated currency
- Reporting currencies use daily rates to convert transaction amounts
- Translation uses period or historical rates to translate account balances

Ledger and Data Access Sets

Release 12 has introduced additional functionality to manage multiple ledgers as a collection. This eases reconciliation and close processes for users that have to work with multiple ledgers.

Ledger sets conditionally group ledgers into a collection. Additionally, Data Access Sets also limit the type of access you can have within specific ledgers. This is in addition to the Balancing Segment values assignment task in the ASM, discussed previously.

Ledger sets

In R12 you can create ledger sets to perform tasks for a set of ledgers instead of having to perform all these tasks individually for each of them one by one.

Ledger sets can be used to perform the following tasks:

- **Translation and Revaluation**: Translate balances and run revaluation across multiple ledgers in a ledger set
- **Open and Close Periods**: Open and close periods for multiple ledgers within a ledger set from a single operation
- **Reporting**: Submit standard reports and Financial Statement Generator (FSG) reports across multiple ledgers in a ledger set
- **Inquiry**: Perform online inquiry on account balances or journals across multiple ledgers in a ledger set from a single view; drill down to the journal details and subledger transaction for each ledger

Ledger sets can be used to allow access to multiple ledgers and perform tasks on this set of ledgers in a single process rather than having to do this for all the ledgers individually.

The ledger sets' functionality enables and facilitates a faster close process for companies that have multiple ledgers (including reporting and secondary ledgers).

 Ledgers must have the same Chart of Accounts and Calendar/ Period Type combinations to be included in a ledger set.

Data Access Sets

Data Access Sets, another new concept in R12, are used to allow secure access to specific segment values. They are similar to the Security Rules that are available in previous versions of the E-Business Suite applications. An important difference between Security Rules and Access Sets is that this allows you to combine the use of a ledger within a single responsibility with an access set, and yet use a subset of some of the balancing segment values in one of the ledgers. It sort of combines and expands on the Security Rule concept across ledgers.

The Data Access Sets can be specific to allow Read or Write access or a combination of both for only the Balancing or Management Segment. Security Rules only allow the availability of a value to use in the transaction for any segment. The following screenshot shows a definition screen for access sets:

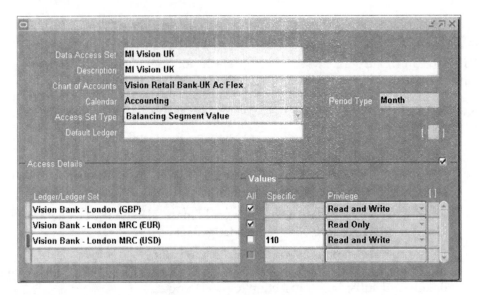

The privileges that can be granted allow inquiry only or both enter/manage transactions and inquiry.

 Using a Data Access Set you can allow full ledger access or access to specific Balancing or Management Segment qualifiers.

Journal entries

Journal entry transaction processes have not changed much. A couple of differences in some of the functionality that can be managed within a journal have been introduced.

Journal entries are typically made at the end of the month to make adjustments to specific balances before financial reports can be generated and distributed.

Journals are always batched, even if you do not choose to use a batch to begin with; the journal name becomes the batch name and the batch contains one journal. You can track the number of journals and the total amount if you use batches, for easier control.

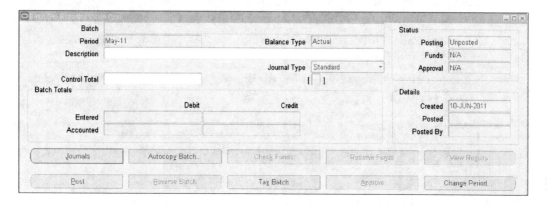

When you enter a journal—either from a batch or an individual journal—you specify the **Period, Category,** and a **Description**; a journal can have only one category, and belongs to a single period.

Once you have entered the relevant information on the Header, you can enter any number of lines for a journal. As long as the debits and credits are equal the journal can be saved but cannot be posted. (You can however, post an unbalanced journal if you have enabled Suspense posting for the ledger.)

E-Business Suite has a unique functionality that allows transacting monetary as well as non-monetary journals. Non-monetary transactions have the following characteristics:

- A special Currency Code is used – STAT
- Do not have to balance debits and credits to post
- Manage to maintain balances for items such as number of people, number of widgets, and other such non-monetary balances

The explanation of the buttons at the bottom of the batch form are as follows:

- **Journals**: To enter journals for this batch
- **Autocopy Batch**: To copy the entire batch (including the journals)
- **Post**: Post the batch
- **Reverse Batch**: Reverse the batch (can only be done after the batch is posted)
- **Tax Batch**: A tax transaction journal entered in GL

- **Change Period**: Change the period of an existing saved, but unposted batch
- **Approve**: Only enabled if journal approval is configured to be used; click to approve
- **Check Funds**: Only enabled if Encumbrance Accounting is configured; click to check if funds are available against a budget
- **Reserve Funds**: Only enabled if Encumbrance Accounting is configured; click to reserve funds
- **View Results**: Only enabled if Encumbrance Accounting is configured; click to review result

 A period must be open to post a journal batch. You can save a journal if either the period is closed or future open; you cannot post unless these periods are open.

The explanation of the buttons on the **journals** form are as follows:

- **Post**: Post the journal/batch. E-Business Suite posts journal batches, not individual journals.
- **Autocopy Batch**: To copy the entire batch (including the journals). If you enter a journal E-Business Suite creates a batch for that single journal.
- **Approve**: Only enabled if journal approval is configured to be used; click to approve Line Drilldown.
- **Line Drilldown**: Allows you to drilldown to the transactional system (AP or AR) if the journal was imported from the subledgers, passing through the subledger accounting layer.
- **T_Accounts**: You can view the **T_Accounts** in the traditional manner using this button.
- **Check Funds**: Only enabled if Encumbrance Accounting is configured; click to check if funds are available against a budget.
- **Reserve Funds**: Only enabled if Encumbrance Accounting is configured; click to reserve funds.
- **View Results**: Only enabled if Encumbrance Accounting is configured; click to review result.
- **Change Period**: Once saved the period cannot be changed on the form; you will need to click this button to change the period.
- **Change Currency**: Once saved the currency cannot be changed on the form; you will need to click this button to change the currency for this journal.

When querying your journals on the **summary** screen the explanation of the buttons shown are as follows:

- **Review Journal**: Review the journal that your cursor is on
- **Review Batch**: Review the batch that your cursor is on
- **Post**: Post the journal (and batch) that your cursor is on
- **Reverse Batch**: Reverse the batch (can only be done after the batch is posted)
- **New Journal**: Open the detail form to enter a new journal
- **New Batch**: Open the form to enter a new batch
- **Tax Batch**: A tax transaction journal entered in GL
- **Approve**: Only enabled if journal approval is configured to be used; click to approve
- **Autocopy**: Autocopy this journal

E-Business Suite allows you to manage journal transactions in multiple ways. The following are a few types that are regularly used:

- **Single/Manual**: These are standard journals that are created either manually or are generated based on transfers from subledgers. An important source for this type of journal is when converting from a legacy system. You can use a specific source and category combination to identify initial balance loads into the system for the first time.
- **Recurring**: Journals that are created periodically can be systematically created based on existing balances and mathematical formulae. A single template can also be created with just accounts and no amounts.
- **MassAllocation**: A unique functionality that allows for a set of groupings of accounts to be used within a set formula to create an allocation across several departments (for example, allocating rent expense across all departments using the space).
- **Elimination**: It can be automated with recurring formulas to eliminate balances at the consolidated level to arrive at appropriate elimination entries, or blank templates can be used.
- You can now also enter a journal entry from the subledger accounting level. This facility is primarily accessed from one of the subledgers: AP, AR, and so on. This is explained in more detail in the next chapter.

 Journals can be entered directly into the subledger and journal level reporting currencies.

Mass Allocations

E-Business Suite allows "Mass Allocations Journals" that works to define a formula that will create a journal allocating amounts from different account balances. The functionality allows you to use monetary and non-monetary balances together to manage allocations in a systematic way.

Mass Allocations use parent and child values that can assist in grouping and collating balances for specific segment values.

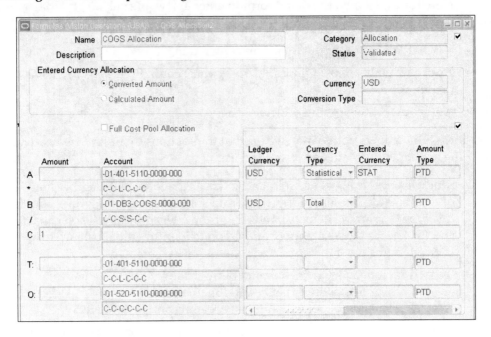

Mass Allocation works on the simple formula of A * B / C:

- The first line in the previous screenshot is the value for **A**—this is the balance you want to allocate.
- The second line in the previous screenshot is the value for **B**—this is based on the balance that you want to allocate—it is the numerator in the formula.
- The third line is the value for **C**—this is based on the balance that you want to allocate—it is the denominator in the formula.
- Each of the lines are combinations of segments and the balances within them; the normal progression is to use the denominator to sum (get the total for the combination) and the numerator to loop (get each value in each segment).
- The last two lines are the target—where you want to allocate the calculated balances and the offset, for the new entry created. (Can be the same as in **A**.)

Posting

Posting is performed on all transactions to create balances that are used to report using FSG reports and review financial results. Posting can either be done from the journal, journal batch form, or from the standard posting form.

Account Inquiry

You can inquire on balances from the GL balances table using the standard Account Inquiry form shown in the following screenshot:

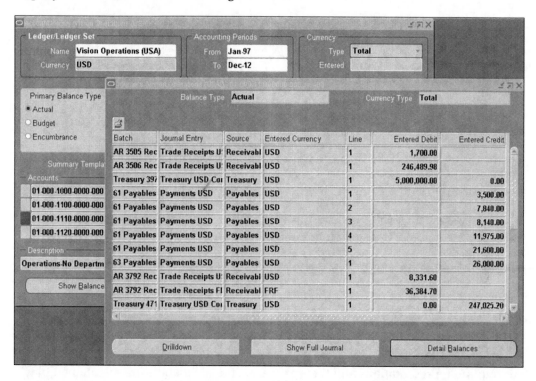

At month-end reconciliation becomes a crucial activity and when information on a specific balance is needed, a drill down to transactions that make up that balance is very helpful. Account Inquiry allows you this functionality to review and manage this need.

E-Business Suite has introduced in 11i (versions after 11.5.10.2 patch), the Account Analysis and Drilldown functions to review balances and drilldown to review detailed transactions.

The following screenshot shows this new functionality also available in R12, along with the added review of the SLA journals that are now part of the subledger to GL transfer:

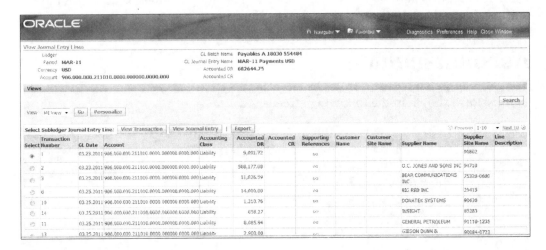

The previous screenshot shows the transaction details from the subledger (Payables in this case) for a given balance. The default view looks different; however, the view can be personalized to include a specific set of columns of data as needed.

In the previous screenshot the columns to the left of **Supporting References** were added by me to make this view more informative.

The **Export** button just above the heading of the lines will export the data to Excel.

Parents, Rollup Groups, and Summary Accounts

Accounting representations and the way transactional balances are maintained play a major role in reporting at the end of a period, quarter, or at year-end.

In E-Business Suite, all balances are maintained for each unique combination of values for the segments in your Chart of Accounts. This leads to a huge number of combinations and extracting and summarizing the data is a monumental task due to the possibility of every combination having a balance.

Balances are maintained in GL for the following dimensions:

- **Currency**: Transacted and Ledger
- **Time**: PTD, QTD, YTD, PJTD
- **Type**: Actual, Budget, Encumbrance
- **Period Type**: User defined (for example, Month), Average Daily

When you enable average balance processing in the General Ledger, the system calculates and stores three aggregate balances for each balance sheet account in your ledger, for every calendar day. The three amounts are the period-to-date, quarter-to-date, and year-to-date aggregate balances. You have to ensure that you also define a daily transaction calendar if you intend to maintain average balances.

Reporting is only done at the most detailed level for exceptional cases and in cases where an in-depth analysis is required. This requirement is met by storing each of the balances at the lowest level of detail.

To enable the capacity to summarize these balances in a manner that is easy to report for both managerial and financial reporting, E-Business Suite has three major functionalities that help in this regard:

- Parent values (with children)
- Rollup groups
- Summary accounts

Parent values are segment values that are a *holder* or *representation* of multiple child values. The parent value is expected to summarize the balances in the child values at run-time. This means that parent values do not hold any balances but calculate them at the time when they are used in a process.

These processes are:

- Financial Statement Generator (FSG) reports
- MassAllocation formulas

These parent and child values need to be managed and maintained as your chart of account segment values change.

 These can be maintained for each segment in your Chart of Accounts.

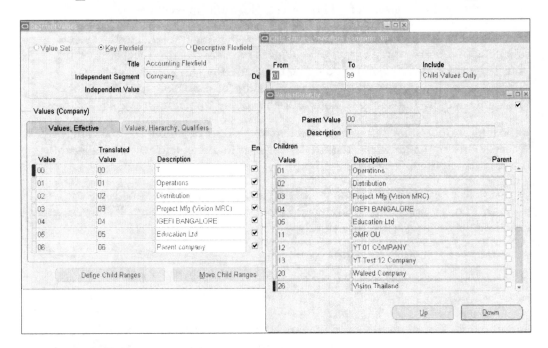

Rollup groups are named parent values that denote an identifier that can be used in the summarization function—summary accounts. These use the parent-child relationship to aggregate summary balances.

Summary accounts actually maintain balances and are the reflection of the rollup groups; these can be used to report and inquire on balances:

- A summary account contains the sum of balances from multiple detail accounts

- It is used to perform online summary inquires, as well as speed the processing of financial reports, mass allocations, and recurring journal formulas

- You can use summary templates to create summary accounts

Summary accounts create an overhead on the journal posting process.

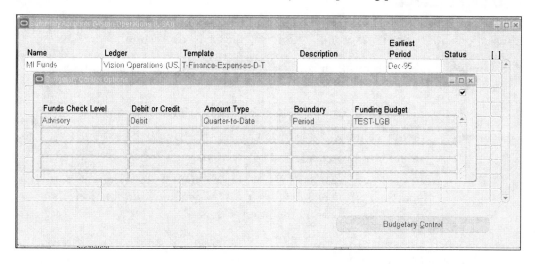

For each segment you can choose from the following options — D-Detail, T-Total, or a Rollup Group.

Detail means that for each of the values in that segment, if there is a transaction the balances will be maintained for each value as a combination of the other segments (which could be Total).

Rollup Group means the same as detail but limited to the segment values in that rollup group.

Total means a summation of the balances for each of the values in that segment.

Topic	Rollups groups	Summary accounts
Balances maintained	No	Yes
Collection of segments	Yes	Yes
Journal Posting impact	No	Yes
Templates	No	Yes
Can Inquire	No	Yes
Can run standard reports	No	Yes
Can run FSG reports	Yes	Yes

Budgeting

E-Business Suite allows budgets to be managed in the same way as normal transactions, for each unique combination of your Chart of Accounts.

You can use summary accounts or rollup groups to manage and maintain budget values:

- Budgets can be directly entered into the application using forms.
- Budget creation requires the creation of the following two elements:
    ◦ Budget Year (can span multiple years).
    ◦ Budget Organization (typically departmental or a group of departments). This will contain all the account combinations that you will create a budget amount for.
- Budgets are not required for all the account combinations, only for those that you need to report budget variances.
- Budgets are managed within Budget Organizations.

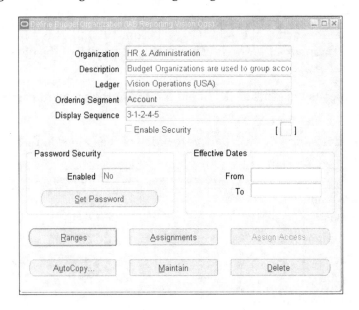

You can also load budgets using Web ADI (a functionality that allows you to manage data using Excel and a plug for Oracle), which will download the Budget and Budget Organization accounts for a span of periods as specified by your template.

	View Context	View Line									
2	Budget	BIS CORPORATE									
3	Organization	Operations									
4	Currency	USD									
5	Period Year		1999								
6	Ledger	Vision Operations (USA)									
7	Data Access Set	Vision Operations (USA)									

Upi Co Dpt Acct Sub Prd	Jan-99	Feb-99	Mar-99	Apr-99	May-99	Jun-99	Jul-99	Aug-99	Sep-99	Oct-99
* List - Account										
01 000 1110 0000 000	-57566.84	9827566.39	-57818.24	-60193.39	-34655.61	0	0	0	0	0
01 000 1120 0000 000	0	0	0	0	0	0	0	0	0	0
01 000 1130 0000 000	0	0	0	0	0	0	0	0	0	0
01 000 1140 0000 000	0	0	0	0	0	0	0	0	0	0
01 000 1150 0000 000	0	0	0	0	0	0	0	0	0	0
01 000 1160 0000 000	0	0	0	0	0	0	0	0	0	0
01 000 1210 0000 000	0	-662960.38	0	0	0	0	5792250.72	1501433.19	0	5818007.15
01 000 1212 0000 000	0	0	0	0	0	0	0	0	0	0
01 000 1220 0000 000	0	0	0	0	0	0	0	0	0	0
01 000 1222 0000 000	0	0	0	0	0	0	0	0	0	0
01 000 1230 0000 000	0	0	0	0	0	0	0	0	0	0
01 000 1231 0000 000	0	0	0	0	0	0	0	0	0	0
01 000 1232 0000 000	0	0	0	0	0	0	0	0	0	0
01 000 1240 0000 000	0	0	0	0	0	0	0	0	0	0
01 000 1245 0000 000	0	0	0	0	0	0	0	0	0	0
01 000 1247 0000 000	0	0	0	0	0	0	0	0	0	0
01 000 1250 0000 000	0	0	0	0	0	0	0	0	0	0
01 000 1260 0000 000	0	0	0	0	0	0	0	0	0	0
01 000 1270 0000 000	0	0	0	0	0	0	0	0	0	0
01 000 1310 0000 000	0	0	0	0	0	0	0	0	0	0
01 000 1332 0000 000	0	0	0	0	0	0	0	0	0	0
01 000 1335 0000 000	0	0	0	0	0	0	0	0	0	0

Multi-currency

E-Business Suite allows users to transact in any currency as long as an exchange rate exists between the transacted currency and the ledger currency.

The ledger currency represents the currency that Oracle General Ledger will maintain balances for your ledger. (This is also referred to as the functional or recording currency.)

When a transaction is entered in the ledger currency and the journal is posted, a balance is maintained for the accounts affected in the ledger currency. When a transaction is entered in a currency other than the ledger currency, the transaction is converted to the ledger currency based upon specific exchange rates available and stored in the ledger currency.

Exchange rates can be maintained for each currency rate type, which are user-definable. There are three seeded rate types that exist in the system:

- **Corporate** (a standard rate used throughout the organization typically for a period of time).
- **User** (entered at transaction time by user).

- **Spot** (for the date of the transaction). You can enter additional types as needed.

Currency			Conversion		
From	To	Date	Type	EUR To USD	USD To EUR
EUR	USD	02.28.2011	Balance Sheet Rate Typ	1.3758	.7268498328
EUR	USD	02.28.2011	PandL Rate Type	1.3649	.7326544069
GBP	USD	02.28.2011	Balance Sheet Rate Typ	1.6121	.6203089138
GBP	USD	02.28.2011	PandL Rate Type	1.61204	.6203320017
GBP	USD	01.31.2011	Balance Sheet Rate Typ	1.5858	.6305965443
GBP	USD	01.31.2011	PandL Rate Type	1.57599	.6345217927
GBP	USD	11.21.2008	Balance Sheet Rate Typ	1.78	.5617977528
GBP	USD	11.21.2008	PandL Rate Type	1.86	.5376344086

Enter by Date Range...

Here are the three essential terminologies that you need to understand that relate to multi-currency processing and their distinct differences:

- **Conversion**: Refers to foreign currency transactions that are immediately converted at the time of entry to the ledger's currency.

- **Revaluation**: A process that adjusts specific asset or liability accounts, which may be materially understated or overstated due to a significant fluctuation in the exchange rate between when the transaction was entered and the time revaluation takes place. Revaluation is primarily performed at period-end.

- **Translation**: A process that restates an entire ledger or balances for a company from the ledger currency to another currency. The cumulative translation adjustment is typically recorded as part of equity. Translation is also primarily done at period-end; revaluation is performed before a translation to accurately state balances in the required currencies.

For translation to work we need to define an average rate for P and L Accounts and a period-end rate for Balance Sheet accounts. This has now all been collapsed into the **Daily Rates** form.

> In earlier versions there was a separate form that managed the rates used for translation; that form and functionality are not used anymore.

Enter historical rates if there is a need to represent a balance for a specific account at a fixed rate.

The Currency Rates Manager enables managing all your currency rate information in one place. You can:

- Enter Daily Rates.
- Upload Daily Rates or Historical Rates from a spreadsheet to the Oracle General Ledger.
- Download Historical Rates to a spreadsheet. You can download for review only or update. If you update, you modify the Historical Rates in the spreadsheet and upload to the Oracle General Ledger.
- Review Period Rates and historical rates using a web interface.
- Create Cross Rates. Cross rates are calculated conversion rates based on defined currency rate relationships. The General Ledger will calculate cross rates based on a Cross Rate Rule you define.

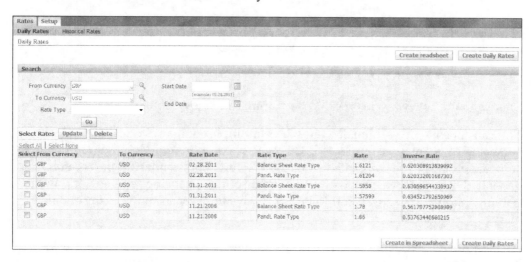

Consolidations

Consolidation is a process that gathers data from various ledgers into a single ledger for reporting and other related processes. In many cases companies use multiple ledgers for various reasons and at the end of the period will want to consolidate them to report in a combined manner in a single currency.

The multiple ledgers could be in different currencies and that would involve additional processes before consolidation can be completed.

The following figure is a pictorial of the tasks before you can consolidate and report:

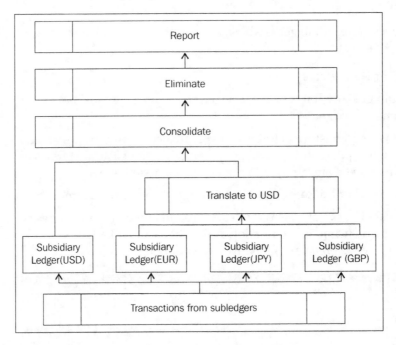

There are multiple ways to consolidate within E-Business Suite.

You can consolidate within a ledger, where multiple company codes (normally balancing segments) are transacted. This type of consolidation does not require a separate process to be completed prior to reporting. The standard reports can be generated to show fiscal reports for each value of the balancing segment, and with parent/child values and/or rollup groups with summary accounts a consolidated view can be generated.

Across multiple ledgers: This type of consolidated reporting requires four tasks before consolidated reporting can be performed. They are as follows:

- Revaluation
- Translation
- Consolidation
- Eliminations

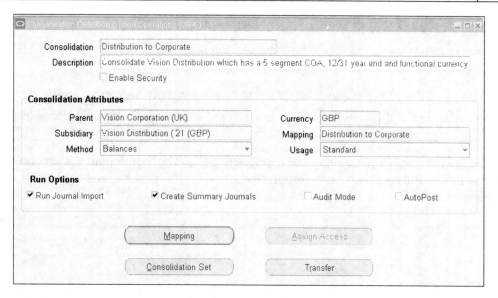

When you define a consolidation you need to define a mapping for how you want to bring the balances (or transactions) over to the Consolidated Ledger (Parent Ledger).

E-Business Suite provides two ways to map the account balances over from a Subsidiary Ledger to a Parent Ledger. They are as follows:

- Segment Rules
- Account Rules

Account Rules: These are used when you map full segment combinations to a different segment combination. This is normally used when you are mapping between ledgers having different charts of accounts.

Segment Rules: These are used when you have to copy or specifically move a set of values for each segment for your charts of accounts. In this case you have multiple options for how you want to derive the segment in your Parent Ledger.

You can choose one of the following (for each segment):

- **Copy Value From**: This is used when you are copying all values from the subsidiary to the parent for a segment
- **Assign Value**: When you are not receiving any value in this segment from the Subsidiary and would like to assign a single value for this segment in the parent ledger
- **Use Rollup Rules from**: Complex consolidations where you are grouping multiple ranges of values from your subsidiary to single parent segment value

Intercompany

There are two ways to manage intercompany transactions in E-Business Suite. They are as follows:

- Within a single ledger with differences in the balancing segment values
- Among multiple ledgers (which will also be managed with differences in balancing segment values)

In the ASM there is a place where you will define the relationship and the accounts to use for the intercompany transactions to be balanced for each given balancing segment value.

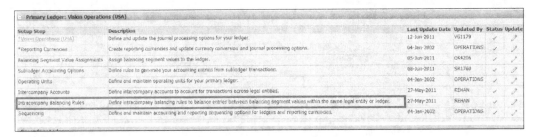

You must define intra-company rules for each legal entity in your ledger.

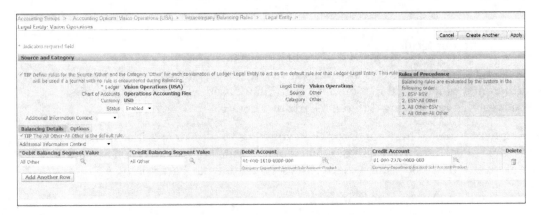

The rule enables automatic inter-company clearing accounts among different balancing segment values. The posting program performs the task of creating additional lines to ensure that each of the balancing segment values can generate an accurate Trial Balance report.

These rules also work for transactions being posted from either AP, AR, or any other subledger, as long as a rule is defined for the source and category combination.

 Using the **Category Other** manages to include all categories from that source in the rule. Using **All Other** in the **Debit** or **Credit Balancing Segment** value includes all values in that ledger.

You can also choose to use a fixed balancing segment value, or have a user-entered clearing balancing segment value.

Advanced Global Intercompany System (AGIS)

AGIS allows you to create, reconcile, and settle intercompany transactions between two legal entities.

This is just a nomenclature to differentiate the transactions that occur between balancing segment values and between legal entities.

The benefit in using AGIS is that you can create AP and AR invoices based on your business needs. If you use the intracompany rules set up as part of the ASM, you cannot create AP or AR invoices for the intercompany transaction.

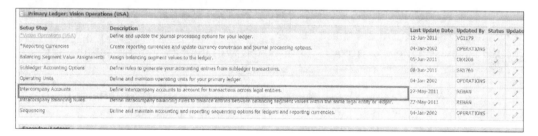

You have to set up the intercompany relationships in the ASM—between legal entities—before you start your AGIS setups. You can also perform these setups from the AGIS responsibility.

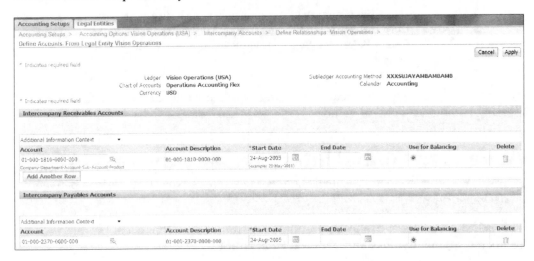

Defining the organization that will connect to an Operating Unit and a legal entity, gives you the basis for inter-legal entity intercompany transactions and related activities such as: invoicing (needs the Operating Unit), transaction creation, review, approval, and reconciliation.

When defining a security for the AGIS you define a combination of an employee, their E-Business Suite user account, and the relevant intercompany organization. This enables them to approve and transact for their organization.

It is required to have an employee (with an Oracle user account) to initiate an intercompany transaction. These are termed outbound transactions.

The transaction can only be amongst ledgers and between two legal entities. You can also specify if the transaction will generate Payables and Receivables invoices.

Your **Home** tab for an inter-company user shows notifications for approval/activity.

The following screenshot shows the main screen that is displayed when you choose the AGIS responsibility:

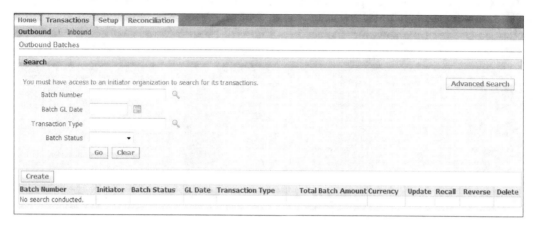

Financial reporting

Standard reports in E-Business Suite do not provide for an income statement or balance sheet. This is facilitated by the Financial Statement Generator (FSG). FSG functionality normally generates output in text format, but with the introduction of BI (XML) Publisher you have the capability to generate these reports in PDF, Excel, and HTML.

Financial Statement Generator (FSG) enables a column and a row combination to generate a report. Primarily the rows show all the data elements and the column can be used for identifying the period for which you are reporting.

One important thing to note is that FSG can only report on GL balances, so the rows will—in most cases—contain a GL Account string (your Account Flexfield segments) and the columns contain a period identifier. This would give you a monthly column for say the balance in your cash account.

Row definition

Rows are used to identify the account balances that would be shown in the report. The following screenshot shows the row definition screen where you can define the characteristics of the row and the account that will be shown.

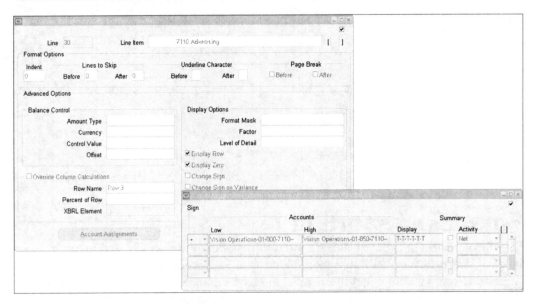

In the Row Set some of the fields can be explained as follows:

- **Line Number** for each row for internal identification.

- **Format Options** allow you to use characters to underline or number of lines you want to skip.

- **Balance Control Options**: This primarily used in the column set — Amount Type, Currency, Control Value, Offset.

- **Display Options**: Format Mask to show how the number will be displayed — with or without decimals or commas, and so on.

- **Factor**: This can be used to reduce the display size of the amount by choosing Thousands, and so on.

- **Level of Detail**: Three levels of detail are available — Financial Analyst, Supervisor, and Controller. Shows varying level of detail of the report based on what is chosen.

- **Display Row**: This should be checked if you want to display this row on the report.

- **Display Zero**: To display the row even if all the balance values retrieved are zero.

- **Change Sign**: Change sign of the value in the balances column for example, Revenue amounts always are credit balances that show up as negative number. You may want to show positive numbers on the report.

- **Change Sign on Variance**: Same as the previous, but on variance only.

- **Row Name**: You can name the row for easier identification.

- **Percent of Row**: Calculates the display in this row based on another row (specified here) as a percentage.

Account Assignments button at the bottom of the row definition form allows you to specify the accounts that the report will use to retrieve data from the GL Balances table. In the account assignments screen, not specifying a Ledger allows the row set definition to be used across ledgers.

The options are available to show **Total**, **Expand**, or **Both**. **Expand** is used if the segment value is a parent/rollup. You can also use **Both** for this type so that it will expand all the values in that parent and show a total. **Total** is used to display only one line item as a total.

Columns

The column is typically used to identify the time element for a report – so the column would show the account balance for a period (based on the intersection of the row and the column). The following screenshot shows the column definition screen. The column can also specify the Ledger that you want to report the balance for. If left blank it allows for the column definition to be used across ledgers.

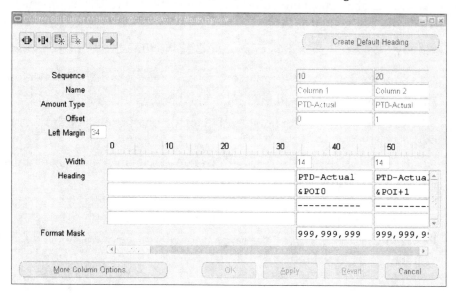

The Column Set has the same characteristics as the Row Set. The Column Builder is also available as a graphical view of the form.

Balance Control Options:

- **Amount Type**: This is used to identify the type of balance (Actual, Budget, and Encumbrance) and the term of the balance (PTD, YTD, QTD, and so on).

- **Currency**: Currency of the balances that you want to report on (can be used on the Row if reporting STAT balances.

- **Control Value**: If a budget is used this is where you would define a Control Value equal to the number of the Control Value definition form, defined as part of the report.

- **Offset**: If the reporting is in columnar format for multiple time periods then you specify each column as an offset from the period you are running for. In the previous screenshot the column 1 is 0, which means it is the period you are running for, **Offset 1** is the next month and so on. If you want the previous month you would use -1.

You can use these additional features to control how the amount is displayed on each row/column.

Content Sets

Content Sets are used to reduce the data content displayed on a report. An example would be if you had a standard report showing the Income Statements for all companies and departments; you would use Content Sets to restrict companies and departments on the report.

Content Sets can be used to manage this without having to write another report:

- **N (No Override)**: Use the display option you entered in the row set definition.
- **RE (Row Expand)**: Expand the range and display all segment values.
- **RT (Row Total)**: Total the range and display only the total for the segment values.
- **RB (Row Both)**: Expand and total the range displaying each segment value and the total for the segment values
- **CT (Column Total)**: Total the range and display only a total for the segment values. This option has no effect on the appearance of your report.
- **PE Report Expand**: Expand the range and create a separate report for each segment value in the range.

- **PT Report Total**: Override the row set segment value range but retain the Expand, Total, or Both display.

 The row options—RE, RT, and RB—are the same as the Expand, Total, and Both options in the row set.

Row Order

Row Order allows control of the correct information displayed for a chart of accounts – Segment Value and Description. In each row, appropriate use of a row order will show segment values and/or description.

The width defines what is displayed on the report.

Report Manager

The capability to generate Excel based reports using Desktop ADI has been discontinued in the R12. Web ADI has replaced Desktop ADI. Web ADI does not allow for reporting functionality like Desktop ADI did. Reporting has been introduced in a new product called the Report Manager.

The concept of the Report Manager is simple and at the same time completely changes what was possible using Desktop ADI. The Report Manager introduced the concept of a single source of truth for reporting.

The Report Manager changes the concept of reporting and availability of data. It allows you to generate a financial report and store it in the database for easy and viewing availability to multiple users. You can generate this for multiple months and it is static (unless regenerated), and can be viewed by multiple users.

Functionality within the Report Manager allows you to create menu/function links to the report stored in the database and assign it to a responsibility for access to users. The functionality also allows you to generate and publish reports that span a period of time (say Jan thru Dec) and allows the user to choose from a LoV to review the periods they need.

There is additional capability within the Report Manager to secure access to viewing reports.

Oracle Web ADI

Web ADI allows for a smoother implementation of the excel integration and a central control instead of on every desktop. There are a couple of settings in Excel (like the old ADI) and in Internet Explorer (new settings) to enable the functionality to work smoothly.

Web ADI can be used to create journal entries and to download and upload Budget data.

For Oracle Web ADI to work with the new functionality you must change some configurations in Excel and IE.

The next section consists of a couple of steps that need to be taken to ensure that Web ADI will work as expected.

Settings in Excel and Internet Explorer for Web ADI

Here is how you would set the properties to be able to use Web ADI to allow you to create the template.

In Excel 2003 follow the given steps:

1. **Tools | Options**.
2. Click on the tab for **Security**.
3. Click on the button labeled **Macro Security**.
4. Ensure the radio button is set to **Medium**.
5. This will always prompt you to enable or disable macros.
6. Click on the tab **Trusted Publishers** and make sure both the checkboxes at the bottom are checked.

In Excel 2007 follows the given steps:

1. Click on the Microsoft home logo and then click on **Excel Options**.
2. On the left-hand sidebar click on **Trust Centre**.
3. Click on **Trust Centre Settings....**
4. Click on **Macro Settings**.
5. Ensure the **Disable all macros with notification** is chosen.
6. Ensure the **Trust access to VBA project object mode** is checked.

Setting in Internet Explorer that is needed to have Web ADI working properly follow the given steps:

1. Click on the **Tools | Internet Options**.
2. Click on the **Security** tab.
3. Click on **Custom level...**.
4. Ensure that the option for **Allow status bar updates** is set to **Enable**.

Summary

What we just finished was the base framework for the E-Business Suite Applications where we discussed an overview of a legal entity and how it constitutes a component for the ledger define process. We also took a peek at the Accounting Setup Manager and highlighted some of the new aspects of the configuration as it differs from previous releases. We also covered some transactional aspects that are essential in understanding the usage of the General Ledger.

In the next chapter, we will discuss the new Subledger Accounting (SLA) engine with emphasis on components, how to use it, and accounting reports.

3

Subledger Accounting (SLA)

Release 12 E-Business Suite introduced the user to a new centralized function called Subledger Accounting (SLA) that works together with Oracle's General Ledger (GL) to provide an integrated accounting methodology. The new centralized accounting architecture addresses the concurrent needs for strong internal controls and global accounting treatments. It offers visibility into enterprise-wide accounting information within a single, global accounting repository and user-driven reporting.

Any organization standardizing its accounting policies needs to document the policy, communicate it to those who must apply it, and ensure the standard policy is enforced. Oracle Subledger Accounting (SLA) lends support for these initiatives by formalizing these and formulating global accounting policies into centralized accounting rules.

SLA is complementary to the account generation tools you may have run on earlier releases of Oracle E-Business Suite. So if you currently use Auto Accounting or Workflow Account Generator for account generation and upgrade to Release 12, you'll be able to continue to use the old methodology until you choose to migrate fully to SLA.

Oracle Subledger Accounting, in combination with Oracle Financial Services Accounting Hub, enables you to centralize accounting data from any third-party transactional system. Together they offer an open repository and a centralized accounting engine for transactional data from third-party sources.

SLA offers a flexible methodology to generate accounting entries by making it possible for the user to configure accounting rules based on virtually any attribute of a transaction.

As an example:

- An expense account for a payables invoice could be derived based on any attribute of that invoice including item, item type, or PO distribution
- The liability account can be based on the supplier, or even broken down into multiple liability accounts by supplier site
- A deferred revenue account on a receivables transaction can be broken down by different lines of business based on the nature of the revenue derived from a Descriptive Flexfield
- You can even define conditional rules such as recording customer invoices to different receivables accounts based on the credit risk of a customer

SLA provides the ability to define accounting rules that derive an entire account combination from various transaction attributes, or you can define separate rules to derive individual segment values of an account combination, or anything in between.

Journal and journal line descriptions are also user-configurable so that you can include any piece of transaction information in them.

In effect the actual accounting entry is created as part of the SLA and not what is specifically entered in the transaction; if you have not modified your SLA rules then what you have entered in the transaction is the default and will also be the accounting entry.

Here is a list of bulleted advantages that SLA provides at a high level that will be addressed in this chapter:

- Controls
    - Online Accounting (Create Accounting from transaction)
    - Preview Accounting (Draft Accounting)
    - Controlled Accounting (Control Accounts)
    - Streamlined Accounting (Replacement Account)

- Accounting Policy Management
    - Comprehensive Accounting (checks for unposted items before closing)
    - Accurate Accounting (reduce reclass by using rules in SLA)
    - Using rules to create two sets of accounting representations for a single transaction
    - Configuration options for SLA processes

- Other functions that are managed in SLA (New functions)

    ° Open Balances Listing (Third Party)
    ° Supporting References
    ° Accounting Reports
    ° Secondary and Reporting Ledgers (different from MRC)

We will now look at the details of how each of these major advantages/benefits is implemented and how to use them.

If you enter a journal in the Subledger Accounting level you have to transfer that to GL as though it has been a transaction created in AP or AR.

Controls

The following section will elaborate on the aspects of each of the topics bulleted earlier and briefly explain how these functionalities can help achieve the controls for your enterprise.

Online Accounting

In the previous versions different processes accounted transactions in each subledger. Changes to accounting entry generating processes were difficult to make, manage, and maintain. In the introduction of Account Generator (part of Workflow) in Release 11, the capability to modify account generation was eased to a certain extent, but this did not encompass all accounting creation processes.

The intention to have a single store of accounting truth and capability led Oracle to release as part of R12, a rules based engine for accounting and a data store, Subledger Accounting (SLA).

In previous releases of Accounts Payable you could see the accounting as you entered them on a transaction line; however, other subledgers may generate these in the background without any specific input from a user. These default accounting representations are more generic and based on configuration options.

Frequently, there are requirements to make changes to the Subledger Accounting (SLA) Rules. If you have not chosen to modify the SLA Rules, then the accounting you see on the Accounts Payable transaction will be the same when you run the Create Accounting process. Using SLA Rules you can choose to modify the outcome of the eventual accounting based on other transactional criteria. These changes are reflected in the SLA level (a new level of journals between Accounts Payable and General Ledger).

These SLA changes are not reflected back to the subledger transaction.

You can choose to view these online when completing/saving your transaction so that you are sure the accounting is accurate. These will only be created once you run the process Create Accounting. This process can be initiated for a single transaction from the entry screen.

Preview Accounting

To ensure that these modifications were right and that other derivation rules are working as expected you can run **Create Accounting** in Draft mode, either from the transaction screen (in all subledgers) or from the standard request run process.

If you run the process in Draft mode, then you are unable to transfer the transaction to GL.

You will see all the relevant accounts in the various lines, but these will only be in the subledger.

The following figure shows the progression of the transactional data flow from the subledger to GL in Release 12:

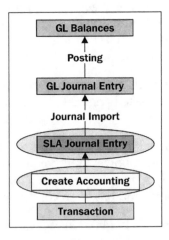

Control accounts

By designating an account as a **control account**, you can prevent manual journals from being transacted using these accounts in GL. You can also designate the control account to be a Supplier/Customer control to disallow entries from being imported from subledgers normally not expected to transact these accounts.

For example, it can prevent the supplier liability account from being updated by the Receivables subledger. This preventive measure can dramatically reduce reconciliation activity during the period-end close.

Additionally, this feature supports tracking of and reporting on control accounts for trading partners, so you can track receivables balance by customer, or payables balance by supplier, by choosing Supplier (or Customer) as a third-party control type. You can also choose **Restrict Manual** to just restrict manual journal entries in GL.

Streamlined Accounting

As is true in many cases there are various reasons when either a segment value or the combination using a segment value is end-dated. In R12 when you end-date a segment value—with the new cascade functionality—it can also end-date the combination(s) that use that segment value. This is not an automatic process, but is propagated by the Segment Value Inheritance Program.

Accounting Policy Management

There are management initiatives that would be best served if these were tightly integrated with the transactional system. The following tasks highlight these aspects to ensure that this control is enforced.

Comprehensive Accounting

In pre-R12 versions the subledgers all transferred to GL and the balancing lines were created after they were transferred to GL. The balancing transactions were primarily a GL activity. Thus, if you had intercompany transactions you would not see the balancing entries in the subledgers. This has changed in R12 and the balancing entries are created in the SLA, which is part of the subledgers.

Access to the SLA journal functionality is through the subledgers and not the GL. You do not have a separate product (or responsibility) that allows access to the SLA; there are functions within the subledger products that allow access to the relevant capabilities, forms, and reports in SLA.

You cannot close the subledgers unless these SLA journals have also been transferred to GL. A new report, Subledger Period Close Exceptions Report, highlights these stuck transactions. This report shows transactions that are pushed form the subledger to the SLA level, but have not made it to the GL. You need to run the Transfer to GL process to transfer them to GL.

Accurate Accounting

Multiple cases exist, and with good reason; to manage accounting due to configuration shortcomings as a default representation and perform reclass activities at the end of the period to achieve accurate accounting representation. This is always the most time consuming part of a close process. The transaction is not the time consuming part; identifying the transactions that effect the balance and need the reclass takes up the most time.

There is always a specific transactional element that is the driver for the reclass entry. Either it is the third party (Customer or Supplier), or the type of transaction, or some other data element on the transaction. With SLA you can now use these data elements to drive the accounting to what it should be, without having to wait for period-end and reclass these transactions in GL.

 Reclass transactions can still be done; however, the transaction drill-down from the balances to the originating subledger will be an issue.

Configuration options for SLA processes

Subledger Accounting rules engine capability. It allows users to see the rules visually in a logical format and make changes easily. Easier is a relative term and helps denote the ease as opposed to managing change with pre-R12 versions.

The following figure shows the progression of the various data elements that help build the accounting engine rules. It shows the names and the abbreviations commonly used within the E-Business Suite world so you can be familiar with these in various documents and knowledge repositories.

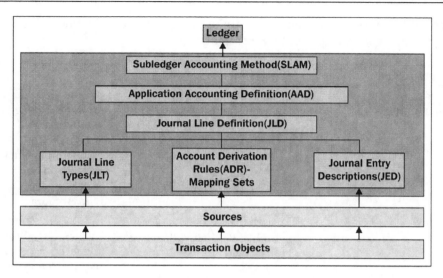

You use the **Accounting Methods Builder (AMB)** to manage your accounting policies and rules, to help build accounting entries that you want to support your business and reporting needs. If you do not have any specific needs then the existing Subledger Accounting Method (SLAM) is sufficient to manage your accounting needs. The standard method (SLAM) for US GAAP is Standard Accrual.

You cannot modify the seeded rules that come with the E-Business Suite implementation; however, you can copy a component, and make changes to it so that it reflects your rules.

Each component has its use and the following list presents a brief description of what each one represents and how it may be used.

Oracle provides seeded events (Payable Invoice, Payable Payments), Event Class (Invoice, Credit Memo), and Event Types (Creation, Cancelation). In most cases these will cover all the Transactions that you will perform. These are called Transaction Objects in the previous figure.

The second layer consists of sources, again pre-seeded for all E-Business Suite subledgers that generate accounting information.

Data type name	Acronym	Description	Use
Account Derivation Rules	ADR	Defines accounts affected: either a single segment, set of segments, or all segments of your Chart of Accounts.	A value that you use for a specific segment in a transaction. Assign the cost center value from the detail transaction line in Assets to the Gain-Loss Account.
Mapping Set		Useful in assigning values to input values that will be used in an ADR.	If you have values such as East, West, and so on, assign a segment value for each.
Journal Line Type	JLT	This element drives how the transaction is built, balance type, side (debit/credit).	Debit or Credit side, Actual or Budget Balance, posting in summary.
Journal Entry Description	JED	Defines what descriptions are pulled to the Header and Line of the journal from the subledger transaction.	Invoice#, Supplier Name, Supplier Site, Transaction Date.
Journal Line Definition	JLD	Manages to bring together all your rules from the previous elements and assigns to an event (transaction).	Need a new one if you change anything.
Accounting Application Definition	AAD	Collate all events for a specific application, for example, Payables.	Need a new one if you change anything.
Subledger Accounting Method	SLAM	Assigns the collection of Application Accounting Definitions for all subledgers to a Ledger.	Need a new one if you change anything.

Additional functions

With the introduction of the new functionality with Subledger Accounting, E-Business Suite has also introduced some new features that enable additional reporting capability and allow for additional capture of data and also enable managing various accounting reports within the SLA.

Configuration

The Create Accounting program submission can be tailored to be specific for each subledger as shown in the following screenshot. This is done in the Accounting Setup Manager (ASM) and is part of your Ledger configuration.

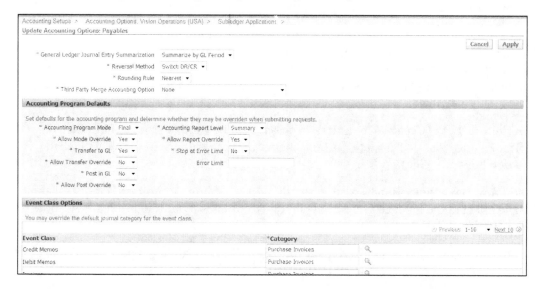

A detailed explanation of what each option on this form means is elegantly provided in the Subledger Accounting Implementation Guide Part No. E13628-04.

This form allows you to control how the Journal entries are created in GL and the default parameters for the Create Accounting Program.

Oracle E-Business Suite has many sources of data that it uses internally to manage accounting representations for transactions. These are rules that majority of the enterprises use to manage their accounting needs. However, when these do not cover requirements in your business SLA's open design perspective and delivery method offers you an opportunity to make modifications to these standard rules.

E-Business Suite provides a method to create Custom Sources to capture these assigning data elements and use them in the SLA rules to drive your accounting representations for a transaction. This change allows you to support the needs and requirements of your enterprise.

Open Balances Listing

In earlier releases the Accounts Payables Trial Balance was generated within a single program at the time of running the Accounts Payables Trial Balance report. It is now generated from the SLA so that the accounting basis is true and accurate and is generated from the central data store, the single source of truth.

A new definition has been introduced to configure and manage data in this report. You can specify a format (BI Publisher) and report definition (Open Balances Listing definition) when you run the AP Trial Balance report. The report definition has the details regarding which account to record (normally AP Trade) and which source (normally Payables).

In Release 12 the Create Accounting Process must be run prior to running the AP Trial Balance and you update the GL Balance and the balance in the subledger to review for reconciliation.

You now have the option to ease reconciliation to include other Journal Sources that have affected the balance of your AP Trade Account as a parameter on the Accounts Payable Trial Balance report.

The definition of what should appear on your AP Trial Balance report (AP Trade Account) is part of the report definition.

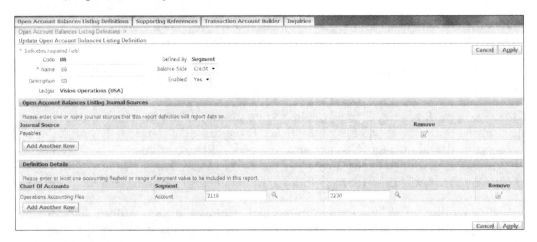

Supporting References

E-Business Suite has introduced a new concept, Supporting References, in Release 12 as part of the SLA functionality that allows for inclusion of additional sources of data elements to maintain balances.

As an example you might want to add a Descriptive Flexfield (DFF) to the AP Distributions form and would then use Supporting References in SLA to maintain balances for each unique value of that DFF.

In addition to having an AP Trial Balance based on your AP Trade Account, you could also have a similar report for each unique value of this DFF. This is maintained in the SLA and is capable of being defined as a rolling balance or one that clears at year-end.

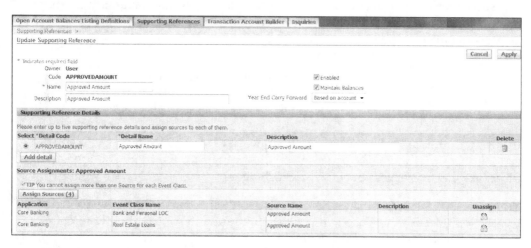

Accounting Reports

All accounting reports now are generated from the SLA. Even though you will see accounting entry related data in the transactions, they are not used for the accounting reports. These are now defaults to the Subledger Accounting Engine (SLA Engine).

If you do not make any changes to your SLA rules these default accounts become your accounting entries in the SLA, which are subsequently transferred to GL.

Since all accounting reports are now generated at the SLA level, changes to SLA rules do not impact Oracle's single source of truth for accounting. Almost all reports that are now generated from SLA are generated using BI Publisher. So these reports can be modified to be generated in PDF or Excel with ease. Further, there is an enormous amount of data in the XML extracts for these reports and the template designates what data you see.

 Data is not populated in the report unless the Create Accounting process has been run for the specific subledger. This process creates the accounting entries in the SLA layer.

Subledger journal entries

You can create journal entries in the subledger level manually. This is an additional method to create journal entries that will generate balances for your accounts. Ideally, accounting transactions (accounting representations of your subledger transactions) will normally be generated based on the Create Accounting program from your subledger transaction.

The subledger layer is an additional transaction layer with the capability to enter manual journals. These will then be transferred and posted to your general ledger as part of your month-end processing.

 These subledger journals are not in your General Ledger and do not effect balances. They will only affect the balances once they are transferred to General Ledger and the journal is posted.

E-Business Suite provides the capability to restrict access to ledgers where you can transact these manual entries. Review the options for the profile option, **SLA: Enable Data Access Security in Subledgers**.

You can also assign Supporting References based on your configuration to these transactions at this time. Based on your configuration the Supporting References can be assigned at header or line level.

 You cannot manually assign Supporting References to journal transactions from the subledger.

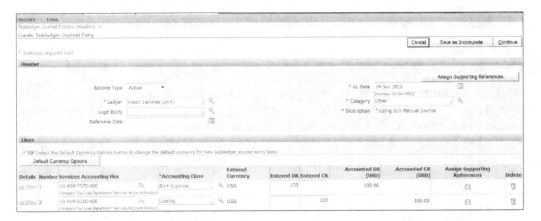

You cannot assign any Supporting References that maintain balances at the header level.

It is recommended that you enter manual journal entries for your primary and secondary ledgers only. Manual journal entries created in the Primary ledger are automatically posted to the reporting ledgers.

Account Inquiry

The Account Inquiry capability has been changed to now use a new form that was introduced in Release 11*i*; you can still use the older form for Account Inquiry but once you start the drill-down process and have to pass through the Subledger Accounting layer, the form shows the java screen as opposed to the standard grey/blue form.

When inquiring on balances you can choose to use the inquiry form or the new Account Inquiry and Drilldown feature to view balances, and drill down to the subledger journals and then to the subledger transactions.

E-Business Suite provides functionality to add predefined fields to your results that show transaction details from the subledger transaction (AP Invoice Number, Supplier Name, Supplier Site, and so on). The default view only shows a certain set of fields, which may be inadequate for many users.

With the export function on the view balances and subledger transactions screen it is easy to generate a download file that can be used as a report, for your balances and related transaction data.

The following screenshot shows an updated view to review transaction data that makes up the balance for the account shown in the header with subledger detail. The **Export** button above the detail panel can be used to download the data in Excel.

Reporting Sequence

E-Business Suite provides a method to manage sequence numbering on journal entry transactions to enable compliance with statutory requirements where all transactions need to be sequenced without gaps.

This was managed with a sequence and an assignment to Journal Categories in previous versions. That functionality has changed; however, R12 contains an additional functionality with sequences assigned to the transactions in SLA.

E-Business Suite now assigns two sequences to journal entries:

- Accounting Sequence is assigned to all journal transactions in the Subledger Accounting layer, when the status is set to **Final**. The Accounting Date (GL Date) is the criterion for determining the sequence to be used.

- Reporting Sequence is assigned to both subledger journal entries and general ledger journal entries when the GL period is closed. The program that assigns the sequences to the transactions is automatically submitted when you close a General Ledger period.

    Reporting sequences are optional.

One important aspect that is new is the capability to alter sequences if they are found to have been incorrectly applied to transactions. A specific process needs to be run that will undo the assigned sequences and then re-apply them after the relevant changes.

Important SLA profile options

Some important profile options are shown here, with explanations of how they affect the processing in E-Business Suite:

- **SLA: Disable Journal Import**: The preferred setting for this profile option is **Yes**. This indicates that Journal Import *always* accompanies the transfer of data from Subledger. Another implication of this value is that, on failure of Journal Import, the data will be rolled back to SLA tables and will not have any resultant hanging data in GL_INTERFACE. Setting this to **No** is not recommended. If this is set to **No** the process will work as in pre-R12 versions and the Journal Import process will need to be manually submitted.

- **SLA: Initial Date for Historical Upgrade**: When upgrading you must determine the initial period to be upgraded. Before running any SLA post-upgrade process you must enter the initial date to be used in the **SLA: Initial Date for Historical Upgrade** profile option.

Summary

In this chapter we discussed Subledger Accounting, covering the components, how to use these components, and what they impact.

We also looked briefly at the controls that SLA provides for accounting Policy Management in a single place, and the additional functionality introduced in R12 including Account Inquiry, drilldown, and the new face of reporting from the SLA.

In the next chapter, you will learn about organizations, items, manufacturers, and so on.

4
Inventory

Inventory means a list compiled for formal transactional purposes. In the U.S. and Canada the term has developed from a list of goods and materials, especially those available in stock by a business. In accounting, inventory or stock is an asset.

The scope of inventory management concerns the fine lines between replenishment lead time, carrying costs of inventory, asset management, inventory forecasting, inventory valuation, inventory visibility, future inventory price forecasting, physical inventory, available physical space for inventory, quality management, replenishment, returns and defective goods, and demand forecasting.

It also involves systems and processes that identify inventory requirements, set targets, provide replenishment techniques, report actual and projected inventory status, and handle all functions related to the tracking and management of materials. This would include the monitoring of material moved into and out of stockroom locations and the reconciling of the inventory balances.

In this chapter, we are going to cover primarily the purchasing, receiving, stocking, and shipping of goods and their accounting impact, and how these are configured to be easily transacted. We will not be covering any specific manufacturing related functionality or tasks.

Here is what we will cover:

- What is an organization?
- How does it affect E-Business Suite framework?
- What is needed to use it for transactions?
- Items and related setups
- Which transactions types use an inventory organization?
- Accounting impact from inventory

Organizations

E-Business Suite uses many types of organizations. These are important to the framework and functionality of E-Business Suite. The following is an example of an organization hierarchy. The organization is a data entity that is truly owned by the HR application/module in E-Business Suite, but if HR is not fully installed, that is you are not using Oracle HR, it gets installed in a shared mode. In this situation most people use the Inventory module to access, create, modify, and maintain organizations. If you had HR installed and were using Oracle HR you would not use this function from Inventory.

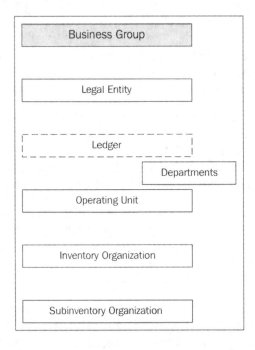

The previous figure is a linear depiction of how organizations are used within E-Business Suite. The following points explain in a little detail what each element means and how it is used:

- The **Business Group** is a default (with the same name) provided on installation and you do not need to create a new one; you can use this default and change the name if needed. No functionality is affected if you change the name. You can create additional business as needed by your enterprise.

The only reason to create a new Business Group is if you intend to use Payroll for different countries.

- The **Legal Entity** is the next level of the organization hierarchy. This was a placeholder in previous versions but has taken on a significant importance in R12. You need to define before you start any other configurations for your accounting system. The Legal Entity configuration is described in more detail in *Chapter 2, General Ledger*.

  In prior versions the Legal Entity was only a placeholder and used sparingly for certain reporting tasks/functions. Beginning with R12 the Legal Entity has evolved into a major owner of various data elements. Banks are now managed and owned by a Legal Entity. This will be explained in more detail in *Chapter 8, Cash Management*.

- Even though a **Ledger** is not an organization it made sense to put it into this figure and explain a little about it as it firms up the organizational structure and functionality in the larger scheme of things in E-Business Suite. To enumerate that this is not an organization, the box is a broken line and is in a different color. The next level is **Departments**. That is a slight anomaly, though it is still termed as an organization and is specifically used in Oracle Projects as project organization.

- The **Operating Unit** is an important part of the subledger implementations and drives the ability to separate data at this level for most subledgers. Data entry is managed by being part of an Operating Unit and cannot cross between two Operating Units for transactional functions.

  Prior to R12, the Operating Units were managed as part of a silo and could not be accessed without changing to a different role (responsibility). This was, in many cases, a restriction that was a problem for many businesses. **Multiple Organization Access Control (MOAC)** was introduced in E-Business Suite R12. With MOAC you can access multiple Operating Units (if configured with the appropriate security profiles) when you are logged in with a specific role/responsibility.

 The Operating Unit facilitates configuration of the subledgers, AP, AR, and so on. However, you cannot complete the subledger configurations without defining an **Inventory Organization** which is the next level in the organization hierarchy.

- Inventory organizations are defined to manage stock levels and perform inventory stock movement transactions. Not all stocked inventory is used for shipments (sales order issue), though all items that are stocked have to be received (purchase receipts) into an inventory organization. Inventory organizations enable you to drive stocking items/materials, receiving and managing them, accounting for them, and shipping/issuing them to external or internal groups.

  The capability to stock materials, manage availability levels, ship to external parties, and account for all of these is an inherent Inventory Management task.

  Accounting is generated by Cost Management for all Inventory transactions, including other related manufacturing, plan, and build transactions.

  We will only be covering the receiving and shipment transactions as part of this book. Configuration and accounting impact related to these transactions will also be highlighted and explained.

- You *must* have a location (address) when creating an inventory organization, or any other organization. E-Business Suite does not intrinsically distinguish between a physical and a logical location. This means that it is not a one-to-one relationship and more than one organization can have the same location.

- Subinventories are sublocations within an inventory organization. Typically an inventory organization reflects a physical location of a warehouse or storage facility. Subinventories on the other hand are logical locations within that physical location that help identify specific areas where materials are stored. This is purely a logical definition. You can further segregate this to be more specific by using locators.

Organizations are classified as one of several specific types and their functionality is driven based on these classifications. The following is an abridged list of the classifications. The ones that we will be discussing in this book are highlighted:

- Business Group
- Company Cost Centre
- **GRE/Legal Entity**
- HR Organization
- **Inventory Organization**
- Operating Company
- **Operating Unit**
- Project Expenditure/Event Organization
- Work In Process (WIP) Organization

The classification determines how the organization will be used. Based on these classifications additional details are captured. The differences are too detailed to be described in this book.

> Detailed information is available in Oracle® Human Resources Management Systems, Enterprise and Workforce Management Guide. Part No. E13511-03. Other organization classification and additional information data is available in the relevant user guides where the classification is used.

An inventory organization is used for master data definition (items and related setups). It is also used for relevant configuration to enable transaction processing. Master Data is defined in the master inventory organization (Master Org), such as Items and transaction defaults. The secondary level of inventory organizations used for transactional purposes is an inventory organization (Org or Child Org).

If you were to define an inventory organization for an implementation to use for receiving and shipping transactions, you would in essence define two organizations—a Master Org and a Child Org.

> You can have multiple Master Inventory Organizations within an implementation, but you can have only one Master Org per Child Org.

As you define an inventory organization there are specific parameters required to be captured for the classification you choose. Based on the Inventory organization classification, multiple details are needed to be captured. The following are a few major data components that need to be captured:

- Link to Ledger, Legal Entity, and Operating Unit
- Configure with accounts for transactional defaults

- Configure with costing organization and costing type

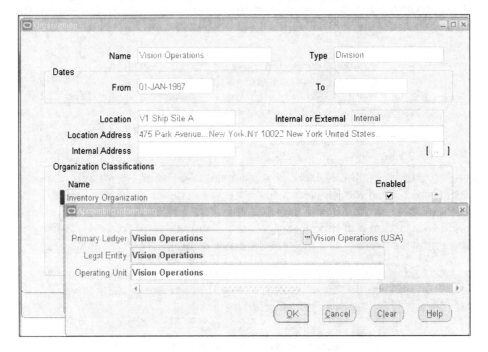

The previous screenshot is a depiction of what is captured when defining an inventory organization to link it to the appropriate primary ledger, legal entity, and operating unit.

With the classification of inventory, the following information (an abridged data set) is captured:

- **General**: This specifies the name of the Org, and the Master organization it is associated with.
- **Costing**: This specifies the Costing method (Standard, Average, FIFO, or LIFO), and related accounts that default to all subinventories and transactions within this Org.
- **Inter-org**: This specifies the default accounts that are related to inter-company transactions. These are however more finitely defined in the shipping networks, which are between specific operating units.
- **Other Accounts**: This is used in related transactions that are performed from within an Inventory.

Items

The Item is a Key Flexfield which means that you can define it in the same way that you can define your Chart of Accounts with multiple segments and values for each if needed. In most cases it is enough to have a single segment where you define that as your Item Flexfield and that also becomes your Item Number.

Items are defined to facilitate transactional and stocking capabilities. They also help identify a specific material/goods item that you will transact repeatedly so you do not have to rely on a description to know what was transacted.

The Item Flexfield is like any other key flexfield and can have multiple segments. When you have multiple segments data entry is inhibited and can be cumbersome; however, the multiple segments allow capture of more than one aspect about the item. There is probably an even split between the use of single versus multiple segments in the Item Flexfield. The usage is eased to a large extent with a single segment.

Item categories

A category is a logical classification of items that have similar characteristics. A category set is a distinct grouping scheme and consists of categories.

Item categories classify items (goods, materials, services, and so on) to ease reporting and accounting derivation and automation. Item categories are normally assigned at the Master level and cascade to all Items in the Child Orgs. You can also choose to assign these categories at the Child Org level.

Item categories are assigned to functional areas as shown in the following screenshot:

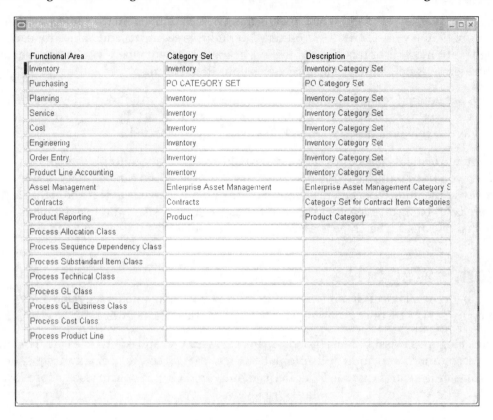

Category Sets are predefined and are assigned to multiple functional areas. The **Inventory Category Set** is assigned as a default to multiple functional areas. This can be changed as part of the configuration step.

Status controls

Items are defined in the master organization only. They have default attributes that apply across the enterprise and are set at the Master level. These are identified as follows:

- **BOM Allowed**: Item allowed to be used in a Bill of Material.
- **Build in WIP**: Item allowed to be used in a Work In Process transaction.
- **Customer Order Enabled**: Item can be ordered on a sales order by a customer.

- **Internal Order Enabled**: Item can be ordered on a sales order by an internal order.
- **Invoice Enabled**: Item can be invoiced. It can be used on an AR Invoice Transaction.
- **Process Execution Enabled**: Item can be used in a process execution transaction.
- **Purchasable**: Item can be used on a Purchase Requisition or Purchase Order transaction.
- **Receipt Enabled**: Item can be received.
- **Stockable**: Item is stockable.
- **Transactable**: Item can be used in a transaction in Inventory.

These attributes are set to true when the status is `active` and set to false when status is set to `inactive`.

Item attributes

There are over 250 attributes for an Item, each specific to a transactional group. These are arranged in logical groups for ease in identifying and managing them. Some of the groups are as follows:

- Main
- Inventory
- Costing
- Order Management
- Invoicing
- Purchasing
- Receiving

Each attribute can be set at either the Master Org or Child Org and for each implementation. Oracle E-Business Suite comes configured with certain default values for each attribute. These default values can be changed as needed to meet the specific business scenario.

Once an Item has been defined at the Master Org level, it must be enabled for transactional purposes in a Child Org. Each Child Org can have transactional differences and these are controlled by specific attributes. Attributes controlled at the Master Org are set to the same value for each Child Org. Attributes controlled at the (Child) Org level can be set for each Child Org.

Items must be received into inventory to stock them. There could be cases where an item is used on a transaction in receiving, but may not be stocked. These could be items such as office furniture, computers, electronics—items that are needed to run any organization. However, to ship any item it must be marked as stocked.

The important attributes, item receipts, stock management, and issue/shipping, that fall under the earlier mentioned groups manage default accounting. We will cover the impact of these attribute settings in *Chapter 5, Purchasing* and *Chapter 10, Order Management*. The following attributes should be considered and reviewed for accurate results:

Tab/Section/Grouping	Item attribute
Main	Unit of Measure, User Item Type, Item Status
Inventory	Inventory Item, Stockable, Transactable, Reservable, Lot Control, Serial Control and Cycle Count
Costing	Costing Enabled, Cost of Goods Sold Account, Inventory Asset Value
Purchasing	Purchased, Purchaseable, Allow Description Update, Expense Account, Asset Category, Purchase and Receiving tolerances, Invoice Matching
Receiving	Receipt Routing, Receiving Subinventory, Allow Substitute Receipts, Allow Express Receipts, Receipt Date - Quantity Controls
Order Management	Customer Ordered, Customer Orders Enabled, Shippable, Internal Ordered, Internal Order Enabled, OE Transactable, Default Shipping Organization, Returnable, RMA Inspection Required, Shipping Sub-Inventory, Shipping and Return tolerances
Invoicing	Invoiceable Item, Invoice Enabled, Sales Account, Invoicing and Accounting Rules

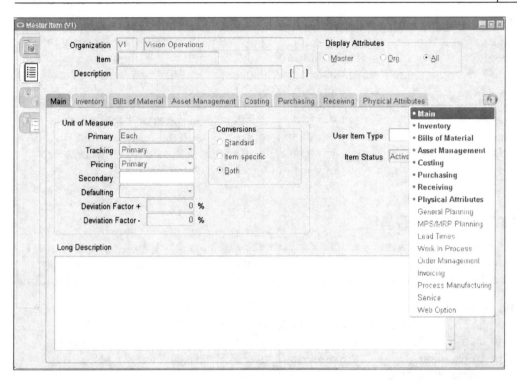

A detailed list of the attribute in each group and their impact is available in the Oracle Inventory User Guide – Part No. E13450-04.

Item defining attributes are specific characteristics that identify the item for a specific functional area and enable transacting in that functional area.

Functional area	Item Defining Attribute
Oracle Inventory	Inventory Item
Oracle Purchasing	Purchased Item, Internal Ordered Item
Oracle Master Scheduling/MRP and Oracle Supply Chain Planning	MRP Planning Method
Oracle Cost Management	Costing Enabled
Oracle Engineering	Engineering Item
Oracle Order Management	Customer Ordered Item
Oracle Service	Support Service, or Serviceable Product
Work In Process	Build in WIP
Bills of Material	BOM Allowed and BOM Type

When you set an item defining attribute to Yes the item is automatically assigned to the default category of the corresponding functional area. For example, if you set **Inventory Item** to Yes the Item is automatically assigned to the default category set for the Inventory functional area. You can also assign multiple categories to an Item.

Item attributes are not easy to manage and maintain; however, with the use of item templates the activity can be eased to a large extent. Having specific item attributes assigned to a template and applying the template to an Item assigns all the attributes to that Item. This ensures that you set all the attributes that you need for that item type, and the attributes for all similar item types are consistent.

Transactions

Oracle Inventory has many transactions that are managed within the product. These transactions are all related to movement of material — receipts into Inventory, issues out of Inventory, or movement within the inventory organizations between locations.

This book will focus on transactions that involve receipts into inventory (purchase receipts) and issues out of inventory (sales order issues). We will also in turn cover material returns both to a supplier and from a customer and related tasks. These transactions will be addressed in *Chapter 5, Purchasing* and *Chapter 10, Order Management* respectively.

Transaction accounting in Oracle Inventory is generated by the Oracle Cost Accounting product and these will be briefly covered.

These accounting transaction created by Cost Accounting are defaults and can be changed using SLA. Please refer to *Chapter 3, Subledger Accounting (SLA)* for details on how the changes can be done.

Transaction configuration

Transactional setup/configuration is an important part of the Inventory configuration steps. The configuration can be classified in the following broad areas:

- **Control Options and Restrictions**: Item revision, locator, lot and serial control, subinventory and locator restrictions, transaction processing mode, transaction managers

- **Processing**: Default subinventory and locators, unit of measure conversions, transaction source types, transaction actions, transaction types, transaction reasons, account aliases, consumption transaction rules, transaction profile options

- **Reporting**: Movement statistics, cycle counts, ABC Analysis

These configurations are enterprise wide and do not specifically affect or relate to any inventory organization and its transactions.

The major transaction sources, types, and actions that we are covering in this chapter (and the book) are already defined and need not be altered or added to. The standard options work well for most companies which process the transactions we intend to cover.

The following list is an abbreviated list of the transaction sources we will cover:

- **Purchase Order Receipt**, will be covered in *Chapter 5, Purchasing*
- **Account Alias Issue**, will be covered in this chapter
- **Return Material Authorization (RMA)**, will be covered in *Chapter 10, Order Management*
- **Sales Order**, will be covered in *Chapter 10, Order Management*
- **Cost Updates**, will be covered in this chapter

There are multiple transaction types that can be performed and they are as follows:

- **Return to Vendor**, will be covered in *Chapter 5, Purchasing*
- **Purchase Order Receipt and Adjustment**, will be covered in *Chapter 5, Purchasing*
- **Sales Order Pick and Issue**, will be covered in *Chapter 10, Order Management*
- **Account Receipt and Issue**
- **Account Alias Receipt and Issue**
- **Standard Cost Update**

A more detailed list of all related Transaction configuration capabilities and their interdependencies are listed in detail in the Inventory User Guide (Part No. E13450-04).

Processing mode configurations are system level configurations that are set for the implementation. These are set normally by a System Administrator at the beginning of the implementation and may be tweaked based on transactional load and other requirements.

These Processing Mode configurations are managed by the following:

- Profile Options
- Transaction Managers

The profile option *INV: Transaction Date Validation* allows transaction dates in past open periods. This is an important option to consider as part of an implementation and when configuring your system.

There are multiple profile options that are related to transaction processing on the forms and allow the user to specify if these transactions should be conducted in online (immediate) or batch mode.

Transaction managers

Transaction managers are background processes that control various aspects of the processing. These are configured by the System Administrator and should not be changed frequently.

These transaction managers cover specific functions within Inventory and a brief explanation of these functions is as follows:

- **Material Transactions**: The material transaction manager immediately executes the material transaction after you save your changes in a transaction window. By starting the transaction manager, you can determine how to effectively show the changes in the balances of your materials in specific locations for reporting purposes.

- **Move Transaction**: The move transaction manager processes move transactions in Oracle Work In Process. You can import move transactions from devices such as portable bar code readers or your custom data entry forms using the open move transaction interface.

- **Resource Cost Transactions**: It is related to the previous manager but addresses the resource allocation and usage for Work In Process transactions.

- **Cost Manager**: The cost transaction manager costs facilitates accounting and is used to create accounting entries.

These transactional managers control specific data flows and can be scheduled at regular intervals. The Material and the Cost transaction managers need to be configured if transactions are generated for non-manufacturing processes such as receiving and shipment processes.

The other two, Resource Cost and Move Transaction Managers, help to process Work In Process related transactions.

Transaction processing

Many transactions are assigned to Inventory by design in the E-Business Suite, but are transacted in other products.

A shipment is normally done on an Order and is part of the transactional flow of an Order being processed. We will briefly touch upon how these are affected by configuration in Inventory, but they will be addressed in more detail in *Chapter 10, Order Management*.

To understand Inventory transactions let us build an example of an organization that has a manufacturing plant and two inventory organizations (and a Master Org), one for **Raw Materials (RAW)** and another for **Finished Goods (FGI)**. These inventory organizations each have multiple subinventories.

For clarity we shall refer to the master as MAS, and the children organizations as FGI and RAW. The subinventory will be assigned to SubInv-FGI1, and so on.

We will assume that both inventory organizations are associated with the same ledger.

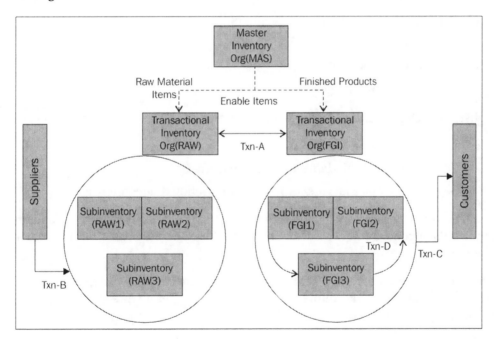

Transactions listed in the previous figure are depicted in this book and reviewed, as per the following information:

- **Txn - A** is an inter-org transfer; this means that materials are being transferred from the FGI to the RAW. Realizing that there are multiple subinventories in each Org, you will need to specify a subinventory when processing this transaction.

- **Txn - B** is a purchasing transaction, a receipt against a purchase order; there could also be a return to vendor.

- **Txn - C** is a shipment transaction that would be processed as part of an order fulfillment and the material is shipped to a customer; there could also be a return from a customer that will also be processed in reverse.

- **Txn - D** is a transfer between subinventories within an inventory organization. If there is a reason to transfer between subinventories in different inventory organizations you will use **Txn - A**.

The following are some reasons to have two inventory organizations from a business perspective:

- Different accounts for material valuation
- Different values (cost/price) for an Item
- Different currency/different ledger
- Different control levels

Further, each Org has multiple subinventories and here are a few reasons why:

- Different accounts for material valuation
- Different locational identities in the system
- Segregating materials and enforcing transactional dependencies

The method to transact transfers between Inventory Organizations for movement of materials depends on whether the Inventory Orgs are associated with the same ledger or not.

If they are associated with different ledgers, then there could be differences in currency, valuation, and accounts. This would also trigger an inter-company accounting processing requirement.

The following profile options relate largely to this particular scenario:

- INV: Inter-company Invoice for Internal Orders
- INV: Advanced Pricing for inter-company Invoice

- INV: Use inter-company AR Tax for inter-company AP
- INV: Intercompany Transfer Price Date
- INV: Intercompany Currency Conversion
- INV: Inter-Organization Currency Conversion
- INV: Advanced Pricing for inter-org Transfers
- CST: Transfer Pricing Option

The profile options described previously are some important profile options that need to be considered if you intend to manage inter-company and transaction processing.

Accounting defaults when transactions are processed are in the following form and this also allows managing and controlling how these transactions between organizations are processed.

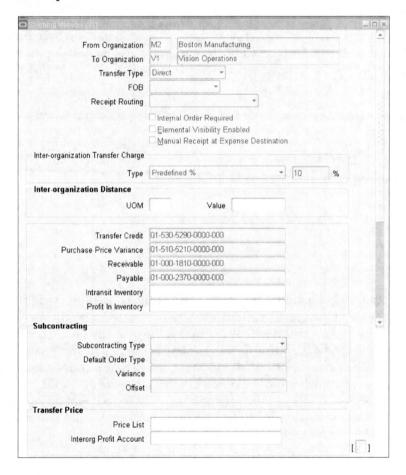

A separate configuration enables true inter-company process flows that include inter-company invoicing and related accounts to manage a more specific movement between ledgers.

Inventory valuation is expected to be accurate and is based on purchase price, price related to building the product (if you manufacturer) and other elements such as labor/resource costs.

To assist in accurate costing (valuation) of an item a process called Cost Update manages to update item valuations appropriately. This process takes into account various elements that make up the total cost and effectively update the cost of each item based on the costing method and the elements configured to build the cost for an item.

The value of a raw material item in stock may be the last purchase price or an average of the purchases in the past specified period. The actual value is dependent on your costing method.

The value for a shippable product (finished goods) is also the purchase price, plus additions of value if any. Or it could be the cost of the raw material, plus the resource cost and other material costs that were used in the process (Work In Process and BOM) to arrive at a finished goods value.

Cost updates are run periodically or can be inherently processed based on the costing method.

E-Business Suite provides multiple costing methods to encompass the requirements for most organizations. These are as follows:

- Standard
- Average
- LIFO
- FIFO

Inventory management includes the review and verification of physical stock levels and these are based on a counting activity performed periodically. When the counting activity is done and if it does not match the quantity on the books, there is a transaction that can be used to adjust the quantities to match and related valuation to be accurate. The transaction that allows this is the physical count adjustment that also drives an accounting entry. The reverse of this adjustment would be done using the issue transaction. This is not the preferred method for accountants as there is no audit trial that shows why this transaction was performed, and it is generally frowned upon by the accounting people.

Cost management

Oracle Cost Management is another product related to Inventory and other manufacturing applications. This does not need to be specifically configured, though the basic configuration is done in Inventory as part of the inventory organization definition.

The data elements that are used to build the value (cost) are defined in Oracle Cost Management. If your enterprise is not a manufacturing company the default setups or minimal setups are sufficient to use in Inventory. Cost management is more relevant when there are manufacturing tasks and the configuration needs to be more detailed.

All accounting is managed and can be reviewed within cost management. Some reports and functions are also available within Oracle Inventory. They are as follows:

- Create Accounting
- Period Close

Summary

The topics covered in this chapter are a review of organizations and inventory transactions that effect non-manufacturing organizations. We also reviewed Items and their related setups with a brief overview of Oracle Cost Management and impacts on Inventory Accounting.

The next chapter is an overview of purchasing and iProcurement. We will walk through purchasing and receiving transactions, including accrual. We will also cover briefly the purchasing close process.

5
Purchasing

We will cover the concepts of procurement in this chapter. Procurement is the process of acquiring goods and services from external parties at the most effective price and possibly over a period of time. This concept obviously excludes one-time purchases that may be made with disregard for the process of negotiation and pricing agreements.

Procurement includes the following processes:

- Information gathering
- Supplier contact and review of offering
- Negotiation and pricing agreement including period wise pricing
- Purchase Order – contract to provide materials/services
- Fulfilment
- Receipt of goods and/or services
- Renewal, as applicable

The first two tasks in the list are manual processes. We will cover the next set of processes that can be managed within the E-Business Suite in this chapter.

Supplier management

Managing suppliers is a major task and most medium-sized companies have this process being managed by the people that create the purchase orders as they are the first to contact the supplier. In E-Business Suite the task of creating a purchase order is assigned to a user who is configured as a buyer in the system. The buyers also negotiate pricing, delivery schedules, and ensure that the company gets the most acceptable pricing for one-time purchases.

In many companies, the onus of creating a supplier is vested in the person who engages with the supplier on the details of the delivery of the product. Normally the creation of a supplier is done by entering data manually; either capturing the data in a paper form or in an e-mail from the supplier to gather the relevant details.

The following screenshot shows an overview screen used to capture supplier information in Release 12:

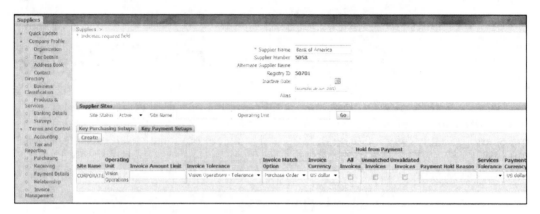

In R12 the supplier form has been merged with the **Trading Community Architecture (TCA)** for a seamless view of all third parties to an enterprise. The TCA tracks suppliers, customers, employees and banks, to name a few entities.

This form changes the concept of how the supplier is created. It has tabs at the side that show the different regions/areas for capturing data.

The overview screen only shows minimal information for the operating unit you have access to. However, when you click on the **Address Book** tab, all the addresses for that supplier are shown. Click on the **Manage Sites** icon to add an address to other operating units as needed.

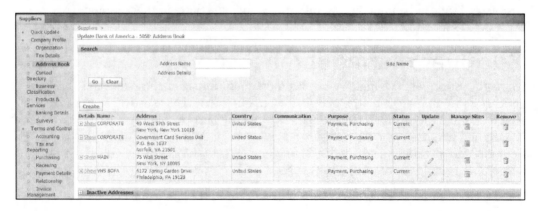

The possibility of duplicates arises frequently. Multiple suppliers either with the same names or multiple addresses pose a real problem. To manage duplicates the supplier merge functionality helps to merge these data entities and resolve the issue. The supplier merge function can be used to merge the supplier, and supplier addresses, including the transactions—purchase orders, invoices, and payments.

In E-Business Suite procurement you can use standard supplier lists to assign suppliers that have been identified as suppliers of specific goods/service products. E-Business Suite also provides approved supplier lists to ease the planning function and can automate creation of planned purchase orders.

Additional supplier management functionality

Supplier management facilitates creation, and maintenance of suppliers, including performance and audit metrics with the supplier hub and the supplier management products.

The iSupplier Portal facilitates self-service transactions between the enterprise and its suppliers. The portal provides a collaborative platform for buyers to manage relationships with their global supply base. It also allows suppliers to receive immediate notifications and respond to events in the purchasing and planning process.

Oracle iSupplier Portal provides the framework that enables buyers and suppliers to communicate key business transactions while enabling the ability to search, monitor, revise, and review purchase order transactions. The portal also allows managing interaction with the supplier and the buyer, including functionality that enables creation of a payable invoice. You can also manage requests for supplier creation from this portal.

Approvals

All procurement transactions, requisitions, and purchase orders require a manual or systematic approval process. In many cases a purchase order does go through an approval process; however, it may not be as extensive as requisition. It could also follow a different hierarchy to support financial and budgeting approvals. Moreover, a purchase order has to be approved to manage receipt transactions.

Oracle E-Business Suite provides multiple methods to manage approvals that are simple hierarchical supervisory role based, or position hierarchy based. The new **Approvals Management Engine (AME)** allows users to use the engine to create hierarchies and branches based on the transaction criteria.

The AME approvals engine has the capability to use the position hierarchy or a supervisory role hierarchy, and extends it with branching logic based on business rules related to each transaction. This allows the flexibility to create complex approval rules to manage appropriate business transactions and spend control.

Both supervisory and positional hierarchies use approval groups and account groupings for each transaction and are configured as shown in the following screenshot.

An approval group has a combination of a document total and relevant accounts that form the approval limit/level. This group is assigned to a job/position depending on the type of approval hierarchy you choose to use. A job/position is assigned to an employee tying all the pieces together with the user.

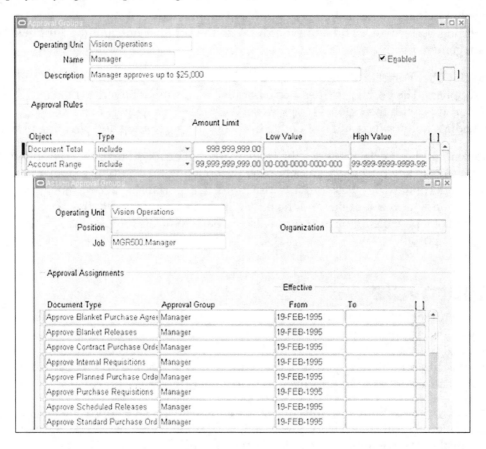

AME can be configured to build its own hierarchy based on transactions, or use the hierarchy built in one of the standard options namely, position hierarchy, or supervisor role hierarchy. Alternatively, AME can be configured to use a hierarchy for each individual transaction or a co-mingling of existing standard hierarchy and one built on the fly depending on individual transaction criteria.

An example of the branching rules provided by AME would be that you can build rules to review the amount of the transaction or the cost centre and branch to require approval from a specific role or person.

> Approvals Management Engine (AME) is available to approve requisition. The engine currently does not support purchase order approvals.

Workflow notifications

Approvals are triggered based on specific rules using position hierarchy or employee supervisor hierarchy. As these approvals progress the method to notify the approver and get approval information back to the requester/preparer is managed using workflow notifications. Workflow notifications can be used from within the application as shown in the following screenshot, or can be configured to use the e-mail system. These e-mail notifications are used to approve, approve and forward, forward, or reject the transaction.

The notification screen shows your requisitions that are approved and can also show other notifications that are sent for approvals.

Click on the box on the left-hand side to select a specific transaction and open it to process the transaction. You have the following choices:

- **Approve**
- **Reject**
- **Forward**
- **Reassign**
- **Request Information**

Workflow is capable of being modified and extended to insert specific business rules to manage document/transaction flow for either decisions or notifications. In the absence of AME you can use the workflow to manage exceptional business cases and modify the approvals hierarchy.

Workflow and AME are further discussed in a later chapter in this book.

Requisitions

Requisitions are internal requests for products and services to be procured from an external source. The requisition transaction is also known as a purchase order request or purchase requisition. A requisition may include an approval process to adhere to budgets and other financial controls. A requisition is not a contract with a supplier to deliver goods or services.

There are multiple procurement activities that companies deal with. They are as follows:

- **Direct Procurement**: Goods and materials mainly for manufacturing activity
- **Indirect Procurement**: Mainly services and consumables—maintenance, repairs, and so on
- **Capital Purchases**: Consist of machinery, computers that will be eventually turned into Fixed Assets

These transactions are managed by issuing a purchase requisition followed by a purchase order, or just a purchase order. Requisitions are converted to purchase order and the purchase order is the contract with the supplier and gets processed for receiving and invoicing.

iProcurement

iProcurement is a web-based product that is relatively easier to use. The transactional process in iProcurement is quicker and more convenient for the user. The following screenshot shows the minimum data entry for an iProcurement requisition transaction. Requisitions can be created in the core application also.

The use of minimalistic entry of data is facilitated by the function of defaults. These defaults can be configured for a user and/or an item. These defaults ensure the transaction is complete and accurate accounting is created. The accounting default for a non-inventory item is managed using expense category accounts. This is explained in more detail later in this chapter. The default accounts for inventory items are normally defaulted to the valuation account for the inventory organization where they are stocked.

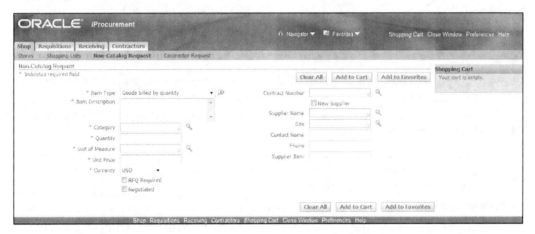

The fields displayed in the previous screenshot are the minimum required to be entered by the user to create a purchase requisition in iProcurement. These values get migrated to the purchase order upon conversion of a purchase requisition.

 Only standard requisitions can be entered in iProcurement.

Another aspect of the ease of using iProcurement is the capability to use Shopping Lists, Stores, and Punchouts.

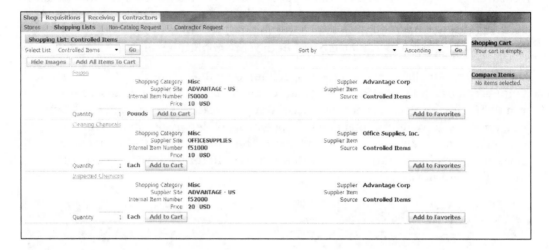

- **Shopping Lists**: These are requisition templates normally used by buyers that relate to a specific set of items which are similar. These could contain supplier information. Personal favorites can be created by a user for an item that is regularly purchased.

- **Stores**: These are mainly a collection of items that are categorized to assist the user in selecting the appropriate set of items. A store is created when you configure item categories.

- **Punchouts**: These are similar to stores, but like an external window into your supplier's portal. The vendor has an agreement with your company to buy certain items at a pre-negotiated price. One can configure the application to get a purchase order created automatically as soon as the purchase requisition is approved. The process of punchout essentially lets you browse and shop on the vendor's website.

Core requisitions

Another method to create requisitions is within the core application as shown in the following screenshot:

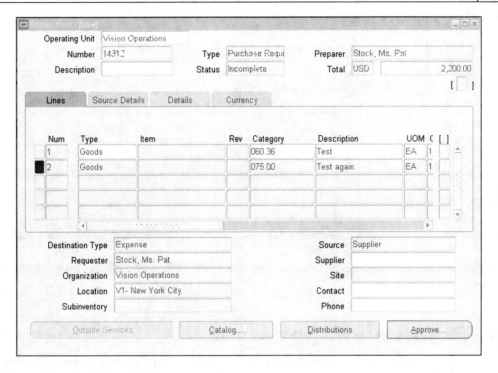

A requisition created using the core functionality provides the functionality enter more information. The user is required to be conversant of the type of information required to be entered for each field. Core applications allow creation of Internal Requisitions. Internal Requisitions are entered to source and supply internal material requirements.

Expense category accounts

The accounting is defaulted both in the core application and the self-service application based on the configuration of expense category accounts.

The process for defaulting accounts is simple. As a requestor you must be configured as an employee in E-Business Suite. A default expense account is assigned to an employee record in Oracle HR.

Account defaulting works as follows:

- The account is defaulted for a transaction from the employee record
- The category accounts (only segments configured in the category) override the default from the employee record

The default accounting derived on the purchase requisition can be changed when entering the requisition.

RFQ and quotations

You can create a **Request for Quotation (RFQ)** from an existing approved requisition or directly in the form used to enter RFQs. These can be sent to suppliers who can send quotations electronically (if configured) for the products/services requested. Alternatively, quotations can be created manually in the system.

These quotation data sets can be copied to purchase orders to process actual delivery and fulfillment of products and services as needed.

Purchasing lets you create supplier lists so that you can predefine groups of suppliers to whom you want to send RFQs. You can establish the approved supplier lists according to the criteria you define (item, manufacturing category, geographic location, and so on) and you can combine these supplier lists to produce multiple copies of your RFQ automatically.

RFQs and quotations are more the norm in manufacturing enterprises where these are automated using sourcing rules. Sourcing rules allow an enterprise to build rules based on location, the item, and other related information that will be used when a material resource plan is run to create requisition transactions to replenish stock.

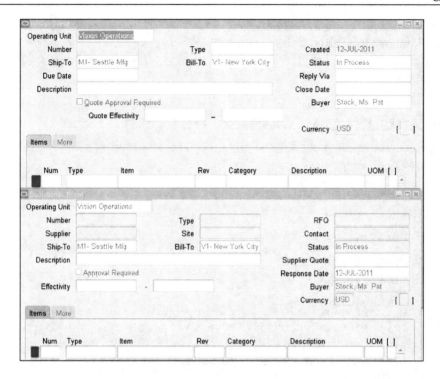

If quotations require approval, the same hierarchies configured for requisitions and purchase orders can be used.

Purchase orders

A **purchase order (PO)** is a commercial document issued by a buyer to a seller (supplier), indicating types, quantities, and agreed prices for products or services the supplier will provide to the buyer. Sending a purchase order to a supplier constitutes a legal offer to buy products or services. Acceptance of a purchase order by a supplier usually forms a one-off contract between the two.

A *buyer* or purchasing agent is a person who purchases goods and services for an enterprise.

A purchase order document allows buyers to communicate their intentions clearly and explicitly to suppliers. Suppliers are protected in case of a buyer's refusal to pay for goods or services.

A purchase order document is the last step of the procurement cycle. The PO is a contract detailing the deliverables and timeline to a supplier. The purchase order document is the only transaction that allows receipts (of goods and services) to be transacted.

Configuring purchasing options

Before you can start using the Purchasing module the following setups or master data need to be completed:

- Suppliers
- Inventory organization
- Item (in some cases)
- Purchasing Options
- Receiving Options

Supplier and items related to Oracle Purchasing are covered in this chapter. Inventory organizations and items have been covered in the previous chapter. As these screens affect the purchasing and receiving activity in the procurement functions we will review some of the important features and impacts of the choices you make.

The **Purchasing Options** form sets the basis for multiple activities that affect the creation and capture of data for purchase orders.

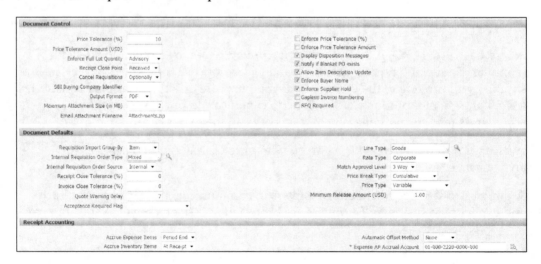

The PO print output can be pdf or text. You can also control the size of attachment size and the attachment file name. The following options assist with managing business rules as part of your business process:

- Allow Item Description Update
- Enforce Supplier Hold
- Buyer Name

Document defaults control how requisitions and purchase orders get their default values. The important ones to note are as follows:

- Line Type for a Purchase Order E-Business Suite provides some defaults, such as goods, expense, or an additional one that can be defined. The important thing to note is that you can default some information from the line type to control how the purchase order is processed. The Goods Line Type signifies that it is an inventory item as long as you use an Item Number and not a description on the PO Line.

- AP invoice creation and matching levels can be managed to reflect your business rules in the transactional flow. A 3-Way match option means that an AP invoice needs a purchase order, and a Receipt for appropriate matching and to allow payment. The various options in E-Business Suite are:

Matching	Requires
2-Way	PO and AP Invoice
3-Way	PO, Receipt, and AP Invoice
4-Way	PO, Receipt, Inspection Acceptance, and AP Invoice

- These options on a purchase order transaction are set on the line, only for tracking purposes and onward processing controls. The impact of each of these options will be discussed and covered in the next chapter.

Receipt accounting options allow the accrual options to be set for inventory and expense items. Ideally the inventory accruals are online at receipt and the expense accruals are at period end. This is the default and the way most companies manage the accruals. This region also allows you to specify the expense accrual account and if you use multiple balancing segment values in one ledger you can choose to use Automatic Offsets. Accrual is discussed in more detail towards the end of this chapter.

You also control the numbering for your procurement transactions on this screen.

Transactions

There are multiple types of purchase order transactions, shown as follows:

- Standard Purchase Order (PO)
- Blanket Purchase Order/Agreement (BPA)
- Global Blanket Agreements
- Contract Purchase Agreement (CPO)
- Planned Purchase Order
- Blanket Releases
- Scheduled Releases

We will cover the Standard Purchase Orders, Blanket Purchase Orders, and Blanket Purchase Releases in this chapter. The others are related to a manufacturing environment. Some enterprises may still choose to use Global Blanket Agreements and this will be briefly covered as an optional type of Blanket Agreement.

A brief description of each type of purchase order is as follows:

- Standard Purchase Orders are created for one-time purchases of various items when you know the details of the goods or services you require, estimated costs, quantities, delivery schedules, and accounting details.
- Blanket Purchase Agreements (BPA) are created when you know the detail, of the goods or services you plan to buy from a specific supplier over a period, but you do not yet know the detail of your delivery schedules. You can use blanket purchase agreements to specify negotiated prices for your items before actually purchasing them.
- Global Blanket Agreements are Blanket Purchase Agreements created for a single organization or to be shared by different business units of your organization. These are created when you have negotiated based on an enterprises' total global purchase volume to enable centralizing the buying activity across a broad and sometimes diverse set of business units. Enterprise organizations can then access the agreement to create purchase orders that leverage pre-negotiated prices and terms.
- Blanket Releases can be issued against a blanket purchase agreement to place the actual order (as long as the release is within the blanket agreement effectivity dates).

- Contract Purchase Agreements are created with your suppliers to agree on specific terms and conditions without indicating the goods and services that you will be purchasing. You can later issue Standard Purchase Orders referencing your contracts.

- Planned Purchase Orders are long-term agreements committing to buy items or services from a single source. You must specify tentative delivery schedules and all details for goods or services that you want to buy, including charge account, quantities, and estimated cost.

- Scheduled Releases can be issued against a Planned Purchase Order to place the actual orders. You can change the accounting distributions on each release if they are different from the Planned Purchase Order against which this scheduled release is being created.

Purchase order transactions need to use a specific approval engine to be completed. This could be any of the approval methodologies as described earlier in this chapter. These were supervisory hierarchy, position hierarchy, and also the Oracle Approval Management Engine.

Purchase order transactions progress through various statuses as they move through the approval process. The status values you will see as the transaction progresses to completion (Approved status) are as follows:

- Incomplete
- In Process
- Requires Reapproval
- Approved

Once the PO is approved, it can be transacted further, with corrections or receipts (of goods/material/services).

If corrections/changes are made a PO revision is maintained within the system, which can be reviewed to see changes made.

Another method to creating a PO transaction involves AutoCreate, which allows conversion of approved requisitions to POs. You can convert multiple requisition lines to a single PO as long as the supplier is the same for all the lines. The system keeps a link to the requisition and ensures that the requisition is not used to create another PO.

However, if you cancel the PO, then the requisition lines can be used to create another PO.

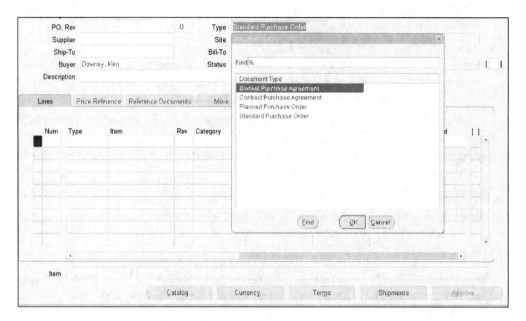

Other purchase orders with different types can also be created using this form, by choosing the appropriate type.

E-Business Suite R12 introduces the Buyers Workbench. This is a consolidated place where you can see your existing transactions and their status.

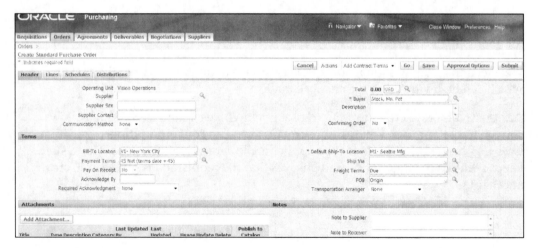

Receiving

The receiving function allows transactions against the PO. As stated previously a PO is a contract between the buyer and a supplier to deliver goods/services for compensation.

The receiving function allows this delivery to be completed, and facilitates the onward flow of the business process, namely, invoicing and payment.

The receiving function allows you to:

- Use routing controls at the organization, supplier, item, or order level to enforce material movement through receiving.

- Define receiving tolerances at the organization, supplier, item, and order level, and order level overriding previous levels.

- Use blind receiving to improve accuracy in the receiving process. With this option, the quantity due for each shipment does not show and quantity control tolerances are ignored.

- Use **Express Receipt** functionality to receive an entire purchase order with a few keystrokes.

- Use **Advance Shipment Notices (ASNs)** to enter receipts in the **Enter Receipts** window.

- Use the Cascade function to distribute a given quantity of an item from a single supplier across multiple shipments and distributions. This function is enabled by a **Receiving Options** checkbox, **Allow Cascade Transactions**, and is available only when you have specified a source and an item in the **Find Expected Receipts** window.

- Record receipt of unordered items based on your item, supplier, or organization defaults. For example, if your organization does not allow receipt of unordered items, you should not be able to enter a receipt unless it is matched to a purchase order (shipment).

- If you set the option to **Allows Substitute Receipts** the system allows the record receipt of predefined substitute items.

There are defaults that allow for controls and other data elements to ease entry of transactions.

Configuring receiving options

Receiving options cover some of the defaults that reflect the transactional controls for the receiving function. Even though the receiving function is truly an inventory transaction it is normally performed during the Procurement process flow to receive material that has been contracted to be delivered via a purchase order.

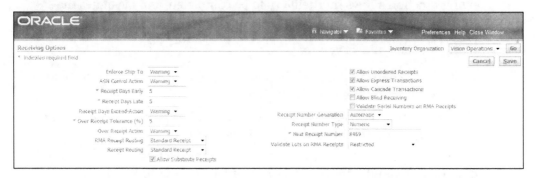

The decision to configure the following data elements affects how the receiving function works:

- Receipt deliveries control
- Receipt transactional tolerances
- Receipt numbering
- Controls on RMA receiving

Receipt Routing, (including RMA Receipt Routing) is an important element to handle how functionality is controlled. The options are as follows:

- **Standard Receipt**
- **Direct Delivery**
- **Inspection Required**

When a receipt is performed the system performs two steps, receipt and delivery to a location. The two steps are performed together when you receive Expense Items, that is, items technically not stocked. All inventory items need to have the two-step process; the **Direct Delivery** choice assumes receipt for an inventory item is performed similar to an expense item, but you must specify information related to the delivery. You can also choose to do the transaction in two steps (Standard Receipt). The **Inspection Required** option forces an additional step for quality control before delivery.

Some others that control elements are as follows:

- **Allow Unordered Receipts**
- **Allow Express Transactions**
- **Allow Substitute Receipts**

Transactions

Receiving transactions are entered based on a PO, once the PO is approved. There are delivery dates normally associated with a PO line and these dates can be used to estimate when the deliveries will be made and also in identifying late receipts. This helps with the analysis of supplier deliveries and their adherence to the company policy.

Receiving can be done using multiple methods. iProcurement forms have a way to enter receipts and these can also be performed using the core application.

The concept of receiving using the web-based method assumes that a minimal amount of data is entered. To manage this it is required that **Receipt Routing** is set to **Direct Delivery** to allow you to enter **Receipts** in the web-based form.

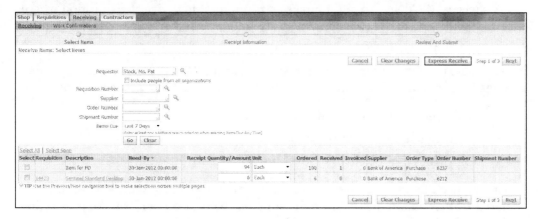

You check the box on the left of the line you want to transact and continue with the steps to complete it.

Using this form you can receive the goods/services with minimal steps.

In the core application there are options to review receiving transactions that allow for a way to perform the additional step to deliver and inspect material.

The following are a couple of profile options that enable and allow for functionality specifically in iProcurement:

- **POR: Support review for Express Receive**
- **POR: Require Blind Receiving**

The standard core receiving form allows similar functions but captures more information as needed by the business.

From both these screens you can use the following functions to perform additional transactions:

- **Receipt Corrections**: Review and correct existing receipt information to ensure that transactions are recorded accurately.

- **Receipt Inspection**: Pick an existing receipt that has been received and perform an inspection transaction. If the item was configured to require inspection it will be enforced; and if the PO was set to have a match approval level of 4-Way this is needed to ensure business rules are applied.

- **Receipt Deliveries**: If the system is configured to transact receipts in a two-step process (Standard Delivery), the initial step would have been to receive the item. An additional step is required to deliver to a location where it will be stocked. This delivery is also required if there was an inspection step performed.

You can also perform **Return Material Authorization (RMA)** transactions using the receipts functionality. This would normally happen in the following situations:

- Wrong good/item was delivered
- Insufficient quality on inspection
- Some parts in the delivered lot could not be used

When you need to return an item to a supplier the process is to request a Return Material Authorization (RMA) from the supplier, before you perform the transaction in the system. This manages a dialogue between you and the supplier to ensure that the item is replaced with appropriate material.

E-Business Suite provides a functionality to allow the system to automatically create a Debit Memo, offsetting the invoice for the delivered material. This is only applicable if an invoice had been created by matching to a PO line. This configuration is available by supplier and needs to be done as part of the configuration for each supplier site. This is covered in detail in the next chapter.

Accruals

Accruals are generated at period end or immediately when the material is received. Typically, inventory items are accrued when they are received, and this is configured in the purchasing options. A single account accumulates the accruals. You can choose a different account for inventory accruals and expense accruals. Expense accruals are generated at period end if they were received, but not invoices.

Inventory accruals are done at the time of receipt, which means that as you receive material that is stocked in inventory (identified by the destination type **Inventory**), the accounting entry will be made when it is received and delivered.

The destination type is defaulted to inventory if you choose an item that is stockable, and cannot be changed. If you choose any other line type, modify, or use an item description, the destination type will default to **Expense** in most cases.

On the other hand, accrual for expense items is configurable based on the three receipt accrual methods:

- None, no accrual is performed
- Accrual on receipt, accrual entries occur when the item is received into inventory
- Period end accrual, at the end of the period an accrual entry is created if a receipt has been transacted

Accrual transactions are tracked and listed in a report called the uninvoiced receipts report.

E-Business Suite provides another set of reports to track inventory accruals. These are as follows:

- AP and PO Accrual Reconciliation Report
- Miscellaneous Accrual Reconciliation Report

For period end accruals, you run a process that creates the events that will direct accounting entries needed for the period end accruals. The create accounting process will create the accounting entries and transfer these to GL. The sequence of steps are as follows:

1. Close AP: If an AP is not closed the next process will not show the current period you are closing in the LOV. This is a required parameter for the process.
2. Run the process Receipt Accruals—Period End.

3. Run Uninvoiced Receipts Report to review accruals:

   ° **Accrued Receipts** parameter set to Y

   ° **Include Online Accruals** if set to Y will also include inventory accruals

4. Run Create Accounting—Receiving (to create and transfer the accounting entries to GL).

These accruals are created with the intention of being reversed as these are called soft accruals. They are accrued as liabilities only for reporting purposes. E-Business Suite will create two journal batches, one for the accrual in the current month and another for the reversal in the next month. This ensures that the accrual batch is reversed in the following month.

Accrual write-offs are part of the accrual process and E-Business Suite provides a transaction to perform write-offs.

 Accrual write offs occurs in Cost Management (though the function is made available in the Purchasing menu). In R12, the write-off function creates accounting entries in GL.

Summary

As part of this chapter, we covered a brief introduction to the procurement products and walked through the transaction capabilities. We reviewed how to create requisitions, how to manage approvals for these and other transactions, how to convert requisitions to purchase orders, and receiving functions.

We covered configuration aspects that relate to transacting purchase orders and receipts. We also briefly touched on accruals and default accounting for transactions in procurement.

In the next chapter, we will cover the next step in the Procure to Pay business process flow and review how to manage expense suppliers, and how to create and manage invoices, Credit Memos, and Pre-payments. We will also walk through a new product in R12, Payments, and review how to configure the payment manager and transacting and managing payments.

6

Payables

The Payables module is the last in the Procure to Pay process flow. It manages invoicing (creating the liability) and payment (clearing the liability).

Accounts Payable is a subledger where the system records what it owes its suppliers (creditors) for goods and services that have been provided. Due to the fact that there is, in most cases, a lag between the time the goods or services are delivered and the time the invoice is received, as well as a period before which the payment is made, this is recorded as a debt (or liability) for the enterprise.

This chapter provides an overview of the following:

- Payable specific supplier considerations
- Creating non-PO matched invoices
- Creating and process expense reports
- Creating PO matched invoices
- Creating automatic debit memos
- Creating payments
- Overview of banks and their use in the payment process
- Considerations during the close process

Suppliers—Payables specific

We discussed the definition of suppliers in the previous chapter, but there are some specifics that are related to Payables only.

In most companies, the purchasing group owns the business process to create suppliers. However, there are payment terms and other related details that are managed by the accounting group, mainly the Payables group. If your organization uses **Electronic Funds Transfer (EFT)**, the treasury group may also get involved to define banks to enable payments to be transmitted directly to a supplier's bank account. Banks are also needed to make check payments and other payment methods.

We will review a few of the Payables specific supplier related configurations that default to transactions to enable accuracy and consistency.

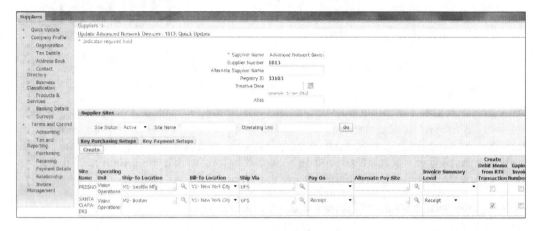

The data you see in the previous screenshot is defaulted from a high-level Payables configuration, but can be changed for a supplier or a supplier site. This previous screenshot shows an overview of supplier information.

- The **Invoice Summary Level** is a functionality that allows for automatic invoicing based on a receiving transaction. If you choose to use this functionality for a supplier, a process called *Pay On Receipt AutoInvoice* creates the invoice based on the receiving transaction.

- The **Create Debit Memo from RTS Transaction** creates a debit memo to offset an invoice that has been matched to a receiving transaction, if the material is returned to the supplier. This happens automatically when you save the return transaction.

- **Hold Management** allows you to control how the invoice is processed for payment. A hold will always hold the transaction for payment, but will account for the transaction (create the liability) unless configured not to do so.

- **Supplier** allows you to specify that an address can be used to transact **Purchase Orders** only, or **Payables** only, or both. You also have an option to specify if this address should be used for RFQs alone.

The following screenshot is a collection of information that can be used to ensure and drive your business rules for transaction processing in AP:

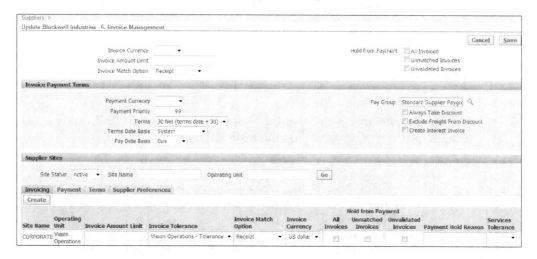

Configuration

The defaults for payables processing are defined in the payables options and these will enable quicker data entry and will cascade down to the supplier, supplier site, and the invoice transaction. These default data elements can be changed.

- Financial options default accounting information. Only the liability and prepayment accounts can be changed for supplier records.

- Payables options default other data elements and control how transactions are processed. The following is a list of a few:

  ° **Automatic Offset**: If you use multiple balancing segment values E-Business Suite provides functionality to enable recording the liability accurately for the appropriate balancing segment.

  ° **Currency** tab: This defines how to process multi-currency transactions. It also identifies the accounts used for realized gain and loss.

  ° **Invoice processing**: It allows a choice of how the GL Date (Accounting Date) is used on a transaction among other defaults.

  ° **Invoice Approval**: Using this with workflow (or AME) is also a choice.

  ° **Expense Reports transaction** options; **PO matching** options for data transformation.

  ° **Payment related transaction processing** options.

Transactions

Transactions in Payables are managed from multiple sources or types as follows:

- Manual entry for non-PO matched invoices
- Manual entry for PO matched invoices
- Credit memos
- Debit memos
- Expense reports (this is a part of the Oracle Projects product and needs a separate process to be submitted to create AP Invoices)
- Interest invoices

Expense reports are special invoices that manage the payments to employees for reimbursement of expenses incurred while traveling or other related activities.

This is a functionality that enables employee expense reimbursements and only employees can use this function. Let us review briefly how to process expense reports, create invoices for them, and process them through to payments.

The following screenshot shows some important setups that must be completed to manage the creation of expense reports in Payables:

A template can be created that has a text item that defaults to accurate accounts for specific expense types. You can also specify separate **Payment Terms** and **Pay Group** to assist in managing the payment cycle for expense reports.

The most important one that should be reviewed is **Automatically Create Employee as Supplier**. The Payable system can only pay invoices, and invoices need a supplier as a data element. Expense reports are created by an employee and unless the employee is created as a supplier in the Payables system an invoice cannot be created. This option enables the automated creation of the supplier from your employee record the first time an Expense Report is transformed to an AP invoice.

You can create expense reports from the core application which is available as part of your E-Business Suite. Internet expenses is an additional product and needs to be purchased separately.

iExpenses

iExpense has a web interface framework (also called Self Service Applications), to enter manage, and monitor your expense reports. There are multiple ways you can enter these transactions. They are as follows:

- Manually
- Import from a spreadsheet template
- Import from a credit card provider

The following screenshot shows the home page for **Expenses** that have been entered for the user. As you can see there are pending expenses and one of the expense reports has been approved and is pending payment:

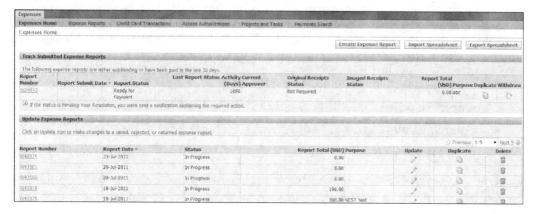

Entering an expense report in this web interface is relatively easy and a spreadsheet template can also be used to create and upload your expense report. When using a spreadsheet you must assign an expense report template before you import it into the system.

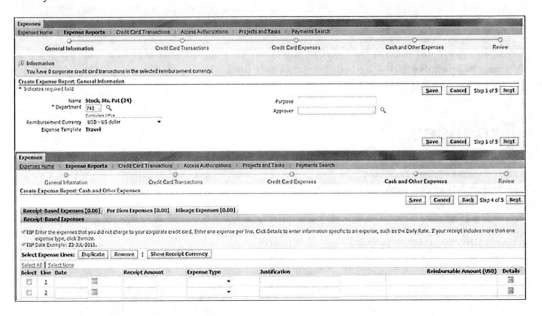

When you create an expense transaction using data from a credit card processor you load the transactions and manage the transactions are created as expense reports.

E-Business Suite provides generic programs that allow you to load data from the major credit card processors.

There are multiple options for payment as follows:

- Employee pays credit card company
- Company pays credit card company
- A combination of both

Generally an employee creates an expense report for themselves. It is also possible to configure iExpense to allow another person (an assistant) to create an expense report on behalf of someone.

iExpense works together with other applications to provide a full array of services devoted to managing and streamlining all aspects of the expense report process:

- Oracle Payables
- Oracle Projects

- Oracle Grants Accounting
- Oracle Approvals Management
- Oracle Application Framework

 iExpense does not support Multi-Organization Access Control; it is associated with only one operating unit at a time.

Approvals

iExpenses can work with standard workflow to manage approvals. This is a single path for approval and is managed with a hierarchy that is built based on a combination of the cost center and the employee. This is defined within Payables. This type of approval is very basic and allows your manager, or his supervisor, to approve your expense report based on the authority they have assigned in the system.

iExpenses also works together with Oracle Approvals Management (AME) and Oracle Workflow to route expense approvals and notifications to cost center owners, cost center business managers, project managers, or award managers. Approval notifications provide managers with all the information needed to make informed decisions, including the reimbursable amount displayed in the approver's currency, and expense lines that were split and charged to their own cost centers.

Invoicing

The first transaction in Payables is an invoice. There are multiple types of invoices that you can create and have been listed in the section dealing with transactions earlier in this chapter.

However, the next process allows you to create an expense report as an invoice so you can pay based on that document. You can pay an invoice as long as the invoice is validated and is not on hold.

Expense report

An expense report must be created as an invoice to be processed for payment. An expense report transaction is not an Oracle Account Payable transaction; it is an Oracle Projects transaction. A process, Expense Report Export, must be submitted to transform these expense reports as AP invoices. The AP invoice created by this process is of the type **Expense Report**. This requires configuration for an employee to be created as a supplier automatically.

Automatic debit memo

Another automated method to create an invoice transaction is when you choose to use the **Return to Supplier (RTS)** functionality. This function is also called "Auto-Invoicing". This feature can be configured for a specific supplier/supplier site. This functionality allows a debit memo to be created when a return to supplier transaction is processed.

This requires a receipt and an invoice to have been created by matching to the PO/Receipt transaction.

The **Invoice Number** for this transaction is the **Receipt Number-OU Number**. The following must be true to create a debit memo in **Payables: Flag**:

- **Create Debit Memo for RTS transactions** is checked at **Vendor** site
- The material is returned to the supplier and not to receiving
- There is already an invoice in AP for the item being returned
- The PO and the original invoice are for the same supplier site
- The supplier site is both a pay and a purchasing site
- The return quantity (debit memo quantity) is not causing the quantity invoiced to go negative and/or the return quantity is equal to or less than the quantity invoiced

Setting the **Create Debit Memo for RTS transaction** flag after the PO has been created does not affect the PO. Only future transactions will be eligible for automatic Debit Memo on returns. You can however, check the **Create Debit Memo** checkbox on the return transaction to manage older transactions.

Pay on Receipt

The Pay on Receipt functionality allows the creation of an invoice based on a receipt transaction. Once the receipt has been transacted in the system the user should run a program, **Pay on Receipt AutoInvoice**, which creates an invoice for the receipt amount in Payables. This program is run from purchasing.

This functionality is typically used in conjunction with the auto Debit Memo (RTS) functionality to manage an easier tracking of the balances with the supplier.

 "Pay on Receipt Auto Invoice" does not adjust for corrections. This functionality is currently not supported. Several enhancement requests have been submitted.

Standard invoices

Standard invoices are created manually and also include those that are matched to purchase order transactions. When matched to a PO, quantity, amount, pricing details, and accounting will default from the PO line being matched. These details cannot be changed on the invoice.

Configurations can default the following data elements needed to complete the invoice processing:

- Payment Method
- Terms
- PayGroup

Some important data elements that effect processing of an invoice transaction are as follows:

- **Invoice Date**: Defaults to the current date and system displays a message if the current period is not open in AP.
- **GL Date**: This is the date when this transaction will be accounted. This has to be in an open period. There are multiple options to default this as follows:
    - System Date (current date)
    - Invoice Date (the date on the paper invoice from Supplier)
    - Goods Received/Invoice Date(Goods Received date is not Mandatory)
    - Goods Received/System Date (Goods Received date is not Mandatory)

- Payment Method, Terms, and Paygroup enable payment processing and can be used to manage the criteria for selecting invoices for payment.

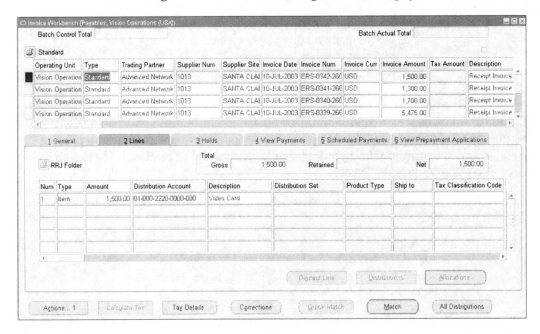

If you are using a 2-Way match process and intend to match to a purchase order, you would enter the purchase order number in the field and click **Match** to find the purchase order line to match. This will pull the information from the purchase order, namely Charge Account, Quantity, Amount, Pricing, and so on, to the invoice.

Credit Memo transactions are the same as Debit Memo, except that these are actual credits with your vendor.

To reverse a purchase order matched invoice line/distribution you will need to use the **Discard Line** button to ensure that the purchase order line is opened back up to match again.

You can match to a purchase order line within any purchase order. If the PO is closed, Payables places the invoice on Hold. The allocation functionality in Payables allows you to record charges appropriately; tax, freight, and miscellaneous charges to each line on the Distribution (or Invoice) so that these charges may be equally distributed to each line having the item cost. This is very important in a situation where you are using Periodic Costing options in a manufacturing environment. It also helps if you want to allocate your other charges to multiple lines on an invoice. The **allocation** button was available in the **Distributions** window in previous releases, but is now available in the main **Invoice Workbench** window.

Procurement card transactions

Procurement cards are credit cards that an organization issues to employees for official expenses. These transactions are imported from a feed that the credit card issuer/provides to the organization. E-Business Suite provides generic programs to manage this import from major credit card processing companies.

Once imported these transactions are staged for employee verification and manager approval. These approved expense report transactions are created as Payables Invoices.

The following are the steps for this functionality:

- Configure Credit Card Program: Associate a credit card issued to an employee and provide any limits that you would want to place on transactions.

- Import Procurement Card Transactions.

- Use the **iExpenses** login responsibility to perform the validation. Review these transactions in the **Credit Card Transactions** tab. Once the employee verification is completed the transaction is routed to the manager for approval.

- Manager approval is required if authorization limits and approvals are configured.

- Review and adjust accounting distributions created based on rules in the system configuration.

- Create payable invoices.

Hold management

Hold management is an important aspect of controls built into the system when transacting PO matched invoices. There are a variety of holds and they can be segregated into two groups as follows:

- Holds that allow accounting
- Holds that do not allow accounting

 All holds restrict payment of the invoice.

System holds are placed by E-Business Suite and cannot be released by the user. You must rectify the error situation and the holds will be automatically released. Holds are placed and released when the "Invoice Validation" program is submitted. Every invoice transaction must be validated before you can process them for payments. Invoice Validation in addition to managing holds also checks for inaccurate and inconsistent data in the invoice and validates accounting information. The validation process also calculates tax and invoice variance.

The following table gives us an overview of how the matching levels work and how holds manage controls in Payables:

Match Option	What	Result
2-Way	Ensures that when creating an Invoice that we have a link to a Purchase Order	You can create an Invoice, but if you choose to have only Purchase Order matched invoices for a specific Supplier, but a hold will be placed denying the capability to make a payment
3-Way	Ensures that there is a Purchase Order and a Receipt transaction that is linked to the Invoice	You can match to the Purchase Order and the invoice will be recorded, but a hold will be placed denying the capability to make a payment
4-Way	Ensures that there is a Purchase Order, a Receipt, and an Inspection Acceptance is linked to the Invoice	You can match to the Purchase Order and the invoice will be recorded, but a hold will be placed denying the capability to make a payment

Approvals

You can choose to use Payables Invoice Approvals, which works with the Workflow Notification and the Approvals Management Engine (AME). The AME works with all E-Business Suite applications and can be configured to manage transaction approvals.

You must do the following to manage approvals for Payables Invoices:

- In the **Payables Options**, in the **Invoice** tab, enable **Use Invoice Approval Workflow**
- If using AME:
    1. Create a business rule, for example **Invoice Amount > 1000**
    2. Enter an approval process, for example to require approval from a group
    3. Create the group and assign members to the group

- Once these setups are complete:

    1. Save the invoice
    2. Run Invoice Validation
    3. Click on the **Actions** button on the **Invoice** form and click **Initiate Approval**

The following types of invoices are not sent through the approval process:

- Expense reports
- Recurring invoices

If approvals are required no payments can be made to invoices prior to approval.

Payments

E-Business Suite Release 12 introduces Oracle Payments a new product to manage payments in a more comprehensive manner. Oracle Payments serves as a funds capture and funds disbursement engine for E-Business Suite products.

Oracle Payments processes transactions, such as invoice payments from Oracle Payables, bank account transfers from Oracle Cash Management, and settlements against credit cards and bank accounts from Oracle Receivables. Oracle Payments provides the infrastructure needed to connect these applications and others with third-party payment systems and financial institutions.

The funds capture and disbursement capabilities of Oracle Payments centralize the collections and disbursement recording in the system.

The user interface is completely new. However, the processing steps have not changed from the previous versions, but the way you perform them has changed dramatically.

The funds capture mechanism is where you have agreements with your Third Parties, customers who will transact direct transfers of funds to Oracle Payments, and these will be recorded according to specified rules. These transactions include the following:

- Bank Account Transfers (EFT)
- Credit Card Payments
- Bills Receivable Remittances

The legacy process of depositing cash in your lockbox and being sent a statement will still remain. This will be transacted as receipts in Accounts Receivables.

Funds Capture functionality within Oracle Payments integrates with various Oracle products. A few are listed as follows:

- Oracle Collections
- Oracle iReceivables
- Oracle iStore
- Oracle Order Capture
- Oracle Order Management
- Oracle Service
- Oracle Service Contracts
- Oracle Receivables

Configuration

The configurations for banks and bank accounts have been moved to Cash Management as a central location. Access can be granted to continue performing this task in Payables if needed. We will cover this in the chapter that will deal with Cash Management.

Oracle Payments elevates the bank accounts to a level above the operating unit to the legal entity.

The configuration for all payment related tasks, other than the bank and bank account information is done in the **Oracle Payments Setup** page. This page contains multiple options to secure and manage validations for payment formats and disbursement methods.

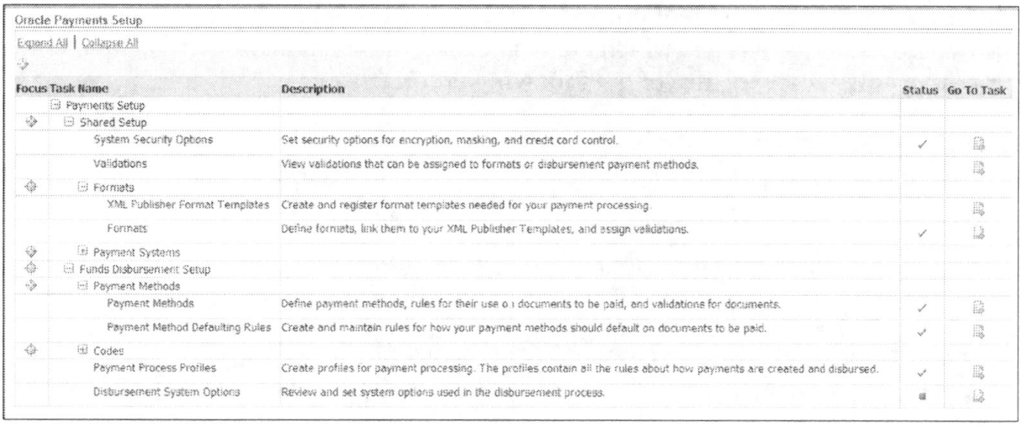

The previous screenshot shows the **Payments Setup** page. This page allows for:

- Managing XML format templates used to generate check formats/layouts
- Configuring payment transmission configuration
- Managing interaction with external institutions enabling you to manage your payments electronically
- Funds disbursement to manage payment formats
- Creating defaulting rules to enable transactional defaulting
- Bank instruction and disbursement codes to manage electronic payment transmission and validation

Payment Process Profiles

E-Business introduced Payment Process Profiles in Release 12 to enable and manage linking a bank and its payment document to a payment process. There are multiple steps that manage payments in R12, and it brings together all the options in a configurable manner.

The Payment Process Profile allows to specify selection of documents payable (Invoices), payments, and payment instructions by Oracle Payments. Payment process profiles also include several types of formatting information for payment instructions and transmissions, including electronic transmission of information to financial institutions.

The selection of valid payment process profiles is determined by the payment process profile's usage rules, which are created in Oracle Payments setup. Payment process profiles allow the use of the following criteria:

- Usage rules based on:
    - ◦ Payment method
    - ◦ Payment currency
    - ◦ Operating unit (first party organization)
- Grouping rules.
- Sorting criteria for the payment documents.
- Limits for the batch.
- Formats for:
    - ◦ Checks
    - ◦ Positive pay file
    - ◦ Remittance file
    - ◦ Payment Registers
- Transmission information for the output.

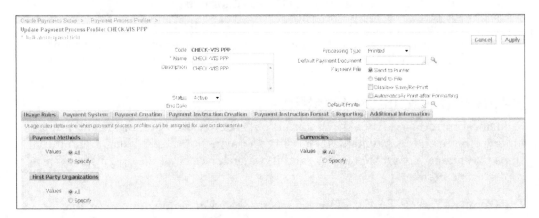

- Specifying a default payment document links this process profile to a bank account that uses the payment document. Leaving this field blank will allow use of this profile with any bank account.

Payment Process Profiles in conjunction with a template can link the selection criteria, grouping methods, and reporting documents to an internal bank account and payment document.

Payment transactions

Once the banks have been configured, you can start your payment processing. Payment processing has been completely redesigned and has a new look and feel. The following screenshot shows the new Payments Manager/Workbench:

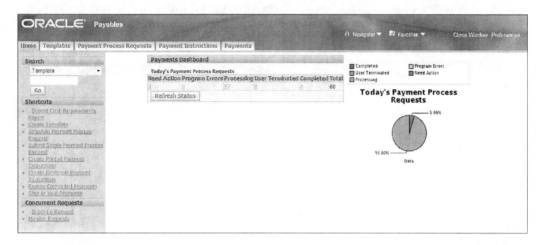

This page is the launch page for the Payments Manager, as it is now called. The start page allows you to review past payment requests and disbursements. It also allows you to submit new single payments or a batch for payment. The links on the left allow multiple tasks related to payments:

- Create a template
- Submit a cash requirement report
- Submit and schedule a payment process
- Create a printed payment instruction (can be used to reprint checks)
- Create an electronic payment instruction (can be used to transmit electronic payment information to the bank)
- Review completed payments
- Stop or void payments
- Monitor and submit generic requests

Payment batches

When payment batches are submitted to process multiple payment documents, the launch page shows the progress and status for each batch. The status for each batch is the same as in pre-R12 versions, but the steps to follow through are different. The following screenshot is the dashboard where you have a count of **3** that is under the column titled **Need Action** and when you click the number, you see those that need action displayed.

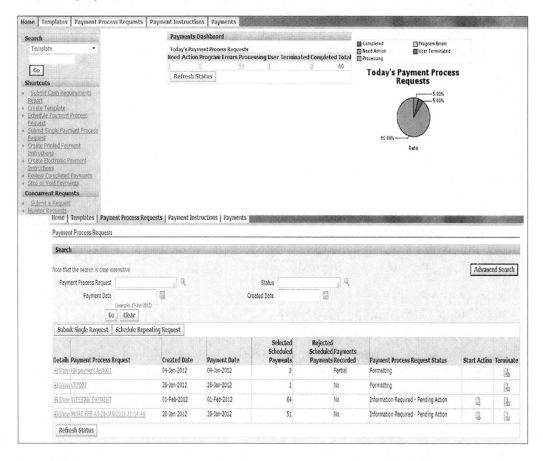

The payment instruction can be best explained as a batch or single payment. The last tab, **Payments**, lists the actual payment documents, that is the checks that have been generated. You can initiate stop payments and void payments for each payment from this tab.

Templates allow you to default multiple criteria that help you select transactions that are selected for a payment batch.

The launch page or portal allows you to create a template that you can apply to a payment process submission. The template allows managing frequently used data elements that streamline your payment process. You can specify:

- Dates
- Paygroup
- Supplier type or payee name
- Payment method and currency
- Legal entities and operating units

The following screenshot shows a generic template definition form:

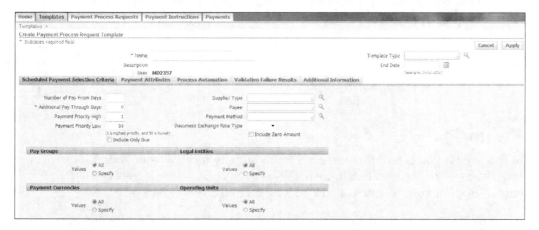

Each tab allows specific data elements to be entered to manage the payment process:

- **Payment Attributes**: Bank account that the payment process uses to generate the payments for this run
- **Process Automation**: The interim reports are generated, payments selected report, payment register
- **Validation Failure Results**: Helps you manage how processing will proceed with the payment batch when there is an error

When you submit a payment batch all the template data assignments will default through if you choose a template. The additional criteria allows to pay a single invoice batch (if you were using batches when entering invoices).

If you do not use a template there are multiple data elements that have to be entered to successfully submit a payment batch.

A template can also be used to create a cash position report. The cash position report will give you the cash required to be able to pay the payment batch selected by the template used. All reports that are generated from the Payments module are in a PDF format by default and you can use BI Publisher (formerly XML Publisher) to change the formats as needed. The check formats that come as default are also in XML and can be modified using BI Publisher.

Quick and manual payments

Quick and manual payments can be processed from the **Invoices** form using the **Actions** button. This is the same as it was in prior releases.

You can use the Payments function or use the Invoice Workbench (based on access) to process these types of payments.

 You can also pay multiple invoices for a supplier by selecting all the invoices to pay and then choosing to pay in full from the **Invoice Workbench Actions** button.

Refunds

In Release 12, you can process refunds that you may receive from your suppliers or employees in the **Payments** window. This allows you to close a credit transaction with a supplier with whom you are no longer conducting business.

A refund closes out an outstanding credit balance, so you are actually making a negative payment for a credit balance. The credit balance can consist of the outstanding balance of any combination of the following documents, as long as the sum is negative and equals the refund amount:

- Invoices
- Debit memos
- Credit memos
- Expense report

AP-AR netting

The Oracle AP/AR Netting is a feature that provides a foundation to create netting agreements and executes an automated netting process so that customers can reduce their debt obligations without incurring bank charges by creating unnecessary payments and receipts.

Oracle AP/AR Netting allows you to net your Payables invoice balances against your Receivables invoice balances for those customers who are also your suppliers.

For example, rather than you and your supplier/customer trading invoices and payments, AP/AR netting allows you to pay the net difference between how much you owe the supplier and how much the supplier owes you.

After establishing a netting agreement with such trading partners, you set up the agreement and associated rules.

The setup steps are listed as follows:

- Netting Bank Account
- Receivables System Options
- Netting batch approver
- Chargeable Subcontracting
- Netting Agreement

 AP/AR netting is restricted to the customers and suppliers of one operating unit. They cannot cross the operating units.

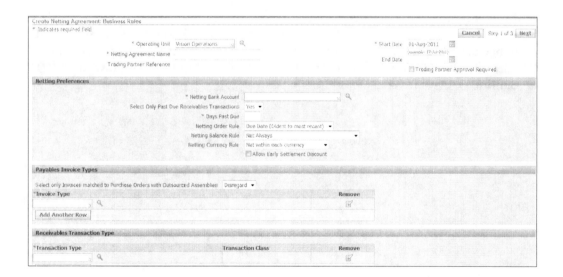

The netting agreement forms the basis on which transactions in AP and AR are selected to format a batch. Next identify the parties involved; these must be sites within the same operating unit.

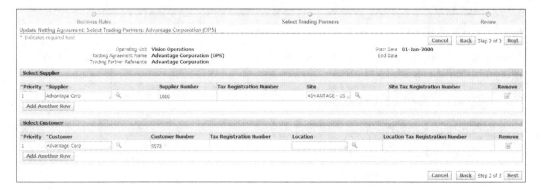

Summary

In this chapter, we reviewed how suppliers are managed in Payables. We also walked through how transactions are created, how the new payments system is configured, and how payments are transacted. We also looked at an overview of AP-AR netting functionality.

In the next chapter, we will review fixed assets. We will discuss Asset Books and Tax Books. We will review how transactions are performed and how to create assets and how they are managed with adjustments, retirements, sale, and other transactions that are processed within the Asset system. We will also briefly cover how to manage accounting changes for specific transactions.

7
Assets

An enterprise is created with the objective of managing its resources to obtain the maximum return on investment. The resources are people, machinery, intellectual property, buildings, land, and various other items. These items are collectively called assets.

People as assets are managed by an HR system that tracks their productivity and costs related to them. The other assets cannot be managed in the same way and need a different approach to track. This is done in E-Business Suite by fixed assets (or Oracle Assets).

Assets can be of two types, tangible and intangible.

Tangible assets can be segregated into two major classes, current and fixed. Current assets comprise the following:

- Cash and cash equivalents
- Short-term investments
- Receivables
- Inventory
- Prepaid expenses

Intangible assets are resources that cannot be physically felt or seen and examples are as follows:

- Goodwill
- Copyrights
- Trademarks
- Patents

Tangible assets that are not current assets are called fixed assets and are generally referred to as PPE (property, plant, and equipment) in many report groupings.

In this chapter, we will give the reader an overview of how an enterprise manages fixed assets. We will discuss the following:

- Asset Books types, how many, why
- Construction-in-Process (CIP)
- Transactions
- Depreciation
- Adjustments
- Disposition

Fixed assets are purchased for continued and long-term use in earning profits in a business. This group includes the following:

- Land and buildings
- Plant and machinery
- Furniture, including fixtures
- Computer hardware and software

As a cost of using a fixed asset, depreciation is charged as an expense. This is done for all assets excluding Land and Artwork. The cost of usage (depreciation) is accumulated in another account as a write-down of the value of the asset cost to a net book value when it is reported.

Configuration

Multiple configuration steps must be completed before you start with configuration in Oracle Assets. They are as follows:

- Flexfields
- Ledgers
- Employees
- Subledger accounting

The following paragraphs show configurations specific to E-Business Suite Assets that are used to track and manage assets.

Flexfields

There are three important flexfields that you need to create and configure as part of your initial setups before you start to use assets in E-Business Suite. These are used to appropriately manage and track the assets in the system for financial and non-financial information. They also enable reporting needs, and are as follows:

- Asset key flexfield
- Asset category flexfield
- Location flexfield

Asset key flexfield

The asset key flexfield is a key flexfield and can be defined with a maximum of 10 segments. It is used to capture additional information needed for your business to enable reporting and other related tracking information. This may be information that is needed but the standard form does not capture. One of the many uses of the asset key flexfield is to track an old asset number. This becomes important for asset records converted from a legacy system into E-Business Suite.

The asset key flexfield is a required step in the configuration so you can define it with one segment. This ensures the structure is built as a requirement for configuration, and having this as a non-required field for entry allows you to proceed easily. This flexfield stores non-financial information for reference.

Category flexfield

The category flexfield is a key flexfield and is designed to have a maximum of seven segments. It is very important and captures accounting related information, which is key to the functionality of Oracle Assets. This flexfield is linked to data that identifies the accounts for cost, depreciation, accumulated depreciation. This also stores information related to the life of the asset and the depreciation method. All these details other than the accounts are defaulted on an asset and can be changed. An asset must be assigned a category to enable accounting and other business rules.

A category is defined as a data element that is used for reporting, especially accounting reports and for managing accounting entries. The categories in assets should reflect the major accounts in your section of fixed assets as represented on your balance sheet.

Most use two segments, a Major and a Minor Category. The asset category flexfield has two qualifiers and they identify each category as major or minor.

Based on these assignments the E-Business Suite has functionality built in for these qualified segments.

Location flexfield

The location flexfield is a key flexfield and is designed to have a maximum of seven segments. This key flexfield has one qualifier for the state (based on the U.S. based reporting requirement for state level property tax reporting).

The location flexfield is used for identifying the absolute location of an asset and is assigned to every asset in the Asset Book.

The following is an example of how the location flexfield can be defined and used effectively:

- State
- County
- City
- Building/Other

This level of detail enables to managing effective reporting for property tax reporting in the U.S. In other countries you may need more level of detail.

 These flexfields are used by all the Asset Books that you define in the system.

System controls

System controls manages the highest level of setup information for the Oracle Assets.

The system controls data set is defined for the whole enterprise. It is not limited by legal entity, ledger, or operating unit. The fields here identify the structure of the flexfields and the corporate name for Oracle Assets.

An important date that is configured here is the Earliest Date Placed in Service. This date identifies the earliest date that can be used to perform any transactions in Oracle Assets.

Take care when making this decision as this cannot be changed once you have saved the data.

Calendars

Fiscal years and calendars are generally intended to be similar to the general ledger and in most cases they are, but in Oracle Assets you must define them separately. In most cases, the fiscal years (start and end dates) and the calendar mirror the ones defined in the general ledger. Since they are defined again in fixed assets, care must be taken to ensure that they are consistent.

 You must have the same period names in Oracle Assets as in Oracle General Ledger. This allows for accurate transaction postings from Oracle Assets to Oracle General Ledger.

Books

Once you have completed the configuration steps mentioned earlier you can define what are called Asset Books. There are three types of Asset Books:

- Corporate
- Tax
- Budget

You can have as many Tax Books as you need, but you have to associate a Tax Book to a Corporate Book. Assets can belong to any number of Asset Books, but to only one Corporate Book.

You can have multiple Corporate Books (generally one per primary ledger).

Corporate Books generally transfer accounting entries to GL, whereas Tax Books typically do not. You can, however, opt to if necessary. In R12 you can associate the Tax Book with a secondary ledger and transfer accounting entries.

Asset categories

Before you transact ensure that you have defined the categories and category details. Category definition (using the category flexfield) enables defaulted asset information that is assigned to that category. The following is an example of a category defined in Oracle Assets:

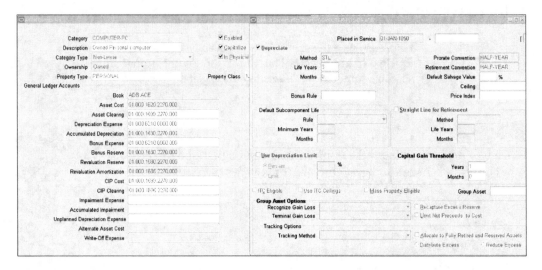

Once the asset category and the location flexfield have been configured you are ready to enter and create assets.

Flexfields allow you to create dynamic combinations, but in this case – for both the asset category and location flexfield it is recommended that these are not created dynamically. This will ensure that the combinations are the ones that make sense.

The following are the steps to ensure that appropriate data is captured:

- Create values for each segment
- Create the valid combinations for each flexfield structure (Category and Location)
- Use these in transactions as appropriate

This is important because these flexfields are used to create accounting (Asset Category flexfield) and property tax reporting (Location flexfield).

Transactions

Transactions in assets are frequently interfaced from the Payables product as a part of the invoicing activity. There are very few cases where an enterprise decides to enter the asset transaction manually in Oracle Assets. However, you can enter assets manually if required in Oracle Assets.

Oracle Assets interfaces data from Payables if the following criteria are met:

- The charge account on the payables distribution lines is an asset or CIP clearing account.
- The **Track as Asset flag** is checked. (This is automatically checked if the charge account is an asset or CIP clearing account.)
- The distribution line is transferred to GL.
- The asset account is defined as a clearing account (or CIP Clearing Account) in an Asset category.
- The GL Date on the distribution line is on or before the GL date you specify in the Mass Additions Create program.
- If the Payables configuration is linked to the same ledger as the Asset Book.

If all these conditions are true, Mass Additions Create transfers details from Payables to Assets.

Another way to create assets is using ADI, from an external source. This method is normally used for conversion of asset data from a legacy system into E-Business Suite.

Mass additions

Records are created in the mass additions table (using the Mass Additions Create program) as part of your periodic processes or during your period-end processing.

Once these interfaced records have been populated as Asset data, certain data elements are required to create an asset.

The process to add these additional data elements is termed as **Mass Additions Prepare**. The additional data provided are as follows:

- Asset category (if not provided on the Requisition, the PO, or an AP Invoice)
- Asset key flexfield information, if required
- Assigment information
    - Location
    - Employee assignment (not required)

- Few other details as needed

  ○ Tag number

  ○ Serial number

  ○ Manufacturer

Once the required information is populated as part of the preparing mass additions process the asset can be created.

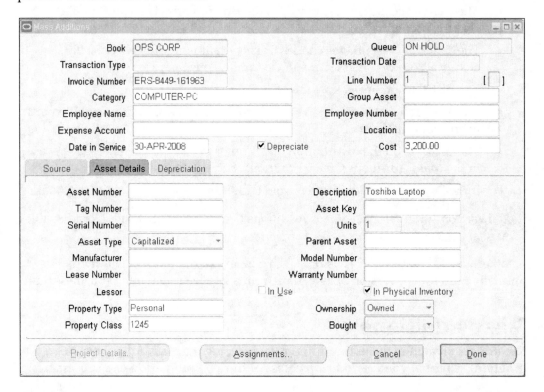

Merge

When multiple lines are transferred from an invoice to the mass additions tables, you might like to create a single asset with the related components. These lines could be a line for the item, tax, freight, or line for computer monitor, keyboard, mouse, CPU. This can be accomplished by merging the relevant lines to create a single asset.

On the **Prepare Mass Additions** form, click the **Merge** button, and all the lines for that specific **Invoice Number** are displayed to merge. You can add other lines as needed from the existing lines that are not processed.

Split

Transaction lines that have been processed from a Requisition or a Purchase Order can have quantities on each line. In such cases, a function in Mass Additions Prepare allows you to split the lines so that each quantity of the item can be created as a single asset. Once you use the **Split** option the number of lines created will be equal to the quantity on the line being split, and the invoice amount will be evenly split amongst these lines.

These lines can now be created as individual assets.

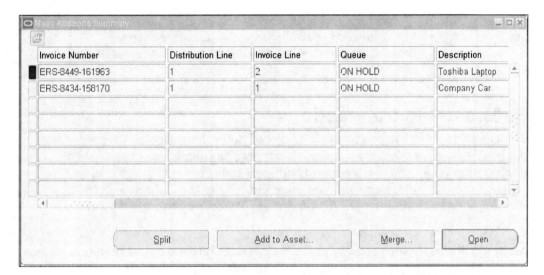

When you split a source line they can only be merged back together (**Unsplit**).

> You cannot merge split mass addition lines. You can, however, post one of the lines to create a new asset, and then add the second mass addition line to the existing asset as a Cost Adjustment.

Adding to an asset

You can add a mass addition line to an existing asset as a Cost Adjustment. This could be done to add a split line or to add a component after the original asset was placed in service.

You can choose to amortize over the life of the asset or expense the Cost Adjustment in the current period. If you have already depreciated the asset before the adjustment is transacted then you have to make a choice, or else all adjustments are considered before the depreciation calculation was made.

Let's better understand the difference between the following two options:

- Expensing the adjustment results in a one-time adjusting journal entry
- Amortized adjustments, spreads the adjustment amount over the remaining life of the asset

 You can set up your amortized adjustments to have a retroactive start date by changing the default amortization start date.

Future dated transactions

You can add an asset with a future date placed in service using the **Prepare Mass Additions Workbench**. This transaction can only be entered in your corporate depreciation book. You cannot enter future assets directly into Tax Books or budget books. Once a future asset becomes effective in the Corporate Book in the designated accounting period, you can use **Mass Copy** to copy the asset into associated Tax Books.

Mass Additions Create program in Oracle Payables forces the date placed in service to be in the current open period, even if the general ledger date and invoice date are in the future. To use Oracle Assets to process future invoice additions, you must set the **FA: Default DPIS to Invoice Date** profile option to **Yes**. This allows you to default the date placed in service to the **Invoice Date**.

Oracle Assets defaults depreciation parameters when you enter the addition transaction via the Prepare Mass Additions window. Future dated asset transactions have default information based on the assignments at the time the transaction was created.

Post Mass Additions

Once you have completed the previous preparatory work you can run Post Mass Additions to create assets.

The available statuses for Mass Addition transactions are as follows:

- **NEW**: When a transaction is transferred from payables or loaded using Web ADI.

- **ON-HOLD**: Changes to this whenever you open the transaction line and save the transaction.

- **POST**: You must manually change the queue to POST either on the **Mass Additions Prepare** form or can set it to POST when loading assets using Web ADI.

- **COST ADJUSTMENT**: This status is set when you are making an adjustment to an existing asset. When you make the link to an existing asset and set the queue to POST the system changes it to COST ADJUSTMENT. This status enables the accurate tracking of the type of transaction on an asset.

- **DELETE**: You can set this to any queue name if you want to delete a transaction from the mass additions table. You must run a process to physically delete the records from the database.

This process to be submitted successfully requires at the very least one transaction to have queue name set to POST or COST ADJUSTMENT.

These following statuses are set by the system and cannot be entered manually:

- **DELETED**
- **POSTED**
- **FUTURE ADD**
- **FUTURE ADJUST**
- **FUTURE CAPITALIZE**

Manual entry

You can also enter manual assets in the system if you do not use Oracle Payables as your integrated system to generate asset transactions.

The manual entry requires you to enter all the asset information and has two options:

- Quick additions
- Additions

Quick entry is an easy way of adding assets to an existing Asset Book, if you do not use Payables or Web ADI to interface transactions into the mass additions tables. The following screenshot shows the quick entry screen:

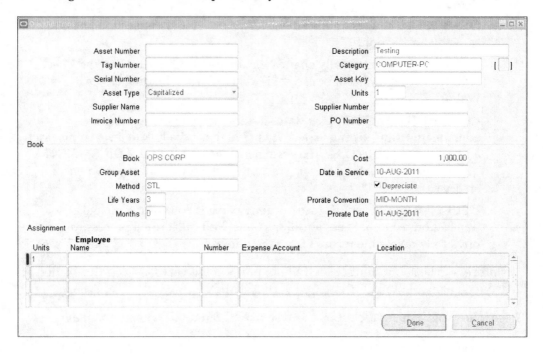

When you are using the **Quick Entry** form you are unable to add source line information such as multiple invoice lines that make up the cost of this asset. However, you can add Cost Adjustments to an existing asset using from payables and the source details will be stored for reference.

You can use the **Additions** form which gives the capability of capturing additional data to reflect your asset accurately. Use the **Additions** form if you are converting assets from an existing system and have other information to add such as the following:

- Source line information
- YTD depreciation
- Accumulated depreciation

You can use Web ADI to add asset information in the process of converting from a legacy system to Oracle Assets.

Short tax years

When assets are acquired as a result of a merger, the first year during which the assets are acquired are typically depreciated during a shorter than normal tax year. It is essential that the acquiring company is able to depreciate the acquired assets correctly during the short tax year.

When you add short tax year assets, you must use either the detail additions or the mass additions process. You cannot use the quick additions process to add short tax year assets. You can define custom depreciation formulas to help you depreciate the newly acquired assets properly in a short tax year.

The following tasks walk you through how to enter and identify a short tax year for an asset. Follow these steps to add an asset using the detail additions process:

- While in the **Books** window, check the **Short Fiscal Year** checkbox to indicate the current year is a short tax year.
- Enter the conversion date. This is the date the short tax year asset begins depreciating in the acquiring company.
- Enter the original depreciation start date of the acquired assets. This is the date when the assets began depreciating in the acquired company.
- Continue adding the asset.

Transferring assets

Assets can be transferred based on changes in the assignment screen. The assignment screen captures and stores information related to the following:

- Change in units
- Employee assignment
- Expense (depreciation) account
- Location

A transfer will be recorded and historical tracking information will be maintained for reporting.

Construction-in-Process (CIP)

CIP assets are created in a similar manner as standard Capitalized assets, and they are adjusted over time with Cost Adjustments to build the actual cost until the asset is capitalized.

Asset numbers are assigned to the CIP asset and do not change when you capitalize the asset.

Standard procedures for cost adjustments (cost additions) to a CIP asset are done through either an interface from payables or a load using Web ADI.

CIP assets have the same category and other associated details that default from an asset category. The only difference is that no depreciation is calculated until they are capitalized. The **Date Placed in Service (DPIS)** is assumed to be the date when the CIP asset is capitalized. This can be changed when you capitalize the asset and ideally before the first depreciation run for that asset.

Asset impairments

Capital assets may incur unexpected or sudden declines in value. When the recoverable cost of an asset is less than its carrying cost, the amount by which the carrying amount of the asset exceeds its recoverable cost is treated as an impairment loss.

To use the impairment functionality you must ensure that Cash Generating Units are set up and the categories have impairment accounts.

After these steps are completed, use the following business process to enter impairment information:

- Assigning Cash Generating Units to assets can be done at the time when impairment is entered
- Entering or uploading asset impairments using Web ADI and updating asset impairments as needed
- Reviewing asset impairment reports
- Posting asset impairments
- Viewing asset impairments
- Rolling back asset impairments
- Deleting asset impairments

Asset impairments are transacted in the Asset Workbench as shown in the following screenshot:

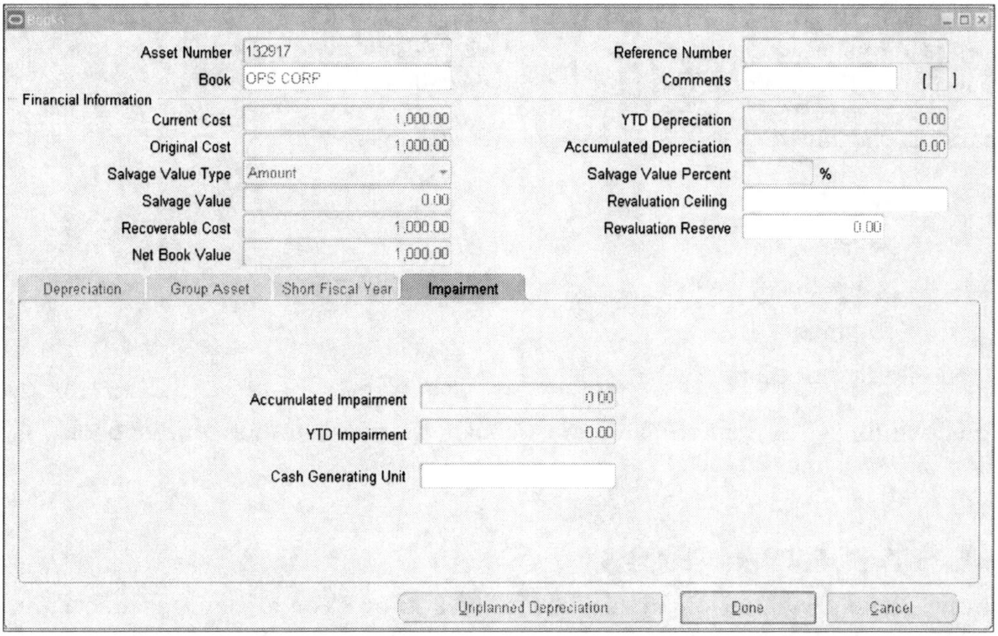

Retirements

Oracle Assets allows you to manage both full and partial retirements of assets. If any asset in the system has multiple units you can retire specific units and the system calculates the appropriate amount to retire.

> You cannot enter a previously dated retirement transaction that crosses fiscal years.
>
> You cannot retire assets by units in your Tax Books; you can only perform partial and full cost retirements in a Tax Book.
>
> You can only perform full retirements on CIP assets; you cannot retire them by units, or retire them partially by cost.

Mass transactions

Oracle Assets recognizes that there are multiple focus shifts in enterprises that result in changes to accounting representations. To allow for this kind of situations and change in business rules Oracle Assets has a functionality to make changes to a collection of transactions. This functionality is called **Mass transactions**.

Mass transactions for the following tasks are available:

- Transfers
- Changes
- Revaluations
- Retirements
- Reclassifications

You can only perform mass changes in a book if the configuration for that book allows mass changes.

Other transactions

Physical inventory functionality in Oracle Assets allows you to manage and ensure that the count of assets on your books is physically present in the enterprise.

This functionality requires:

- A unique identifier, which can be either the asset number, tag number, or serial number
- The location
- The number of units

You can enter physical inventory data into the system manually or use Web ADI to load this data for comparison.

You can also perform the following processes in Oracle Assets:

- Manage maintenance schedules for your large long-term assets
- Store and manage Insurance details

There is no functionality to perform additional tasks based on these maintenance and insurance details. They can only be used to report from. Functionality exists where you can update the completion of a maintenance schedule.

You can calculate estimates for insurance premiums, but this for reference purposes only.

Tax Books

You can have multiple Tax Books to manage your property tax requirements. You must have a Corporate Book assigned to each Tax Book. You can have only one Corporate Book per Tax Book; however, you may have multiple Tax Books.

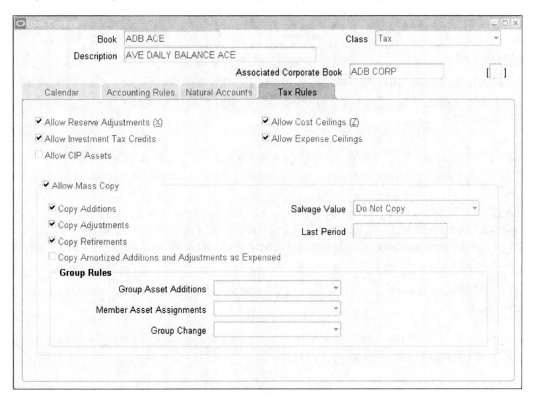

Assets are typically transferred from a Corporate Book to a Tax Book using a standard system process as part of your period end activities. You may choose to make an initial transfer and continue to update the Tax Book with periodic transfers on a regular basis.

The data elements that are copied when you use the copy function are as follows:

- Cost and original cost
- Date Placed in Service (DPIS)
- Capacity and unit of measure, for units of production assets
- Salvage value, if you configured to copy salvage value for this book

The financial information, current cost, original cost, and date placed in service are shared between these books.

The remaining depreciation information comes from the default category information for your Tax Book according to the asset category.

 Initial Mass Copy does not copy any transactions on CIP assets or expensed items.

Use Periodic Mass Copy in each period to keep your Tax Book up-to-date with your Corporate Book. You must run Periodic Mass Copy sequentially for each month for the fiscal year.

 The Tax Books and the Corporate Book can have different fiscal years.

The Periodic Mass Copy program copies addition, adjustment, retirement, and reinstatement transactions to your Tax Book from the current period in the associated Corporate Book. Adjustments are copied only if you choose to do so as part of your book definition.

In the U.S. according to GAAP rules the following transactions can be managed in the Tax Books:

- Investment Tax Credits (ITC)
- Adjusted Current Earnings (ACE)

Depreciation

Oracle Assets contains multiple depreciation calculation rules for standard straight line method depreciation. Other generic depreciation methods used world-wide are also available and can be used to manage assets out of the box.

You can also define additional rate tables and formulas for specific requirements that your business might need.

When running depreciation you have an option to close the period for a specific Asset Book. Once a period is closed for an Asset Book it cannot be re-opened again.

The rollback feature is built into the system, and is not a separate process. When you make an adjustment to an asset after calculating depreciation, the system performs a rollback for that asset. You can then rerun the Depreciation calculation (for that one asset) and any others you may have added.

You must not have closed the period to be able to perform this adjustment.

You can run depreciation projections that are estimates of the actual depreciation expense. You can project the depreciation expense for any depreciation book.

You can run depreciation projections only for the current depreciation parameters set up in your system. If you need to project depreciation for scenarios other than your current setup, you can run the what-if depreciation using different parameters provided at runtime.

You can use the what-if depreciation analysis to forecast depreciation for a group of assets in different scenarios without making changes to your Oracle Assets data.

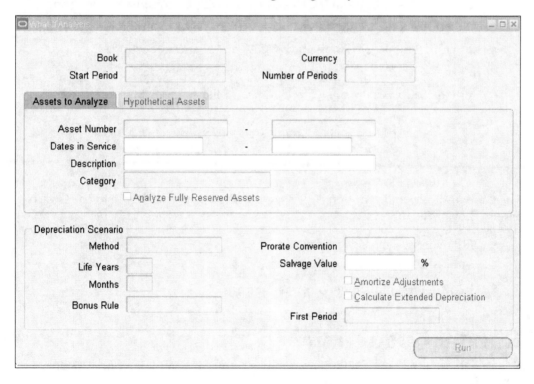

Group depreciation

The group depreciation feature enables you to set up logical groupings of assets based on regulatory requirements and your own business needs. These logical groupings of assets are referred to as group assets. Group depreciation also handles complex transactions for group assets and their member assets.

In many countries, local property tax regulations require companies to depreciate assets in a composite or aggregate form (in a group). The group depreciation functionality addresses the requirements of depreciating assets in groups.

Depreciation is computed and stored at the group level, and is known as group depreciation.

Group Depreciation accommodates many of the composite or aggregate depreciation requirements imposed by the following global regulatory requirements:

- United States Telecomm (FCC) and Utility (FERC) compliance reporting
- United Kingdom Writing Down Allowance (WDA) compliance reporting
- Canada Capital Cost Allowance (CCA) compliance reporting
- Japanese group asset financial and compliance reporting
- Indian group asset management and compliance reporting

 You must allow Group assets for your book in the **Book Controls** window before you can create group assets and use the functionality.

There are multiple configuration choices you make when you choose to use Group assets. They are as follows:

- CIP members and depreciation
- Allow member asset tracking
- Allow inter-company member assignment

Capital budgeting

You can enter budget information manually, or you can maintain your budget information in another system and upload the information using the budget interface. You can prepare and analyze your budget information on any feeder system and then automatically transfer it into Oracle Assets. You can use capital budgets to project depreciation expenses for your assets.

Accounting

As in past releases all the transactional steps remain the same, but the accounting is not created when the depreciation process is run. The accounting is created by the Create Accounting program and is consistent with all other subledgers in the E-Business Suite.

The basis for accounting in Oracle Assets is different from other products. The following table is a high-level overview of how accounting is derived in Assets for all the events:

Account	Source	Notes
Depreciation Expense	Asset Assignment	All segments for Chart of Accounts are sourced from here
Cost of Removal Clearing, Gain & Loss	Book Controls	Only account segment
Deferred Depreciation Expense & Reserve	Book Controls	Only account segment
Net Book Value Retired Gain & Loss	Book Controls	Only account segment
Proceeds of Sale – Clearing, Gain & Loss	Book Controls	Only account segment
Revaluation Reserve Retired Gain & Loss	Book Controls	Only account segment
Asset Clearing	Category	Only account segment
Asset Cost	Category	Only account segment
Bonus Depreciation Expense & Reserve	Category	Only account segment
CIP Clearing & Cost	Category	Only account segment
Depreciation Reserve	Category	Only account segment
Revaluation Reserve	Category	Only account segment
Revaluation Amortization	Category	Only account segment

As you can see in the previous table the rules for the sourcing and creating the account combinations is specific to the type of account. The rules can be listed as follows:

- The balancing segment is always sourced from the Depreciation Expense account from the assignment form.

- The values for all other segments other than the Balancing segment and Account segment are sourced from a default account string that is provided as part of your Book Controls configuration for each book.

- The logic to build these is part of the SLA, and prior to R12, was in the workflow process FA: Account Generator. By default in R12 the SLA is used for account generation unless you set the **FA: Use Workflow Account Generation** profile option to **Yes**.

 If you are upgrading from prior releases the upgrade process sets a profile option to continue using the Workflow and does not switch the account generation to SLA.

Summary

In this chapter, we reviewed how to manage assets that are owned by an organization. We also walked through how to transact, depreciate, and manage the cost and financial adjustments to these assets.

Accounting is managed using the new subledger accounting module introduced in R12; however, the changes made to any workflow Account Generator in pre-R12 versions will be used as is in R12 if performing an upgrade. This can later be transitioned to R12, SLA, for consistency.

The next chapter will cover Cash Management as a corollary to managing the Assets covered in this chapter.

There are multiple aspects, the major ones being Bank Account Reconciliation reporting for Cash Position and Forecasting.

Other transactions include managing Transfer of Cash between accounts that can be managed with a single repository for easier control.

8
Cash Management

Cash management is the task of managing the cash flow in the enterprise. This can be accomplished with the help of an integrated system that tracks all your payables and outstanding receivables balances, and provides you with a net cash flow. The task of managing cash can be broken down into the following broad areas:

- Managing information of financial institutions that you do business with
- Integrating with external financial institutions to make and receive payments
- Reconciling payments and receipts from within your financial system
- Projecting cash position with a cash flow

There are multiple methods to manage these tasks. These tasks are managed sometimes with the help of your financial institutions' web presence, but for a large enterprise the capability to manage should be within its control. This is ideally provided by a financial system that the enterprise uses to capture, manage, and track its own financial and operational transactions.

In this chapter, we will review how to perform all the tasks that will help in getting the enterprise in a position to integrate systems to manage all interactions in a seamless manner. This will include the following:

- Configuration for managing banks, bank accounts, and access to these accounts
- Managing the integrated data transfer between the enterprise and the financial institutions
- Creating templates and reviewing cash flow positions
- Reconciliation for payment transactions

It is important that the processes of managing banks, bank accounts, and their usage are managed in a central location. In the current environment with multiple methods that are electronic, the integration of the systems between your enterprise and the financial institutions has to be secure and easy to manage.

E-Business Suite provides cash management as an enterprise solution that helps you effectively manage and control your cash cycle. It also provides comprehensive bank reconciliation and flexible cash forecasting capabilities.

Bank reconciliation is performed by loading bank statement information from your bank and reconciling against transactions generated within Oracle Payables. These are for payment documents—checks, EFTs, and so on, which have been generated in Oracle Payables.

While you are reconciling payments, you can also create miscellaneous transactions that relate to charges and interest that are part of your bank statement.

You can also reconcile receipts in an automated fashion if you use the automatic receipts functionality within E-Business Suite.

Cash forecasting is a planning tool that helps you anticipate the flow of cash in and out of your business, allowing you to project your cash needs and evaluate your company's liquidity position.

Using sources from other E-Business Suite applications and from external systems, you can generate cash forecasts from previously defined cash forecast templates. Integration with E-Business Suite and other external applications provides you with an enterprise-wide cash information and management solution.

Configuration

There is very minimal configuration in this product. But the most important aspect that is now part of Cash Management in R12 is the maintenance of banks and bank accounts. This also includes creating the payment documents that will be used to make payments to suppliers and other related configuration that will drive accounting to the appropriate ledgers.

You now define banks, bank branches, and bank accounts in Oracle Cash Management.

Bank setup

Bank setups are now part of Cash Management and must be managed with the new **User Management (UMX)** functionality for access to bank accounts for transactions and maintenance of the banking information.

Before you begin defining any bank accounts (or for that matter banks and bank branches), it is important that you understand how the bank account access for maintenance is granted to legal entities.

Bank accounts are owned by Cash Management and are assigned to a legal entity, with access to transact in an operating unit (Oracle Payables or Oracle Receivables).

To grant this access you must use the User Management responsibility, and grant access to legal entities to allow them to manage and transact. These access grants are made to responsibilities that allow maintenance and transaction access to operating units within that legal entity.

Bank account details created before access is granted cannot be used in transactions.

The bank access is granted using the User Management responsibility under the SYSADMIN user. You must log in as SYSADMIN to perform and complete this task.

The following screenshot shows the access that can be granted:

- **Use**
- **Maintenance**
- **Bank Transfers**

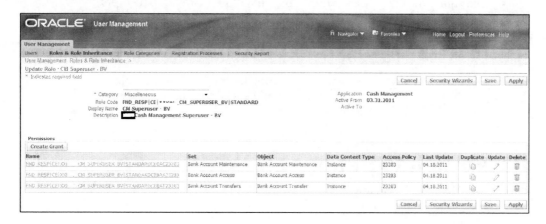

The note 435654.1 on Metalink gives an excellent step-by-step task list regarding appropriate configuration for banks in R12.

Cash Management integration

Cash Management integrates with primarily Oracle Payables and Oracle Receivables to help with reconciling payment transactions from payables and receipts from receivables.

Accounting entries that are related to transactions that are created when Cash Management clears, reconciles, or reverses transactions is managed by payables and/or receivables. No accounting entries are generated in Cash Management. All accounting entries are created within the Oracle Payables or Oracle Receivables products respectively.

Receivables integration

Oracle Receivables allows creation of automatic receipts that can be cleared using Cash Management.

The following are the highlights of what you can achieve with Cash Management integration with receivables:

- Clear and reconcile receipts
- Undo the reconciled status of a reconciled receipt
- Undo the cleared status of a cleared receipt
- Navigate to receivables where you can create or reverse receipts
- Create miscellaneous (non-invoiced) transactions, such as interest, debits, and credits

 If you use automatic clearing for receipts in receivables, receipts are only cleared and are not reconciled against a bank statement.

Payables integration

If you are using payables, and want to reconcile payments you must use Cash Management, to do the following:

- Clear and reconcile payments
- Undo the reconciled status of a reconciled payment
- Undo the cleared status of a cleared payment

- Record miscellaneous transactions that are on your bank statements such as bank charges, or bank errors
- If you plan to use Cash Management to record miscellaneous transactions, you must install and set up receivables, since miscellaneous payments in Cash Management are actually *negative* miscellaneous receipts
- Open the Payments window to enter the payables payments

Payroll integration

Integration with Payroll allows you to do the following:

- Reconcile your payroll account with your bank statement
- Undo the reconciled status of a reconciled payroll payment

Treasury integration

Cash Management integrates with Oracle Treasury through the Reconciliation Open Interface. Using Cash Management, you can do the following:

- Update bank account balances in Oracle Treasury
- Reconcile Treasury settlements against your bank statements
- Undo the reconciled status of a reconciled Treasury settlement

Bank Reconciliation

Bank Reconciliation is the task of matching your payments to a bank statement and ensuring that the checks you have issued have been cashed. This process is called Bank Reconciliation in E-Business Suite.

The following are the steps you perform to manage this task:

- Load bank statements
- Run auto-reconciliation process
- Manage and clear other payment transactions that have not been accurately matched by the automatic reconciliation process
- Run create accounting from payables

E-Business Suite provides standard templates that can be used to load the data from a bank statement. Templates are available for the following:

- BAI2
- SWIFT940
- EDIFACT

Bank transaction codes

If you want to load electronic bank statements or use Cash Management's Auto-Reconciliation feature, you must define, for each bank account, the transaction codes that your bank uses to identify different types of transactions on its statements. You should define a bank transaction code for each code that you expect to receive from your bank.

Open interface

Oracle Cash Management uses the reconciliation open interface to reconcile Treasury settlements. Treasury settlements appear as open interface transactions in Cash Management windows and reports. If you already reconcile open interface transactions from your proprietary applications, you can use the Reconciliation Open Interface to reconcile Treasury settlements as well as the external transactions.

Cash forecasting

Cash forecasting is a tool that integrates within the E-Business Suite and with external data sources to allow an enterprise to manage cash flow into the business based on configured templates. These templates are configurable and you can choose the products/applications you want to integrate selectively.

A template contains cash forecast specifications, and the number and type of rows and columns to create custom forecast templates. Templates determine the presentation of sources (rows) and forecast periods (columns) for your cash forecasts. An important aspect is the forecast period types, either GL periods or days.

The source information from the following shows the inflow of cash:

- Receivables customer invoices (based on due date)
- Receivable customer receipts, historical and uncleared – unapplied on account
- Uninvoiced sales orders
- Opportunities that have not been converted to orders

- GL revenue budgets
- Treasury
- External sources
- User-defined inflow

The source information from the following show the outflow of cash:

- Payables invoices
- Payables payments – historical and future payments
- Expense reports
- Payroll expenses (historical)
- Purchase orders – not invoiced
- Requisitions
- GL expense budgets
- GL encumbrances
- Treasury
- External sources
- User-defined outflow

Oracle Projects also integrates with Cash Management enabling you to build a template to impact cash flow, including project related transactions in receivables and Order Management, Project Billing Events, and Project Budgets. You can also build an outflow using similarly related transactions in payables.

The following screenshot shows how cash forecast would look if it was run to gather information from sources based on the template:

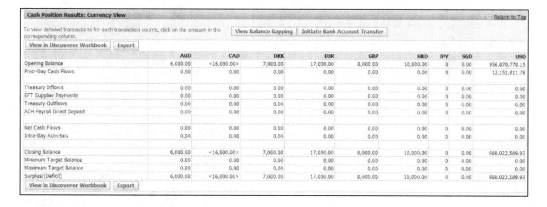

Managing bank account balances

Bank account balance maintenance and reporting are supported for all internal bank accounts that are defined in Oracle Cash Management. For each bank account, you can keep track of multiple bank account balance types including:

- Ledger
- Value dated
- 1-day float
- 2-day float
- Projected month-to-date average
- Year-to-date average

Reporting tools are available to view all this centrally stored balance history for trend analysis.

These data details can be uploaded using the Bank Statement interface that has been briefly described as part of the *Bank Reconciliation* section in this chapter. Use the Bank Statement Loader program to complete these activities.

Cash Management also enables you to verify interest amounts charged or credited by banks based on the balance history and user-defined interest rate schedules. Maintaining interest rate schedules in the system and calculating interest for your interest bearing account enables this functionality.

Cash positioning

Cash positioning is a planning tool that helps you view your daily cash position by currency or bank account. Cash positioning allows you to project your cash needs and evaluate your company's liquidity position.

Cash position differs from cash forecast in that, it includes your bank balance and statement information.

Forecast Results By Transaction Source

TIP To exclude a row, uncheck the Include checkbox and click the Recalculate Summary Cashflows button.   Export

Add Row or Column | View in Discoverer Workbook

Include	Row Number	Source	Description	Feb-04	Mar-04	Apr-04	May-04	Jun-04	Jul-04
☑	2	Supplier Invoices	AP Invoices	<139,385.00>	<10,405,813.01>	<2,194,299.37>	0.00	0.00	0.00
☑	3	Customer Invoices	AR Invoices	3,841,850.38	17,503,717.63	0.00	0.00	0.00	0.00
☑	4	Purchase Orders	Purchase Orders	<3,140,524.14>	<3,227,082.12>	<1,527,621.00>	<1,571,070.00>	<1,534,331.00>	<1,518,331.00>
☑	5	Purchase Requisitions	Purchase Requisitions	0.00	0.00	0.00	0.00	0.00	0.00
☑	6	Sales Orders	Sales Orders	1,203,543.33	0.00	0.00	0.00	0.00	0.00
☑	7	Payroll Expenses	Prior Period Payroll	0.00	0.00	0.00	0.00	0.00	0.00

Recalculate Summary Cashflows

Summary Cashflows	Feb-04	Mar-04	Apr-04	May-04	Jun-04	Jul-04
Cash Inflow	5,045,493.71	17,503,717.63	0.00	0.00	0.00	0.00
Cash Outflow	<3,279,919.14>	<13,632,895.13>	<3,721,920.37>	<1,571,070.00>	<1,534,331.00>	<1,518,331.00>
Net Cashflow	1,765,574.57	3,870,822.50	<3,721,920.37>	<1,571,070.00>	<1,534,331.00>	<1,518,331.00>

Cash transactions

Cash transactions would denote that cash is being paid for services or products. In the cash transactions of Cash Management this is not the case. These transactions are bank account balance transfers.

Transfers

You can create these transfers manually so that they are reflected in the appropriate place to enable you to use Cash Management (or Treasury) as your bank balance reporting/maintaining system.

You can also create bank transfers automatically if you are using cash positioning and choose to use pooled bank accounts. There is a process that can be leveraged in Oracle Cash Management called *cash leveling*. It creates a transfer to level balances across pooled accounts and if you choose to do so creates an automatic funds transfer transaction.

An important profile option to note when performing cash transacting is **CE:Bank Account Transfers**. The value in the profile option determines where the fund transfers are transacted — Oracle Cash Management or Oracle Treasury.

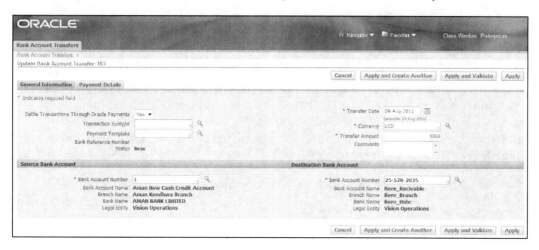

Accounting for these transfer transactions is processed via Oracle Payments (Payables) and subledger accounting to GL. The various statuses for these transactions are as follows:

- **New**: The transfer has been created but not validated yet.
- **Validated**: The transfer has been created and validated. It is ready to be manually authorized for settlement.

- **Invalid**: The transfer has failed validation.
- **Rejected**: The transfer is rejected by the user who is performing manual authorization.
- **Settlement in Process**: The transfer has been authorized for settlement and sent to Oracle Payments.
- **Settled**: The transfer was successfully processed by Oracle Payments or it did not require settlement through Oracle Payments.
- **Failed**: The transfer failed processing in Oracle Payments.
- **Canceled**: The transfer has been manually canceled by the user.

Accounting entries can only be created when the status is either **Settled** or **Settlement in Process**.

Cash flows

Cash flows can be used to create accounting entries from Oracle Cash Management. Cash flows (to create accounting entries) can be created from the following:

- Bank account transfers
- Sweep transactions
- Cash leveling
- Bank statement cash flows

These transactions are currently performed by many organizations, and are performed manually. The basis is a bank statement or advice from the bank. Bank statements can give you all the data related to transfers between accounts, sweeps, and other bank charges. These line details can be used to create journal entries directly from Oracle Cash Management.

You can also include cash flow as a source in cash positioning activity.

Summary

The chapter on Oracle Cash Management allowed us to review the setup and configuration of banks and bank accounts. The tasks and functionality that we discussed also showed the integration that Oracle Cash Management has with other E-Business Suite modules such as Oracle Payables, Oracle Receivables, and so on.

Oracle Cash Management can also capture data to enable tracking and review of cash positions and cash forecasting aspects.

Funds transfer capabilities are easily streamlined by getting information from a bank statement. You can use this data and create the accounting entries to keep your general ledger and bank balances synchronized.

In the next chapter, we will discuss another module that is closely linked to Oracle Cash Management and has been developed as a separate module in R12 – Oracle Treasury. You will review managing cash and the investments that are made in financial instruments, namely, equities, hedge funds, foreign exchange transactions, and other deals. Functionality also exists to perform risk management of investments and track trends. Treasury can also perform funds transfer between companies (legal entities) and bank accounts.

9
Treasury

Prior to the release of Oracle R12, Treasury was part of Cash Management. The functions that you can perform in Cash Management and Treasury are similar though they are two different products in R12.

Treasury allows you to manage Cash, Investment Portfolio, and also gives you the capability to create journal entries based on inter-fund, inter-entity, and inter-bank transfers.

Oracle Treasury also enables management of interest accruals and charges. Specific configurations drive how these transactions are created. Templates allow data to be captured for reporting and manage positions for cash, funds, and portfolios.

Configuration

Generally, you set system parameters during your initial implementation, but you can review and modify them, as needed, later. Many Oracle customers find that as their processes mature, configuration changes are necessary. The following activities can be managed using configuration options in Oracle Treasury:

- Portfolio codes
- Confirmation templates
- Journal entry actions
- Deals for bond and stock issues
- Company and counter-party profiles (counterparty is generally a bank)
- Policies—deal and product types, limits, and hedging policies
- Limits

The following screenshot shows the configuration steps to define deals and their subtypes; these help in managing an investment portfolio:

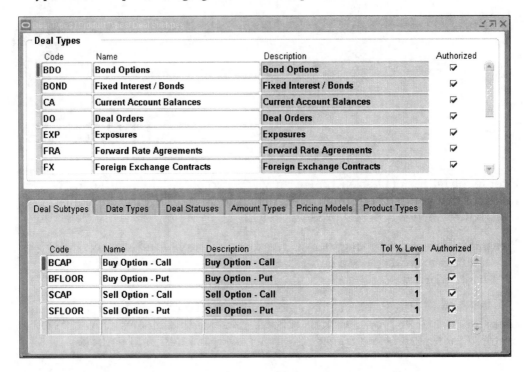

A deal is a specific investment vehicle that you can use to manage your funds. Treasury allows you to track deals and manage activity against a deal so that you can review all the information in a single place.

You can set up deal types including stocks, bonds, registering certificates available for issue, setting up payment schedules, defining your exposure types, and setting up hedges.

This allows an enterprise to manage all their investments and be able to review and manage risk in a central place.

Limits can manage controls and allow configuration specific thresholds to be placed on transactions for counterparties, companies, currencies, dealers, and so on.

Every deal you enter into has an element of risk. If you enter into a fixed interest rate loan, there is a risk that the interest rate will drop. If you buy a large amount of foreign currency, there is a risk that the currency will lose its value. Use limits to define the tolerances for deal-related risks.

Tolerances can be defined to manage thresholds (to name a few) as follows:

- Term limits
- Sovereign limits, related to a country
- Currency
- Counterparty or groups of counterparties
- Daily transactional limits
- Dealer based limits

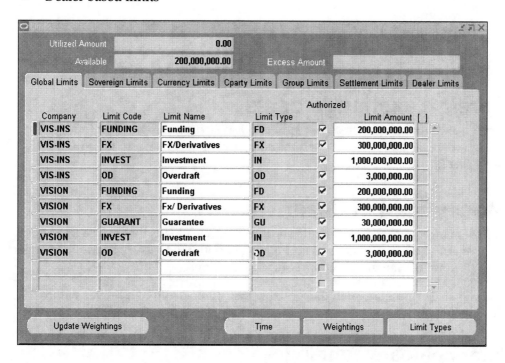

Company	Limit Code	Limit Name	Limit Type	Authorized	Limit Amount [ ]
VIS-INS	FUNDING	Funding	FD	☑	200,000,000.00
VIS-INS	FX	FX/Derivatives	FX	☑	300,000,000.00
VIS-INS	INVEST	Investment	IN	☑	1,000,000,000.00
VIS-INS	OD	Overdraft	OD	☑	3,000,000.00
VISION	FUNDING	Funding	FD	☑	200,000,000.00
VISION	FX	Fx/ Derivatives	FX	☑	300,000,000.00
VISION	GUARANT	Guarantee	GU	☑	30,000,000.00
VISION	INVEST	Investment	IN	☑	1,000,000,000.00
VISION	OD	Overdraft	OD	☑	3,000,000.00
				☐	
				☐	

As part of the configuration you can also assign/restrict access to specific companies and products to applications' users to perform certain transactions in Treasury.

As part of the configuration you can also choose from the various deal type components that are available in the treasury system.

Transactions

Transactions are dealt with based on the type of activity you intend to perform. You may or may not transact all the types of treasury activity a large enterprise engages in, but the functionality to perform these transactions is available:

- Foreign exchange deals
- Money market deals
- Trade equities
- Hedging deals
- Bank balance management
- Settlements

Foreign exchange deals

Foreign exchange transactions use spot and forward rates to transact (buy/sell) foreign currency amounts between the company (enterprise) and the counter party (bank).

Money market deals

Money market transactions include short term money loans that can be used by companies. These can be entered and managed with the treasury portfolio to ensure a single point of view for all your money transactions.

You can also transact in related negotiable instruments and derivatives within this functionality.

Inter-company funding

You can use inter-company funding to manage the debt and investment relationships centrally between a company and the parties that are part of its inter-company group.

 If you enter into an inter-company funding deal with another company, journal entries are automatically created for both companies.

Journal entries are generated for each company based on the **Journal Entry Actions** screen. This has been addressed later in this chapter as part of the *GL Transactions* section.

Use the bank account interest rates window to set up the default interest rates that you want to use for your inter-company funding deals. You can use the standard global interest rates for inter-company funding.

Global interest rates are the default for inter-company funding rates for transactions for a company and account balance range. These are for a combination of company, party, currency, and account balance range.

 If an applicable specific interest rate exists, that rate is used in place of any global interest rates that may exist.

You can also use open interfaces to load frequent funding deals. Alternatively, if they are available in electronic sources such as bank files or other third-party applications, use the XTR_DEALS_INTERFACE table and the deal interface summary window to import the deal details.

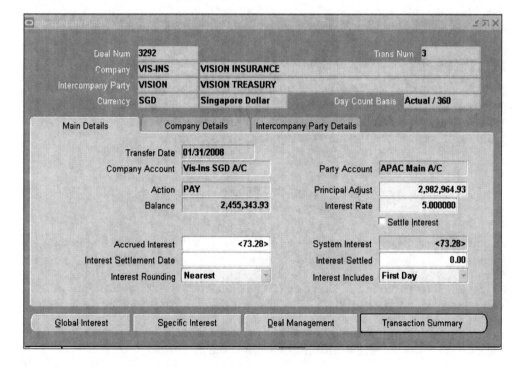

These transactions help the enterprise manage and track all funding related information in one place and easily aggregate all the information for effective reporting.

In addition to the inter-company funding you can also perform the following within money market deals:

- Short term money
- Wholesale term money
- Retail term money
- Negotiable securities
- Discounted securities
- Fixed income securities
- Derivatives
- Forward rate agreements
- Interest rate swaps
- Bond options
- Interest rate options

Equities

Equity is a share of stock that your company either invests in or wishes to track. You use the equities deal type and related windows to set up stock issue information, purchase, track, and resell shares of stock, process cash dividends, and settle, revalue, and account for stock investment activities in other companies.

 The purpose of the Treasury equities functionality is to manage your company's investment or trade in stocks issued by other companies.

You can purchase stocks for the type stock issue codes you have defined in the system and only those authorized can transact these deals.

You can use the open interface load process to load market rates/values and then revalue your existing portfolio holdings for equities to arrive at the current value.

You can also enter and manage dividends on equities you own to track all relevant transactional data for these portfolios in a single place.

Any changes to the value, position, or ownership of equities create journal entries based on how you configure the journal entry actions.

Hedging

Hedging is the process of trading and transacting two opposing investment vehicles to ensure that the loss is minimized due to the net effect of managing monies in both of these investment vehicles.

The end result is that losing money in one investment may be diffused by the other investment gaining (best case scenario). The net result is a gain nevertheless.

Oracle Treasury can manage hedging transactions using currencies if the enterprise has receivables and payables in multiple currencies. You can use input from these products to identify your risks and also be able to use that information in preparing your hedge portfolio.

You can also manage forecast hedgers within Oracle Treasury.

Bank balance management

Oracle Treasury enables managing your bank balances, reconciling them, and also managing transfers between bank accounts.

You can manage and maintain your balances in the system and review these in Oracle Treasury. However, bank balances are only loaded using Oracle Cash Management. You have to transfer them from Oracle Cash Management to Oracle Treasury. The *Transfer CE Bank Statement to Treasury* process makes the data available in Oracle Treasury for reporting and other transactional tasks.

You can manage the balances and also enter information to allow the system to calculate interest for those accounts that have interest bearing balances.

Interest rates and other charges are managed within a portfolio and pricing model to calculate accrued interest. Subsequently, when bank balances/statements are loaded into the system these will net out with actual interest generated and credited to your account by the financial institution.

Bank reconciliation is managed within Oracle Cash Management and not in Oracle Treasury. When statements are loaded with interest and charges in Oracle Cash Management, these can be made available in Oracle Treasury to report and track balances.

The following screenshot shows how the bank balances are maintained and managed in Treasury to synchronize with the GL balances for your enterprise/entity:

Balance Date	Name	Type	Account Number	Legal Entity	Bank Name	Bank Branch	Currency	Ledger Balance	Available Balance	Value Dated Balance	1 Day Float	2 Day Float	Projected Balance	Average Closing Ledger MTD	Average Closing Ledger YTD	Average Closing Available MTD	Average Closing Available YTD
12/31/1997	Primary Checking Account-202	Bank Account	1233349-484877	Vision Corporation	Bank of America	San Francisco	USD	<57,336.82>									
12/31/1998	Primary Checking Account-202	Bank Account	1233349-484877	Vision Corporation	Bank of America	San Francisco	USD	<573,025.61>									
01/31/1999	Primary Checking Account-202	Bank Account	1233349-484877	Vision Corporation	Bank of America	San Francisco	USD	<668,829.01>									
02/28/1999	Primary Checking Account-202	Bank Account	1233349-484877	Vision Corporation	Bank of America	San Francisco	USD	<719,639.24>									
03/31/1999	Primary Checking Account-202	Bank Account	1233349-484877	Vision Corporation	Bank of America	San Francisco	USD	<771,061.43>									
04/30/1999	Primary Checking Account-202	Bank Account	1233349-484877	Vision Corporation	Bank of America	San Francisco	USD	<823,665.48>									
05/31/1999	Primary Checking Account-202	Bank Account	1233349-484877	Vision Corporation	Bank of America	San Francisco	USD	<875,274.23>									
06/30/1999	Primary Checking Account-202	Bank Account	1233349-484877	Vision Corporation	Bank of America	San Francisco	USD	<927,211.15>									
07/31/1999	Primary Checking Account-202	Bank Account	1233349-484877	Vision Corporation	Bank of America	San Francisco	USD	<982,455.67>									

Interest rates are maintained by external loads in Oracle Treasury to manage deal, brokerage, and other charges. These can be applied to account balances, deals, equities, and other investments to get true cash position analysis.

You can also review your liquidity position using the Oracle Treasury module as long as all data has been entered manually or using external feeds into the system.

Settlements

Settlement is the validation/approval process for the transactions that you have entered as part of the deal management process or any other transfer or charge and interest that may be calculated.

Transaction validation

Any transaction that you have entered must be validated before you can account for it. The process validating these transactions is managed by a system option that you choose to configure accordingly.

Settlement and accounting can only be performed after the transaction has been validated.

Settlements are normally conducted to review and approve/authorize specific transactions that lead to the following two tasks:

- Payment initiation
- Accounting entries

Authorization is a required step before these two tasks can be initiated. This is important to appropriately manage both the legal liability to make a payment and/or create an accounting entry to reflect a liability in your books.

Accounting actions

The Journal Entry Actions manage how these accounting entries are created.

For each applicable company, you define the journal entry actions for a combination of the following:

- **Deal Type**
- **Deal Subtype**
- **Product Type**
- **Portfolio**

The following screenshot shows a transaction for a combination of these elements that will create an accounting entry. You will notice that all the elements for creating a journal entry have to be specified in this screen.

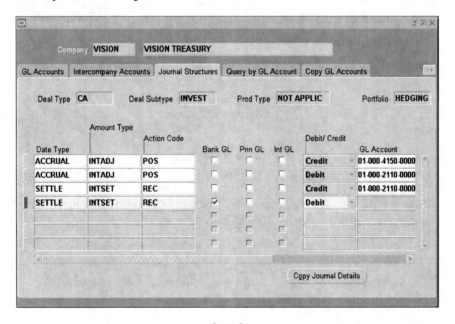

The date type drives the date of the journal entry. The following are the date types available:

- **ACCRUAL**: Accrual date
- **COMMENCE**: Rollover date
- **DEALT**: Dealt date
- **RATESET**: Rateset date
- **REVAL**: Revaluation date
- **SETTLE**: Actual settlement

The amount type is the amount that is used for the journal line. The following amount types are available:

- **CCYREAL**: Currency exchange
- **CCYUNRL**: Currency exchange unreal
- **FACEVAL**: Face value amount
- **INITIAL**: Inital principal
- **INTADJ**: Accured interest
- **INTRFND**: Prepaid interest refund
- **INTSET**: Forecast interest
- **PRINFLW**: Pronicipal
- **REAL**: Realized gain/loss
- **TAX**: Tax amount
- **UNREAL**: Unrealized gain/loss

Depending on the activities that you are performing you may use all or part of these dates and amount types.

The action type denotes a posting or a reversal and is a list of values that you can choose from.

You can specify the GL account that should be used or you can use one of the checkboxes to specify an existing account to use from a related setup/configuration:

- Choose **Bank GL**, if you want the journal action to refer to the general ledger number related to the company's cash flow bank account
- Choose **Prin GL** if this is an inter-company funding deal, direct journal actions to either the principal, or the interest general ledger account
- The last two checkboxes are only available for non-accrual and non-revaluation date types

Journals created from Oracle Treasury do not use the SLA layer to create journals in GL. These transactions are processed directly into the GL Interface table.

 Oracle Treasury has not implemented SLA yet, and therefore drill down capability is not available from journal transactions generated from Oracle Treasury.

A more detailed instruction set and steps for creating various accounting entries are available on MetalinkNote - ID 1328696.1, as well as related documents that are contained within that note.

Summary

In this chapter, we reviewed some of the basic functionality within the Oracle Treasury product.

Deals are termed as any one of the following; they are managed within the Oracle Treasury with appropriate accounting entries and payments:

- Foreign exchange deals
- Money market deals
- Inter-company transfers
- Equities
- Hedging
- Bank balance management

Oracle Treasury is closely integrated and uses data elements that are owned by Oracle Cash Management. Using these two products together is an effective way to benefit from the complete functionality these two products provide.

In the next chapter, *Order Management*, we will review how to manage sales orders and fulfill them with a normal streamlined process that allows products and services to be placed on order and shipped to customers.

10
Order Management

Order Management allows users to manage orders for products and services (including warranties) that the enterprise either manufactures or contracts to build and/or assemble. There are situations where the order is provided by a consumer, the shipment is done via a partner, and the enterprise processes the order transaction.

Order Management is a wider area than just this module. Multiple integrated products work with Order Management to give you a full suite of order processing and fulfillment capabilities for your enterprise.

This chapter covers the following topics:

- Order Management: Order Capture and an overview of related processes
- Order Fulfillment using Oracle Shipping Execution
- Basic Pricing

Other modules typically used in order processing are mentioned, only where they are relevant to the discussion and when a full system process or function description is needed. These may include:

- Quote Management
- Advanced Pricing
- iStore
- Release Management
- Configurator
- Global Order Promising
- Manufacturing related modules: Cost Management, Work In Process, Bill of Material, and so on

- Trade Management
- Service Contracts
- Install Base

Other modules integrated with order processing covered in this book are:

- Inventory
- Receivables
- Purchasing

Before processing orders in your system the following must be in place; these are related configurations in other modules, some of which are covered in this book:

- Items (Oracle Inventory).
- Customers, including credit rules. The customer must have a Ship To site and a Bill To site.
- Price list.
- Salesperson (optional but desirable).

 Though optional, the salesperson is an important data element that can drive accounting representation, sales compensation, and other reporting requirements. A default named *No Sales Credit* is available.

Items

You need items because your customer places an order for those items or products that you either build, manufacture, assemble, or buy to be resold with value-added components. These may also include services such as warranties and extended warranties.

In any of these cases these (and other related items) need to be defined and available for use when processing an order.

Chapter 4, Inventory described how inventory works and how items are defined for transacting in either Purchasing or Order Management.

In Purchasing, you can have a Purchase Order that does not have an item. These are referred to as expense Purchase Orders. Examples of these could be office supplies, furniture, and so on.

In the case of a sales order you *must* have an item. It is also a must to have specific attributes checked (or enabled) to be transactable in Order Management.

The following is a screenshot of the tab where order related attributes are managed. The screenshot shows a few key attributes that need to be checked to enable the item to be used on an order transaction:

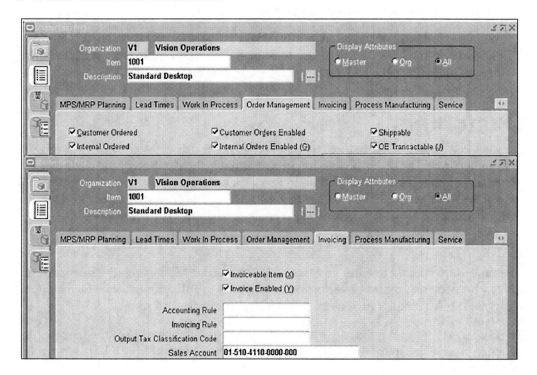

Trading Community Architecture

Customers (as suppliers now) are managed and owned by the **Trading Community Architecture (TCA)**. This framework enables the management of master data in a single location. This framework started in early 2000 and is completed with Release 12. So when you create a customer, the following is the hierarchy of data you enter:

- **Party**
- **Account**
- **Address**
- **Site**
- **Business Purpose**

This is true for all master data managed by TCA, including employees, suppliers, customers, and banks.

The party is not where E-Business Suite transactions occur. The transactions are performed at the account level. A party account is identified as a customer for transactions in Oracle Order Management and Oracle Receivables. It also identifies the supplier for Oracle Purchasing and Oracle Payables.

The details of TCA are not covered in this book. For more information on TCA and the technical and framework design please refer to the Trading Community Architecture Reference Guide (Part No. E13569-04) or User Guide (Part No. E13570-04).

Customers

For many organizations, creating customers is a choice driven by the business process at the enterprise. The order processing group initiates the creation of the customer due to a customer related transaction. In this situation, the customer data is entered for use in Order Management to ship material. This same customer is invoiced for the material shipped. However, you can also create a customer in Receivables.

Your organization's business process determines where the customer is created.

Customers are needed to enter any transaction in Order Management—sales orders, quotes, agreements, returns after processing an order, and a return transforms into a receivables transaction—such as an invoice, credit memo, and so on.

There are certain aspects that are managed on the Receivables side of the fence, or to be more precise, in Credit and Collections, where they manage credit limits, payment terms, and other processing and reporting related identification for customers.

Customer profiles

Profiles for customers are used to apply business rules related to credit worthiness, credit limits on transactions, payment terms, creation of standard statements, and so on.

Use customer profiles to segregate customers into groups for strategic purposes, and also to manage transactions and for reporting.

 E-Business Suite provides a default customer profile. This is assigned to each new customer if you do not choose to assign one specifically.

It is recommended that you create specific customer profiles for your organization that meet your business requirements. This should be done before you start creating your customers in the system, so the profiles can be set appropriately for the customers as you create them.

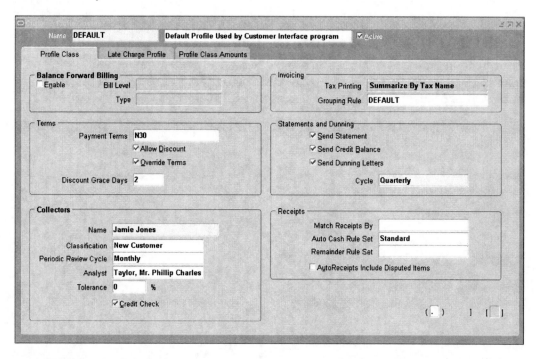

In addition to using profiles to manage customer groupings, you can also modify the profiles for a specific customer. Furthermore, you can apply that modified profile to the following:

- All customers assigned this profile
- Only those that were assigned but were not modified
- Do nothing (no changes that you made are reflected in the already assigned profiles to customers)

 Profiles are only assigned to Bill To sites. These sites are explained when we discuss customers addresses later in this section.

Credit balances can be managed by currency and are used to control booking order transactions. Both open order lines and open invoice lines are checked against the threshold for each currency. The orders can be put on hold (not processed) till the credit level is changed or outstanding transactions are closed.

Customer addresses (sites)

Each customer must have an address to be used on a transaction in either Order Management or Receivables. In Receivables, you only need to have a Bill To site, but in Order Management you will also need a Ship To site.

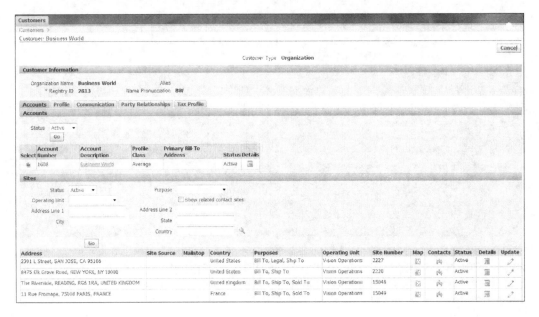

What are sites? Sites are another name for addresses and the site types (Bill To, Ship To, and so on) indicate business purposes or use for a particular addresses. One address can be assigned multiple business purposes.

A partial list of business purposes is as follows:

- Bill To
- Ship To
- Sold To
- Statement
- Dunning

Salespersons

Salespersons are people that sell your products and services and in most companies these people are tracked for sales they closed.

Order Management tracks and monitors salespersons in order to credit the appropriate individuals for closed sales transactions. Order Management uses this to generate appropriate sales credits for the sale.

There are other uses to capture the salesperson on a sales order, and it is an organization's business process that will drive the capture and usage.

There are certain prerequisites and configurations that are necessary for salesperson assignments. These assignments occur in Resource Management. It is outside the scope of this book and chapter to go into details of all the steps but the following are the important prerequisites:

- Define an employee
- Define the employee as a resource
- The resource needs to be created as a salesperson

Salesperson records can also be used to drive accounting information in Receivables transactions. This is optional but is an important aspect for revenue accounting in many enterprises.

 Oracle provides a default salesperson called **No Sales Credit** to use on transactions if you choose not to use salespersons.

Price lists

Price lists are another required aspect for entering and transacting an order. Advanced Pricing is a separate product that Oracle licenses to businesses with complex pricing methodologies and mechanisms.

However, Basic Pricing can be used within Order Management without having to procure the Advanced Pricing product family.

A detailed comparison of the differences between Basic Pricing and Advanced Pricing is available in the Order Management Implementation Manual (Part No. E13406-04). All items that are transacted on an order must be on a price list. The price list must be the one that you chose for the order. The price list for the order is first captured on the Order Header, but can be changed for each line if needed.

You cannot change price list default pricing without defining discount rules.

 You can also control who can change prices on an order line with a profile option that allows or disallows discounting. A discount still must be defined to change the price.

Order capture/entry

Order Management provides an end-to-end solution for processing a simple quote through the negotiation process and automating the transition of the quote to a sales order document and to fulfillment of that order.

A quote can pass through various stages from its initial preparation to fulfillment (as a sales order or sales agreement). These stages include preparing a draft, negotiating with a customer, obtaining internal and external business approvals, versioning, and converting the quote to an order.

Oracle Order Management includes a workflow process to support the activities that occur within a negotiation process, such as internal approval and customer acceptance. This enables creating and managing quotes during the negotiation phase and transforming the quote to a firm order after internal and external approvals.

 A quote is transacted as another order transaction with a type of quote instead of a Sales Order.

There are differences in tasks and processes that are not supported for a quote transaction. The following cannot be managed/transacted for quotes:

- Holds
- Scheduling
- Copy return transactions
- Independent line process flows

The following are a few important considerations for a transaction type when entering an order. To process an order (or a quote) you will need to define a transaction type to manage a couple of the activities that will happen on the sales order transaction, as follows:

- **Document Type**: Sales order or agreement
- **Order Category**: Mixed, order, or return
- **Fulfillment Flow**: To drive processes around completing the transaction with or without approval
- **Credit Check Rules**: To manage credit checks and rules to put order on hold if needed
- **Shipping Defaults**: To identify where the items ordered will ship from
- **Invoicing Details and Accounting**: This defines invoicing parameters and COGS accounting

Once the transaction type is created you can start using it to enter an order. The default source is always manual if you are entering on the screen, but there may be other sources that could be used for importing orders from external data sources. These also require a transaction type with the previous details.

The **Quick Order** screen allows users to enter a manual order quickly and efficiently. Oracle Order Management provides defaulting rules to allow data entry to be managed as a seamless process.

A customer record also contains the basic information you can default to when creating an order transaction. A hierarchy is available on how these data elements are sourced in a transaction. This is important when you are automating or need to bring efficiency into the order capture process.

The following is a list of data elements needed to complete an order booking activity:

- Order transaction type
- Order number
- Customer
- Price list
- Salesperson
- Item (on the price list specified)
- Quantity ordered
- Warehouse (Inventory Organization) from where the order should be fulfilled

In the following screenshot the tabs represent data elements that are required based on various situations when a transaction is entered in Order Management.

- If the item is a *Service Item* type on a specific line the tab **Services** allows data to be entered

 Service Contracts and Order Management integrate to create contracts for service and extended warranties sold on an order.

- If the transaction is a return transaction the **Returns** tab will be activated and you will have to enter specific data for the return transaction
- **Pricing**, **Shipping**, and **Addresses** tabs are all used for either an order or a return transaction

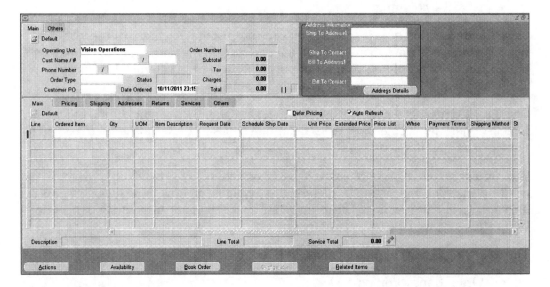

Back to Back orders

Often there are situations where you want to satisfy customer demand and you do not stock or build that product. Instead you must procure it from another source before you can ship it to the customer.

In this case, you can use a process called the **Back to Back order** process. Back to Back orders involve creating a sales order and requisition simultaneously. You process the Sales Order to fulfilment when you receive the product from the supplier.

The steps for this process are as follows:

1. Enter the item on the sales orders line.

2. Run the AutoCreate Requisition concurrent program or you can initiate it for a single order by using the Progress Order action on the sales order.

3. Run the concurrent program Requisition Import to create the purchase requisition tied to the sales order line. You can either manually submit the Requisition Import concurrent program, or you can schedule it to run periodically.

4. A Purchase Order is created, approved, and sent to the supplier.

5. Once the PO or release is received, the items are recorded in inventory and a reservation is automatically made to the sales order line.

6. The sales order can now be pick-released, shipped, and invoiced just like other orders.

Drop-ship orders

When a customer orders products, these are fulfilled/shipped from your warehouse. In cases when you do not have the product in your warehouse, drop-ship orders can be used to fulfill these orders.

To fulfill these orders, create a drop-ship transaction. A drop-ship transaction is a sales order that is fulfilled by raising a purchase on a supplier who will provide the product to the customer directly. The sales order and purchase order are linked in the system.

The following are the steps to create this type of transaction:

1. Create an order in Order Management. Drop shipments are marked with the source type **External** in Order Management.

2. The purchase release concurrent program in Order Management creates rows in the requisition import tables in Purchasing.

3. Purchasing's requisition import process creates requisitions.

4. Requisitions are converted to approved purchase orders. This is where a supplier purchase order is linked to the sales order for the delivery.

5. The purchase order transaction is received when the supplier sends the notification of delivery to the customer. This task can be performed manually or automatically using the **Advanced Shipment Notices (ASN)** functionality.

6. Once the receipt is completed the sales order status changes to **shipped** for the line linked to the Purchase Order.

749139.1 on Metalink is an excellent resource to understand the necessary steps to create drop-ship transactions as well as understanding how these are processed.

Sales agreements

A sales agreement is defined as an agreement with a customer having specific characteristics between you and the customer. These characteristics may include the date range of the agreement, the items, the price for the items, the quantity of each item that the parties committed to, as well as other attributes, such as freight or payment terms. Once a sales agreement is entered for a customer, multiple releases (shipments) against the sales agreement may be processed over a period of time within Order Management.

Tracking information is also accumulated for sales agreement such as quantity fulfilled, and dollar value fulfilled of released lines. This information will be used to view status of orders executed against a sales agreement.

Sales agreements interface with Oracle Pricing to price sales agreement lines, default pricing information, and provide special pricing for sales agreements.

Sales agreements can also be amount based and not necessarily for a set of items. The amount may be consumed for any items that the customer might purchase.

Order Import

Order Import is an Order Management open interface that consists of interface tables and a set of APIs. Order Import can import new, changed, and completed sales orders or returns from other applications such as a legacy system or other order capture mechanisms.

The orders may also come from any source such as EDI transactions that are processed by the Oracle e-Commerce Gateway.

Internal sales orders are also created using this same mechanism for internal requisitions transacted in Oracle Purchasing.

Order Management checks all the data during the import process to ensure its validity. Valid transactions are converted into orders with lines, reservations, price adjustments, and sales credits in the base Order Management tables.

Return Material Authorization (RMA)

This process allows you to enter, update, and process customer returns of products that you shipped to the customers.

RMA transactions are processed with or without credits, so that you can specify if you want to give the customer credit for the return, which creates a credit memo. This credit transaction will be applied to the invoice automatically in Receivables. If no credit is expected the return transaction will only return the material to your warehouse.

 The automatic credit memo application to the invoice only happens when you copy an order to an RMA or use the order number and line reference on the RMA transaction.

There are multiple seeded process flows that can process your returns, shown as follows:

- Return for credit with receipt of goods and approval
- Return for credit with receipt of goods
- Return for credit only
- Return for credit only with approval

There are specific configurations necessary to process RMA transactions. There are multiple steps and setups involved in completing RMA transaction. The following are some major criteria to be configured:

- Return order flows (workflow processes, seeded ones are available)
- Receiving returned goods
- Invoicing (credit) activity
- Item attributes
- Oracle Order Management transaction types (order category must be *Return* or *Mixed*)
- Return reasons (defaults available)

RMA transactions can be created in multiple ways. One of the easiest ways is to copy from an existing order that was used to ship that product.

You cannot successfully complete this transaction flow if the order being copied has been invoiced and the invoice has been paid.

Generally, the invoice transaction is defined to only hold a positive balance, so applying a credit memo when the balance is zero will not be successful.

Item Orderability

Item Orderability is a functionality that limits the List of Values for items in an order transaction to those items that can be transacted in that organization. This is driven by rules that you configure to manage the list accessible to the user. If you do not configure any rules then all the items are listed in the LOV.

 This functionality was introduced in E-Business Suite Release 12.1.

Configuration

There are multiple configurations that help manage the order capture functionality and processing of transactions. The following is a list of some of them along with a brief description:

- **Order Types**: Identifies the type of order and process flow (workflow) the transaction will follow. The order type also defines some transaction defaults, credit checking, invoicing activity and tax calculation, timing, and functionality.

- **Process Constraints**: There are multiple processing constraints that are provided with Oracle Order Management. A processing constraint is a restriction or availability of a specific task such as changes and deletion. These can be modified to align with your business needs.

- **System Parameters**: This defines the basic criteria driving access to item information, the main one, and other related aspects used for transaction processing.

- **Workflow**: Seeded default workflow processes are available that allow generic processing of standard orders. These can be modified to include business rules that may be relevant to your organization.

- **Credit Checking Rules**: This enables a business to control order acceptance for customers who are overdue on their payments or have a high balance before processing the order.

- **Pick and Ship Rules**: This determines how picking and shipping activities will consolidate a selection of orders when the picking/shipping activity is performed. A report is generated that can be used to pick the specified items.

- **Account Generator**: Account Generator is the pre-R12 version of the accounting engine that allows the system to generate a COGS account when the shipment is complete. The default COGS account is on the item, and can be overridden by the Order Type.

You can modify the COGS account generation with a change using modifications to SLA in R12.

Configure to Order (CTO)

There are various cases where standard configurations are not acceptable to some customers, and some products cannot be preconfigured for sale. Enabling Confgure to Order (CTO) allows the creation of orders with various options and components to build the product at the time of placing the order.

 Basic configurations can be managed using Order Management and Bills of Material products; for complex configurations, Oracle Configurator a separate product may be needed.

The following are a few optional facilities that you can use to accept orders for maximum flexibility:

- Assemble to Order (ATO)
- Pick to Order (PTO) Item (Kit)
- Pick to Order (PTO) Model
- Hybrid, a combination of PTO and ATO

Order actions

There are multiple actions that can be performed on an order, some at entry and others after booking. Process constraints configuration allows or disallows actions based on rules that are seeded or defined by you for your business.

All order transactions must be booked before they can be transacted further. These include the following:

- Credit Check
- Picking Items
- Shipping Items

Other actions can be performed at specific times either before or after booking or at pick time. The following is a list of some of these actions:

- **Additional Order Information**
- **Reservation**
- **Scheduling**
- **Progress Order**
- **Tax Calculation**
- **Applying changes**
- **Pricing updates (Repricing)**
- **Applying attachments**
- **Sales Credit**

A complete list of these actions is available in the *Order Management User Guide (Part No. E13408-04).*

Shipping execution

Shipping execution is part of the standard functionality. It is available with your license of Inventory and Order Management. Shipping execution enables the enterprise to ship and fulfill your customer orders.

Several steps are required before shipping tasks may be completed. They are as follows:

1. All users must be granted a role to allow them to perform the task.
2. A role is assigned to the user in Order Management. A seeded role is available for normal shipment activity.
3. Shipment methods must be defined.
4. Freight carriers must be defined.

Shipment consists of two steps before the transaction moves into accounting as follows:

- **Picking**: This task requires the user to enter warehousing and shipping method information
- **Shipping**: This task completes the action of sending the products to the customer, by putting this on a truck or other transportation vehicle for the delivery and capturing the shipping details

After these are complete the Create Accounting process generates the accounting entries to record the Cost of Goods Sold (COGS) for the products shipped.

The steps to complete an order form booking to invoicing are as follows:

1. The status for the lines that have shippable items changes to **awaiting shipping** once the order is booked
2. For items that are not shippable the status changes to **fulfilled**
3. The next task of picking an order line creates delivery lines
4. Delivery lines can be grouped together for shipment
5. The product(s) on the line(s) are reserved once they are picked
6. The system automatically reserves these products without reserving specifically before this task
7. The delivery lines for multiple orders can be combined together on a single delivery task
8. Multiple delivery lines can be combined to efficiently use your shipping methods
9. These could be for different customers, and your freight carrier will need documentation as where to deliver them
10. This is done with the help of shipping documents printed after the delivery is confirmed (or closed)
11. Shipping documents can be used to complete the ship confirm task, which manages accounting and reduction of product value/inventory quantity
12. When the line status changes to **fulfilled**, the line proceeds to the next step/action, that is, invoicing

Your business has important choices to make regarding shipping and invoicing. You can:

- Invoice each line as it is fulfilled
- Invoice each set of lines as they are fulfilled (grouping)
- Invoice only when all lines are fulfilled

If you choose the first option you will likely have an invoice for each line on the order, assuming that invoicing is immediate. Most customers would like to receive a complete product that is usable. The second option allows for invoicing for a group of lines or a complete product. The third option allows invoicing to progress only after all the lines ordered are fulfilled.

Order Management provides functionality to manage these by using ship and fulfilment sets:

- **Ship Sets**: This functionality ties all the shippable lines together and sends them to the interface tables for invoicing once all the lines included in a particular ship set are fulfilled
- **Fulfilment Sets**: This functionality ties together all the lines on an order that should be invoiced together, including shippable and non-shippable products

Fulfilment Sets can be easily explained with the following example:

- An order contains five lines of products, with two additional lines for support and service respectively. The first five lines are shippable products. The last two are not shippable.
- To process the first five lines together and fulfill them at the same time use a ship set to group them together.
- The next two lines are not shippable so you cannot use a Ship Set. These are service items and would only be credible if they were invoiced once the products were at the customer site.
- Use a fulfilment set to connect all seven lines together so they process together to invoicing.

Arrival Sets are another important functionality that has been introduced in R12 to ensure that all the material shipped arrives at the customer location at the same time.

> Multi-line orders can have multiple Ship Sets and multiple Fulfilment Sets. You can have lines in Ship Sets and Fulfilment Sets at the same time. You may also have lines in Arrival Sets and Fulfilment Sets at the same time. However, you cannot have lines in Ship Sets and Arrival Sets at the same time.

Accounting

A shipping task is executed as part of the Order Management menu stack, but is actually a function that is managed and performed in the Inventory product. This is important to note because no accounting transactions flow to General Ledger from Order Management. The system creates an accounting entry to register the Cost of Goods Sold (COGS), and this is sent to General Ledger from Cost Management (from Inventory in prior releases).

When the quantity is decremented from your Inventory the accounting impact is recorded in your books by the COGS accounting event.

This task of decrementing the inventory value in your books and creating the accounting for an order shipment is performed after *ship confirm* transaction is complete.

Summary

In this chapter, we reviewed how to capture order information from your customers for products that you stock. We also reviewed ways in which to procure and ship to your customer some products that you do not keep in stock or did not have enough of levels to fulfill the order.

You also had an overview of the configuration and master data elements required to create an order, including customers, pricing, and salesperson.

In the next chapter, you will review how these order transactions are financially tracked to collect and manage revenue aspects for financial reporting.

11

Receivables

Oracle Receivables allows you to manage all your receivable transactions based on orders and service contracts that may have been transacted in other modules. Most invoicing (and credit) transactions are sourced from Order Management, Service Contracts, and Oracle Projects.

The capability exists to create manual transactions and import/create invoice transactions (including Credit Memos) from external non-Oracle systems. Oracle Receivables also manages cash receipts and applications. This chapter intends to lead the reader through a modular approach for configuring, creating receivable transactions, and applying cash to manage the account receivables and collection activities in an enterprise.

This chapter discusses the functional tasks of receivables and collections, including:

- iReceivables
- E-Business Tax
- Trading Community Architecture
- Receivables
- Collections (Advanced Collections)
- Bill Presentment Architecture

The products listed previously form part of the activity of a receivables department workload and not all will be covered in detail, though we will touch on each of these to help the readers understand how the products work together.

We will focus on the following three tasks that are more receivable centric in this chapter:

- iReceivables
- Receivables
- Advanced Collections (only to the extent it affects using Receivables)

iReceivables

Configuration for iReceivables consists of various options that you select based upon the business processes for your enterprise. These configurations allow users to manage and view their data in specific ways that have meaning for them. You can choose to build forms that are most suited for each user so that it gives them the opportunity to review the data that is most relevant to them.

You can view customer aging and account information from a single screen and make payments for open transactions. This is the only transaction that can be initiated from within iReceivables.

Configuration drives rules that can change form layout and data shown for specific customer/customer sites.

By clicking on the **Account** tab you can view all transactions. When a transaction number is clicked on you can view the activity on that transaction.

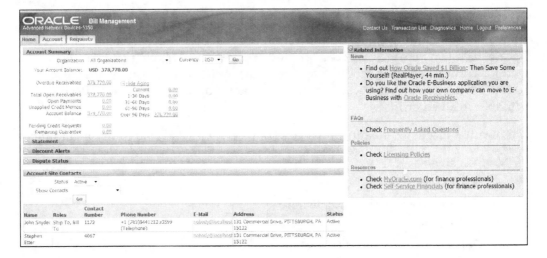

E-Business Tax

E-Business Tax is the new rules based tax engine that allows for multi-country taxability on transactions. The new module still requires loading of tax rates from a service provider to manage accurate tax calculation.

The configuration for this is discussed in detail in *Chapter 13, E-Business Tax (EBTax)*.

The configuration for tax calculation to work properly in Oracle Order Management, Oracle Receivables, and Oracle Service Contracts requires accurate addresses with appropriate jurisdiction information.

The key aspects of the new tax engine are as follows:

- Jurisdiction and Address Validation
- Requiring rules to apply (or not apply) taxes to receivables transactions

Both the previous tasks are performed as part of the configuration for E-Business Tax.

Choosing to validate addresses in your implementation enforces address validation for all addresses in the system, customers, suppliers, and banks. If you choose to validate U.S. addresses on State, County, City, and Zip, then all addresses have to be accurate based on the combination loaded from the service provider.

The following screenshot shows the validation enabled and the suggestion from the list of accurate combinations loaded from a service provider. This suggestion will only be shown if the address entered is inaccurate.

This validation enabling is done in the Trading Community Architecture framework.

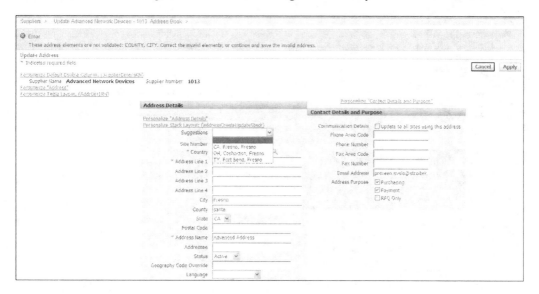

Trading Community Architecture

Trading Community Architecture (TCA) is the new name for all trading partners, suppliers, customers, banks, and employees.

This new framework stores and tracks the data of all these entities.

TCA is a new product released in a prior release of E-Business Suite. In R12 this has been formalized and now owns all the partners that the enterprise deals with. This leads to a difference in the technical and functional aspects of how these data sets are managed in R12.

The most important reason to bring up the TCA is to explain briefly how address validation is managed. The following screenshot shows a depiction of how address validation for U.S. addresses can be configured:

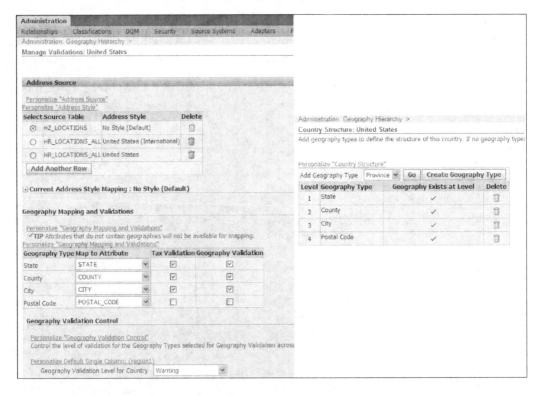

You can manage the structure and the validations using these screens individually.

Receivables configuration

Oracle Receivables system has multiple configuration options that drive how the system works and manage transactions. We will review the major aspects with a brief explanation of what they accomplish and their impact.

Oracle Receivables configuration is operating unit specific. You must configure Oracle Receivables for each operating unit. Based on your access you may be able to perform setup for multiple operating units within a single responsibility.

System options

System options are defined per operating unit. They store data that defaults to transactions related to accounting and general processing rules.

Use system options to specify the following:

- You need a salesperson for an AR Invoice
- Where your territory flexfield is defaulted from
- Your default country
- Customer and customer site numbering
- Write-off limits for receipt write-off

Descriptive Flexfields

Descriptive Flexfields (DFFs) are used by E-Business Suite of applications to store additional information that the system does not naturally capture in a data entry sequence.

Oracle designed its E-Business Suite to use DFFs in numerous modules to aid its customers with capturing and tracking specific data through the system. DFFs also help ensure validity and link to the original transaction. One of these is the line transaction flexfield. This tracks information related to the originating transaction created from Order Management, Projects, Contracts, and so on. This flexfield can also be used to track any information you may want to pass through the standard interface when generating invoices from external systems or as part of data conversion.

The other flexfield that is relevant to Oracle Receivables is the Territory Flexfield, used for reporting and tracking transaction purposes.

Remit-to address

When you enter any transaction you *must* have a remit-to address that defaults on the receivable transaction at the time it is saved.

> It is important to note that without a remit-to address configured you will not be able to enter an invoice. Additional setups are discussed later in this chapter.

You must also ensure that when you create a remit-to address, it must cover all the countries that you have customers in; there is no default!

If you have multiple remit-to addresses based upon states or countries, which may be true, create an address and assign the country/state that you would want to default on the transaction.

In addition to the remit-to address you also must define/configure the following to manage your transactions:

- **Payment Terms**: This helps define when the invoice becomes due on your aging.
- **Accounting Rules**: This allows to manage creation of specific accounting lines based on business rules. Is is used mostly in revenue recognition scenarios.
- **Batch Sources**: This helps drive transaction numbering and manage how to access and identify data from external systems including Oracle products.
- **Document Sequencing**: This defines the numbering sequencing.
- **Transaction Types**: This assigns status for transactions and can default accounting specifics to individual transactions.
- **Approval Limits**: This is used to approve adjustments and write-off transactions per business rules.
- **Receivable Activities**: This is used for managing accounting for receivables transactions per business rules.

Transaction types are used to manage default accounting for transactions by using AutoInvoice rules to generate segments in your transaction.

AutoInvoice (AutoAccounting)

AutoInvoice configuration is a mechanism that allows you to manage value generation for each of the segments in your Chart of Accounts. AutoAccounting provides flexibility to create accounting entries with appropriate values for each set of accounts that affect your receivable transaction. The benefit of using AutoInvoice is that it has been used in Receivables for a long time prior to the introduction of SLA, and many users are familiar with how it works. There are a few shortcomings which can be addressed using SLA rule changes if needed.

The major construct of AutoInvoice is that each of the accounts listed can be individually created for each segment based on specified sources for the value in the segment:

- **Receivables**
- **Revenue**
- **Unearned Revenue**
- **Unbilled Receivables**
- **Tax**
- **Freight**
- **AutoInvoice Clearing**
- **Bills Receivable**
- **Factored Bills Receivable**
- **Remitted Bills Receivable**
- **Unpaid Billed Receivables**

The following are the sources that can be used to get the value for each segment in the accounts listed previously:

- **Transaction Types**
- **Salesreps**
- **Standard Lines** (Item in most cases)
- **Site** (Customer Bill To site)

There are additional sources that are specific to the accounts:

- Taxes
- Remittance banks

AutoInvoice has been retained in Release 12, ensuring backward compatibility and ease of transition for users from earlier versions of E-Business Suite.

These sources create the default accounting that is shown on the accounting distribution lines. However, if you make changes to the SLA rules, the default accounting is overridden by your SLA rule changes.

You can get very creative and source each segment from a different place (including constant/fixed value) as shown in the following screenshot:

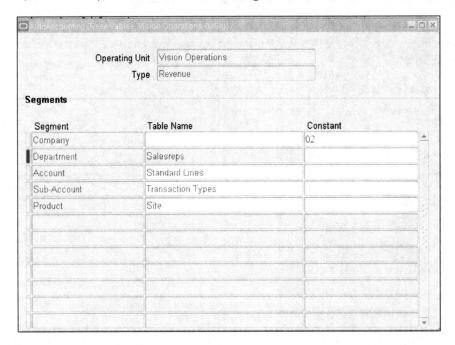

 You can also use memo lines to default one side of the accounting for an invoice/credit transaction. These override the AutoAccounting rules for the account type, typically the credit side.

Approvals

Invoice and debit memo transactions do not necessarily need approval; however, credit memo can be approved per business rules with the use of Oracle Approval Management Engine.

An invoice or debit memo is normally generated as an activity to collect after the task of delivering a service or product has been initiated; so an approval seems redundant. However, a credit memo affects the outstanding balance of an invoice or a debit memo and needs to be appropriately controlled. There is also an audit requirement to manage transactions that impact account balances.

Other approvals that can be managed are adjustments to transactions, including receipt write-offs. Approvals are managed by an amount limit applied to the user performing the adjustment. If the initiator does not have the limit to create the adjustment, any other user with the appropriate level of approval can approve the adjustment. There is no hierarchy inherent in this process.

Receipt write-off transactions are similar in nature to adjustments processing.

Both adjustments and receipt-write-offs, need definition of a Receivables Activity to manage the accounting.

 A system level write-off limit is set for an operating unit. This configuration is often missed and creates a problem when you want to perform your first write-off transaction.

Customers

Customers are required to enter any transaction in Oracle Receivables, such as an invoice, credit memo, debit memo, and so on.

In many cases, customers are entered into Order Management as a part of an initial sales transaction for shipping material. However, you also create customer records in Oracle Receivables.

The task of creating and managing customers is the result of your organization's business process decisions. You may not have the capability for creating customers in Oracle Receivables. There are certain aspects that are managed on the Receivables side of the fence, or to be more precise, in the credit and collections group, where it is typical to manage credit limits, payment terms, and other reporting related identification for customers.

Transactions

Transactions are created in Oracle Receivables from shipment details or other related services delivered to customers. There is an accounting requirement to create receivables transactions soon after the shipment, service, or other related activity has been completed.

In some cases invoicing is delayed based on local statutory requirements, but for now let us assume that the activity which initiates invoicing has been satisfied and the invoice will be created.

AutoInvoice, described in the previous section, impacts all transactions creation (invoices, debit, and credit memos). Transaction types and batch sources are required to manage creation of any of these transactions.

Transaction types define the accounting (as related to your AutoInvoice definition), type of transaction, and if these should be accounted and open for receivables.

Batch sources define the numbering sequence and the ability to capture additional information related to transaction creation when AutoInvoicing is used. As mentioned earlier a large percentage of transactions are created automatically in Oracle Receivables. Consequently, batch sources manage all the derivation methodology to arrive at the data elements needed to create a complete transaction.

One of the major aspects of the creation of these transactions is the derivation of the GL date and, in some cases, invoice date. The following are the two principal choices that drive this date:

- For goods shipment related transactions the source for the GL date is the date the item is shipped
- For other transactions the GL date is the date when the process to create the transaction is submitted

The major items other than derivation information for all data elements are listed as follows:

- Document sequencing
- Default transaction type
- How to manage a GL date in a closed period
- Salespersons and related salescredit

Invoices and debit memos

Invoice and debit memo transactions are created for all billing activities. They generally have a positive balance (or are expected to). These are created when you want to bill a customer for goods or services provided.

When creating manual invoices with accounting rules for spreading revenue across multiple periods you must be sure to enter the **Accounting Rule** (which does not default) before you leave the first screen.

When entering the accounting distribution you may also need to enter the accounting segments manually based on your AutoAccounting rules.

Credit memos

In addition to automatic creation, you can generate credit memos from an external source:

- Stand-alone (On Account) credit memo
- Credit memo related to an existing invoice/debit memo

The first kind is available for application to an invoice or appears on the account balance as an open credit.

The second kind is applied to the invoice when you initiate it from an existing invoice form, as shown in the following screenshot:

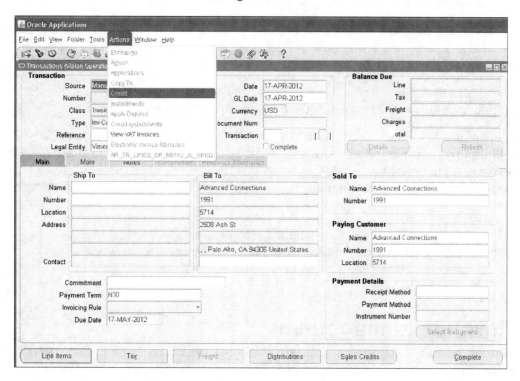

As mentioned in an earlier part of this chapter, credit memos transactions can have approval automation based on the Approval Management Engine functionality. The existing workflow allows for an approval mechanism with the use of Approvals Management Engine.

Adjustment transactions

An adjustment transaction is used to reduce the receivable balance for a customer, as an example, to offer a discount or write-off a balance that they are not willing to pay.

An adjustment transaction cannot be entered independently, it must be initiated based on existing transaction. Once you enter an adjustment transaction, based on your limits, the transaction may await approval.

Adjustment transactions can be made to a single line, the whole invoice, or to the tax amount only. The accounting for these is managed through receivable activities that must be chosen when entering the adjustment transaction.

Commitment transactions

Deposits and guarantees are generally created when you want to track customer commitments for goods and services in the future.

A deposit is a payment made in advance for goods or services that you intend to provide to a customer. The deposit is applied to the invoice when it is generated and reduces the balance by the amount of the deposit.

The application of the deposit (also labeled as a commitment on the screen) creates an (internal) adjustment to reduce the open receivable balance.

A guarantee is similar to a contract. You record a guarantee transaction to track billings to a customer for reporting purposes. You use the same field to attach/ associate a guarantee for a customer on an invoice. It is just used to track business with the customer and does not impact the receivable balance for the customer.

You are no longer required to apply a deposit when you create the invoice (a restriction in pre-R12 releases). You can now use the **Tools | Apply Deposit** option to apply deposits.

Revenue management

In prior releases of E-Business Suite when you defined an accounting rule to defer accounting over a period of time, or did not recognize the revenue immediately, there was no easy method to make changes after the transaction had been posted to GL.

Beginning with R12 Oracle introduced Revenue Management (and this has been back-ported to the latest release of 11*i* as well). This new product allows revenue to be managed as the business progresses and changes to recognition become evident. The functionality allows for manual changes to the revenue schedules and also supports external triggers to manage revenue.

In addition, functionality is also available to enable revenue recognition based on contingencies you define and assign to specific customers.

Predefined contingencies listed may be used immediately. These contingencies reflect business policies for the enterprise as to when revenue can be recognized:

- Refund policy
- Payment terms policy
- Credit classification

These contingencies allow the user to manage revenue based on events. An event can be described as a receipt application to an invoice.

This allows for a more flexible and manageable revenue accounting that is based on revenue recognition policies at the enterprise level.

Additional revenue contingencies can be defined as needed.

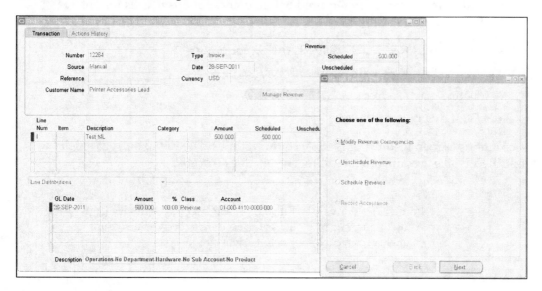

Bills Receivable

The Bills Receivable functionality allows aggregation of outstanding receivable balances for a customer and assigns them to a remittance agency or a bank to be able to receive money ahead of the due date from the bank or remittance agency. This helps the enterprise secure short-term funding.

E-Business Suite supports multiple types of Bills Receivables that can be transacted in the system:

- Signed
- Unsigned
- Promissory notes (customer-issued Bills Receivable)

Oracle Receivables allows you to create Bills Receivable transactions in multiple ways:

- In a batch mode using the **Bills Receivable Batch Creation** program, the transactions to be picked up must have a payment method of **Bills Receivable**
- Manually
- Exchange an open invoice from the **Transactions** window

A few configuration tasks are required before you can manage Bills Receivable transactions. They are as follows:

- Define Bills Receivable related AutoAccounting
- Define Bills Receivable transaction types
- Define batch sources
- Define customer drawee sites

Accounting is managed using AutoAccounting rules. The initial entry is a debit to a Bills Receivable account and credit to a receivables account.

 Receivables derives the Bills Receivable account segments from AutoAccounting and inherits the account's receivable account segments from each transaction exchanged.

Receipts

Receipts are cash receipt transactions and manage closure of open receivable balances.

E-Business Suite allows the user to enter two types of receipts in the system. They are as follows:

- **Standard Receipts**: Those related to customer invoices
- **Miscellaneous Receipts**: Those not related to customer invoices

Receipts can be entered once specific configurations are completed. The configurations that must be completed before you can enter receipts are as follows:

- Define Banks
- Define Receipt Classes
- Define Payment Methods
- Define Receipt Sources (to batch receipts)

The banks define where the money is going to be deposited and the account that should be impacted when a receipt is saved.

The payment method identifies the receipt transaction by how they were paid. Examples are check, wire, and so on.

The Receipt Sources allow you to batch the transactions together so these are easier to manage for reconciliation.

The receipt batch is not a mandatory configuration, unless you are transacting automatic receipts.

Receipt classes

Receipt classes cover a wide range of data elements that enable transaction processing.

The basic types can be listed as follows:

- Manual
- Automatic
- AP/AR Netting
- Bills Receivable

The receipt class ties a bank and a payment method together. The payment method is what you choose when you create a receipt.

The receipt class also links the payment method to accounting entries if there was a discount on the payment.

Other discounts given to customers due to short payment and disputes are managed by an adjustment transaction.

Once you save a receipt class you cannot change bank related information or accounting information. The accounts default from the bank for various accounting entries and can be changed only when entering for the first time. These cannot be changed once the receipt class and payment method are saved.

You can have multiple payment methods attached to a receipt class. The payment method can be linked to a different bank account.

The following are the stages that a receipt goes through as it is entered and fully applied:

- Entered and saved; status is **Unidentified**
- Entered and saved with a customer name and not applied to invoices; status is **Unapplied**
- Entered and saved with a customer name and applied partially; status is **Applied** for the amount applied and **Unapplied** for the remaining amount
- Entered and saved with a customer name and applied partially; remaining amount put on **On Account**; status is **Applied** and **On Account**

Accounting entries are specifically different for each stage and can have the same or different accounts as configured.

 Receipts always have two stages as they are entered and applied. These two stages are unapplied and applied. Related accounting entries are always created.

Receipt reversals

You can reverse and reapply receipts to the correct debit transaction if you perceive that there is an error in the initial application. Receivables allows you to create two types of reversals:

- **Standard**: This reverses the accounting created by the initial application and reopens the open balances that were closed by the application.

- **Debit Memo Reversals**: This reverses the receipt application but does not reopen the invoice. Instead Oracle Receivables creates a new debit memo transaction with the amount that was closed with the initial application of the receipt.

Miscellaneous receipts

Miscellaneous receipts are cash receipts that you enter to account and manage non-invoice related cash transactions.

These could be cash you received against interest, or for another reason that is not related to your core business of product sales or services.

Configuration required for miscellaneous receipts are as follows:

- Define banks
- Define distribution sets
- Define receivable activities

The last two tasks drive how receivables accounts for these cash receipts.

 You cannot create a debit memo reversal for a miscellaneous receipt.

Automatic receipts

Additional setup is required to enable automatic receipts generation. Automatic receipts are generally termed as receipts you create within your system, based on an agreement with a regular customer. You send a remittance advice to the customer's bank to withdraw the required funds when transactions become due.

Automatic receipts are created by selecting invoices to include in your batch. A receipt class with a creation method of Automatic is required. You can also specify additional selection criteria such as currency, due dates, and range of customer names. The create automatic receipts program picks up all complete transactions that meet this criteria and creates receipts to close out these transactions.

Automatic receipts have the following statuses, which indicate whether they are complete:

- **Started Creation**
- **Creation Completed**
- **Started Approval**
- **Approval Completed**
- **Started Format**
- **Format Completed**

For automatic receipts to be complete and to have funds transferred to your bank account you have to remit the receipt information to the bank and then you can clear these receipts as part of your bank reconciliation process to ensure that you have received the money.

Once complete the information needs to be sent to the bank (remitted) so your bank can request and have funds transferred from your customer's bank account.

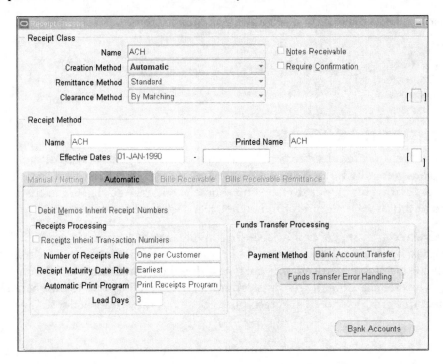

Automatic receipts are the only receipts that can be auto-reconciled using the Cash Management Bank Reconciliation process.

You can also use the Automatic Clearing functionality and program in Oracle Receivables to clear your receipts, but not based on bank statement information. If you want to clear and account for your receipts only after the bank has the money from your customer's account, then you have to use the Cash Management clearing process.

Notes receivable

You can also manage notes receivable and promissory notes as part of your receipt transactions. These transactions are managed as future-dated receipts. These work similar to an automatic receipt in that they must be submitted and remitted to the bank to receive the funds. The difference between this transaction and automatic receipts is that notes receivable transactions are created manually most of the time.

Credit card payments and refunds

Credit card payments are treated similar to automatic receipts and the invoice is created, and the automatic receipts program creates the receipt. The information to create these transactions is based on the credit card information provided along with the initiating transaction. The initiating transaction may be a sales order or an invoice.

Refunds can be processed for credit payments made in excess or for credit memos generated against invoices that have been paid by credit cards.

The following are some prerequisites to manage this process automatically:

- Define a Receivable Activity with **Refund** as the type
- Configure how to manage refunds for credits
- Configure Oracle Payables
- Configure Oracle Payments

You can also create manual refunds in the **receipts** window. The functionality works with payments to generate a refund request. This can also be managed with workflow and approvals if needed.

Chargebacks

When a receipt is paid for an open balance for a customer invoice, you can close this particular transaction and create a new transaction called a chargeback as a new transaction with an open balance.

You can control the due date for the chargeback transaction based on the configuration you choose in the **System Options** form.

 To manage Chargebacks you must review/define a transaction type called Chargeback and a Receivable Activity called Chargeback.

Prepayment

A new functionality introduced in E-Business R12 allows you to manage prepayments for goods and services that you supply or perform for a customer.

Prepayments are automatically applied to invoices when they are created using AutoInvoice, by a post process program that is spawned as part of the AutoInvoice set of programs.

 You cannot create prepayments manually. A feeder system must initiate the creation and the transaction is created in Oracle using an API.

To use prepayments, specific business process practices must be followed. These impact how the initiating transaction is processed, and how the order is processed and fulfilled. When the invoice is created it has to be marked as prepaid with relevant information to identify the prepayment transaction. The post process matching program applies the prepayment transaction to the invoice.

If you intend to use the automatic clearing house or credit card to manage prepayments you must ensure that Oracle Payments Funds Capture functionality is configured appropriately to handle these transactions.

You can also enter and apply cross currency receipts in receivables, based on a profile option that allows this activity. If this **Profile** option is not set to **Yes** the system assumes that all receipts will apply funds in the invoice currency only.

QuickCash

You can use predefined rule sets to apply receipts to customer open balances using AutoCash rule sets and minimal information provided at the time of receipt entry.

Once the data is created you can use the **QuickCash** screen to review how these customer payments will be applied. Once you are satisfied with the review run a process to apply the receipts, Post QuickCash.

Lockbox processing

Lockbox processing is an automated way of acquiring your receipt data from your bank in a specified file format and then using rules to apply them to your receipts.

This function eliminates the need to enter all the receipts that the bank received from your customer and then apply them to the relevant invoices manually.

The steps to accomplish this task are as follows:

- **Import your receipt transactions**: This picks up the data from your bank in a prespecified format and loads it into an interim table
- **Validate data in interim tables**: This validates data; is available to appropriately match customer invoices
- **Post QuickCash**: This applies and updates your customer balances

There are multiple rules associated with the process to identify the customer and transaction by this receipt. The last step in this process appropriately applies the receipt.

If no match is found then the receipt is created as an Unidentified Receipt.

Discounts

When applying cash receipts to customer balances Oracle Receivable provides multiple discounting options. There are also options to deal with partial payments and short payments on open balances:

- **Earned discounts**: This is a discount that the customer is entitled to based on the payment terms; normally for early payment of open balances
- **Unearned discounts**: These are similar to the previous type, but are assigned specifically after the grace period for the early payment has passed

- **Discount on partial payments**: A choice whether to provide a discount to your customer for partial payments
- **Tiered discounts**: These are based on payment schedules and their due dates for early payment

Receipt write-offs

In many cases there is a necessity to write-off receipts due to the following:

- Excess payment for an invoice
- Small unapplied amounts that remain after applying a receipt to an open balance

You have an approval process similar to adjustments that manages your receipt write-off transaction.

 There is a system-level threshold that you cannot cross for receipt write-off transactions.

Receivable activities with the type of receipt write-off drive accounting for receipt write-off transaction.

Collections

In Release 12, Oracle Advanced Collections is the product and engine that manages collections and related activities. Oracle Receivables integrates with Oracle Advanced Collections to provide you with a complete collections management solution. With this integration, all collections activities take place from within Oracle Advanced Collections.

Advanced Collections provides a simpler process flow where users work primarily within one main screen to easily review accounts, take promises, and process payments, adjustments, and disputes, all while recording the interaction with the customer.

In previous releases collections was part of Oracle Receivables, but in Release 12 collections processing has been moved to become part of the Oracle Advanced Collections product. Users can still perform simple collection tasks within Oracle Receivables but specific configurations must be performed.

Collections features for receivables are best illustrated by the following screenshot where all the functions and facilities to manage transactions are integrated:

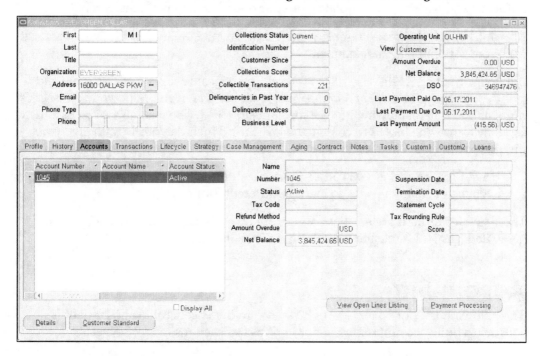

There are additional configuration steps required to make the collections functionality work with its basic functions. These are as follows:

- Link your user ID with an employee
- Set up the employee with collector roles
- Use the CRM Resource Manager responsibility to perform the previous task
- Collections responsibility is a separate responsibility

Document printing

Customer invoices, and statements including dunning letters are not provided as standard formats that can be used out of the box.

These are generic text formats that must be modified to an acceptable format by third-party software with your logo and your format.

However, with the release of **Bill Presentment Architecture (BPA)** and **BI Publisher** (formerly XML Publisher) capabilities Oracle has now introduced an easier method to format and use specific templates for your documents to your customers.

BI Publisher can be used to manage and extend any document format, with standard MS Word for template management.

Bill Presentment Architecture (BPA) is a user manageable capability to format and print your invoice document. On the invoice screen is an icon beside your transaction number that will display the invoice format using BPA. The formats can be modified as easily as moving blocks to change the layout and include your logo to give your invoice document a business look.

The benefit of BPA is that you can easily create different templates and assign these to customers or customer sites to manage different formats.

These invoice formats are easily viewed from iReceivables online and can also be generated using BI Publisher for printing, e-mail, fax, and so on.

Accounting

The following is a brief overview of how accounting is generated and content is sourced to build account segments for various transactions in receivables:

- Invoice, debit memo, credit memo, commitments use the AutoAccounting rules, transaction type, and memo lines
- Adjustments, receipt write-off, Charges use Receivable Activities
- Chargeback uses the transaction type
- Receipts uses receipt classes and Receivable Activities

Accounting created in the Oracle Receivables product is a precursor to the new SLA feature in Release 12. Modifications in the SLA level can change these accounting entries.

AP/AR Netting

Oracle AP/AR Netting is a feature that provides a foundation to create netting agreements with flexible definition of business rules and association of trading partners. It executes an automated netting process so that customers can reduce their debt obligations without incurring bank charges by creating unnecessary payments and receipts.

There are specific configurations that must be performed before you can execute the AP/AR Netting functionality. These are as follows:

- Netting bank account
- Receivables system options
- Netting batch approver
- Chargeable subcontracting
- Netting agreement

Summary

This chapter included a review of major billing and receipt application activities. These activities enable business users to manage their receivables and revenue recognition in a systematic manner.

Other transactions to reduce or close open receivable balances were also reviewed.

In the next chapter, we will review how to manage credit rules and aspects of dealing with customers. We will also discuss how credit review and checking affect transaction capabilities within Oracle Order Management and Oracle Receivables.

12
Credit Management

This chapter discusses managing credit rules and profiles. In addition, there is a discussion about the new Credit Management product and its integration with Order Management and Receivables. This integration helps organizations function more efficiently and optimizes the credit and collection subprocesses. Credit Management was introduced in the later releases of 11*i*, and enables businesses to manage customer ratings and helps interaction to avoid bad debts. Payment profiles help related decisions they make about their customer base.

The perspective of Credit Management is to allow an enterprise to manage the cash flow in the company.

- How much credit do you extend to your customer who is shipped a product?
- How often do you ship to them?
- What is the threshold of an open account when you will not allow shipments to a customer?
- What benefits do you extend to a customer who pays on a regular or timely basis?
- When would you choose to have a customer pre-pay for shipments to them?

These are a few questions that come to mind when you think about Credit Management, though these are not what are commonly reviewed as the questions you would ask! This is because in relation to the E-Business Suite these are disparate tasks that are commonly not performed within a single product.

These tasks are still disparately positioned as functions in various modules/ products—Order Management, Receivables, and Credit Management. However, for this book it is appropriate to combine all these perspectives into a single chapter and focus on the credit and collections department in a company.

The following is a list of data elements that we will consider for this chapter that drive the functional requirement of a credit and collections group:

- Customer payment terms
- Credit check rules
- Credit checking
- Credit scores

When you start the discussion about payment terms you are assuming that the customer already exists; however, that choice is the first one that a credit and collections group makes to get a customer on board. The company may already be in the system as a prospect or there may just be paperwork related to the customer.

Oracle Credit Management helps in providing a seamless integration with Dun & Bradstreet (D&B) — a premier credit rating agency — from within your system to allow you to engage in efficient credit (and risk) management processes. D&B have been the premier credit rating agency to track and gauge the credit worthiness of multiple enterprises across the country and enable their users to make an informed decision about their choices with customers.

Payment terms

Once the customer is accepted on board, which may include certain information exchanges and other documentation, the crucial decision of the payment terms to extend the customer becomes imminent when the first transaction is processed.

You could choose to have default payment terms for all customers and let this be the first payment term all customers are granted when they become a trading partner in the system. The credit and collections group may choose to change the payment term assigned based on recommendations from credit rating agencies that provide more current marker information about the customer.

Payment terms on a customer are defaulted from the following places:

- Agreement payment term
- Customer ship to payment term
- Customer invoice to payment term
- Customer payment term
- Price list payment term

Defaulting rules are defined in the sales order. The initiating transaction affects an activity which in turn involves a payment term. This can be changed to suit the business needs at your organization.

 The system stops when it reaches a valid value at any one of these source locations.

Typically most companies use the default from the customer invoice-to (Bill to).

This will be your first encounter with credit management to grant your customer a credit of Net 30 days to pay for products shipped. This extends credit to your customer for 30 days, impacting your cash flow.

In addition, you may also require the customer to pay with a specific payment method.

Credit check rules

Credit check rules are designed to check open balances for a customer before you can commit and transact another transaction with that particular customer. This enables your enterprise to avoid extending too much credit to a single customer and incurring a serious risk management problem.

 Credit checking for transactions only occurs on order transactions in Oracle Order Management and not for invoices in Oracle Receivables.

Credit rules are defined in Oracle Order Management and are assigned to order types and the credit rules are checked at various times during the processing of an order. These are assigned by you as per the business rules at your organization.

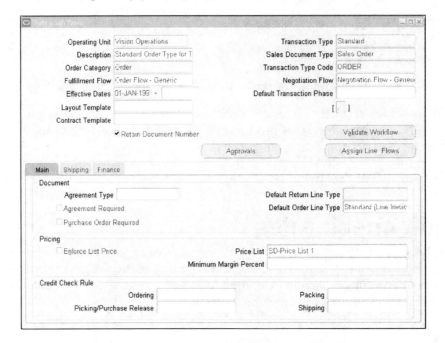

In the form shown in the previous screenshot, where a transaction type is defined you specify when the credit rule will be invoked. Accordingly the rule will be applied at each stage and check credit validity of the customer—taking into account his open balance. The tasks where credit check rules can be applied/checked are as follows:

- Ordering/booking
- Picking/purchase release
- Packing
- Shipping

Credit rules are defined and you can specify what amount you would like to have as the credit limit. You can also specify the balances you would like to have the threshold checked against. These are shown in the following screenshot for clarity:

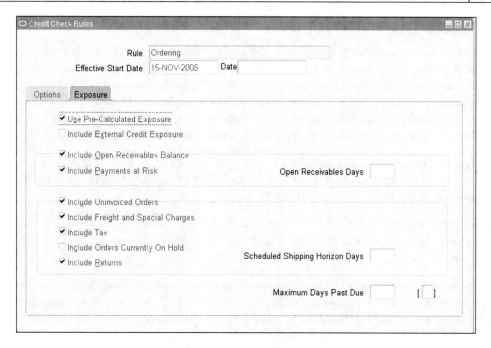

You may elect to perform your credit rule check at a different time in your order process cycle to ensure that you have the most recent transaction balances for your customer.

Pre-Calculated Exposure

Exposure summary information is used only during the credit checking process if you have selected the **Use Pre-Calculated Exposure** checkbox within the **Exposure** tab on the **Credit Check Rules** window.

Order Management enables you to rebuild a credit exposure image periodically (with orders, invoices, and payments) for all customers or customer sites for all possible credit rule definitions.

You build pre-calculated credit exposure data by running the **Initialize Credit Summaries** program.

Credit checking

Credit checks are performed as part of the order processing workflow and all orders go through the process regardless of a credit rule being defined or not. In most cases the credit check rule is successful and does not fail. The failure of a credit check rule puts the order on hold. This means that the order cannot be processed further. This will direct your attention to review the reason for the hold, and ensure that the customer has enough credit to cover the open balance once this order is processed.

Credit checking is normally performed on order transactions at four levels as mentioned in the previous section. The system puts the order on hold, preventing any other activity from being performed.

As part of the credit check rule you can define how you want the rule to work, on an order or a line level. Then the order or order line can be put on hold as per your configuration.

When an order is put on hold the system is capable of restricting access and allowing only specified users to release the hold. This configuration functionality enables the order to be progressed to the next level of activity based upon rules and security. You invoke the functionality from either of the following places:

- Defining a credit check rule.
- Assigning it to an order transaction type. (This only places the rules in a position to be used when the functionality is invoked.)
- Customer profile tab, a checkbox enables credit checking for the customer Bill To site.
- Another place where credit check can be invoked is by enabling the payment term for credit checking.

 Profile amount limits for each currency you transact orders in must be defined for a customer profile to aid the credit check rule to arrive at a threshold value.

Once these pieces are in place the credit checking process provides you with a control mechanism to manage your credit exposure appropriately.

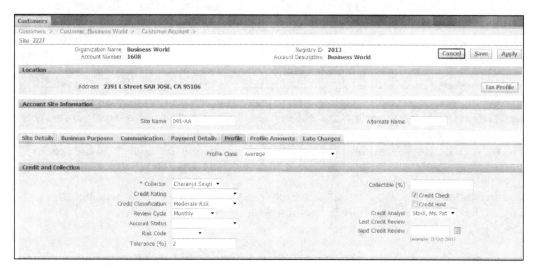

As noted in the previous screenshot you can check the **Credit Check** checkbox, which launches a credit check process on all order transactions based upon the rules you defined in the system. If an order transaction fails a credit check process, a hold is placed on that order. If you check the box labeled **Credit Hold** on the customer site, the order transaction is on hold immediately when the transaction is saved. It does not process a credit check function.

Use the header level credit check rule option if most of your orders have lines that are shipped to the same address. If the order lines are shipped to multiple addresses, use line level credit checking.

In subsequent R12 releases the line level credit check functionality has been enhanced to manage lines for the same Bill To site. Only the lines that are over and above the threshold are put on hold.

This fine-tuning of the credit check functionality is managed by an OM System Parameter, Credit Hold Sequence for Order Lines.

Credit Management

Oracle Credit Management provides a global, standardized system that lets you implement credit decisions based on credit data collected from your business-to-business customers and prospects. Credit reviews are automated by the Credit Management workflow process.

Automated periodic credit assessments include all activities from the initial credit review request and creation of the credit application, to credit scoring and analysis, to the final implementation of credit decisions. This enables you to have a consistent approach to your credit guidelines and manages automation to a large extent. It also allows you to schedule automated credit reviews periodically to reduce the risk to your enterprise.

Credit Management also facilitates manual credit reviews for those that fail the automated process through features such as online case folders, easily generated what-if scenarios, and integration with Dun & Bradstreet.

How are credit reviews initiated? Oracle EBS provides your enterprise with multiple ways to initiate credit reviews. A few are described as follows:

- An order entry clerk places an order in Oracle Order Management that causes a customer to exceed its current credit limit
- Six months have passed since a customer's last credit review date, automatically initiating a periodic credit review
- A credit analyst manually enters a new credit application for a prospect
- A credit review is initiated by calling the Credit Review API from an E-Business Suite integrated product or from non-Oracle EBS systems

Once initiated, a credit review can either be completely automated, or managed by a skilled credit analyst. You control how credit reviews happen when defining your credit policies.

For the specific order transaction a related hold will be placed based on the credit checks rules; the workflow can initiate a credit review by passing the relevant data elements to the Credit Review API.

The Credit Management product allows you to manage specific data elements. These data elements are the necessary configuration steps. They support the credit policies and business rules framework that your enterprise uses for an efficient credit review process. Some of the tasks are listed as follows and we will walk through some of them for clarity:

- Maintaining customer data
- Populating transaction data

- Defining scoring models
- Defining checklists
- Gathering data points
- Assigning automation rules
- Setting up credit recommendations
- Setting up credit decision approval policies
- Reviewing credit management performance

The credit management process works with the initiation of a credit review. A credit review can be initiated manually or by using the API provided by Oracle.

Initiating a credit review creates a folder for the review where all related information can be accessed.

Managing customer data

You assign a credit classification and a periodicity for a credit review with first time customers or prospects.

Credit Management integrates with Dun & Bradstreet (D&B) to extend availability of data during your credit review. This is in addition to the historical data you might have within your system for existing customers.

 Before you can purchase products from D&B, you must first enable integration between the E-Business Suite and D&B form within the Oracle Trading Community Architecture.

You can use the Assign Customer Credit Classification program to add or update the credit classification for a customer. Use this when you first start using credit classifications or when you want to update multiple customers.

Credit classifications are updated based upon reviews as the credit analyst approves and uses the recommendation that the review has provided. You can also assign credit classifications in an automated fashion based on your business rules and approval mechanisms.

In addition to these external sources of credit review data that enhance the use of your historical data, you must ensure that your historical data is collected in specific tables as a summarized set of information to be used during credit review.

Oracle Data Quality Management (DQM) and Oracle Trading Community Architecture work together to assist in reviewing and help define matching rules to identify critical customer information from D&B to use in the system.

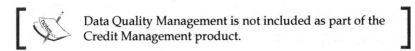 Data Quality Management is not included as part of the Credit Management product.

Scoring model and checklists

A scoring model is a set of data points that are used to arrive at a relative score for the creditworthiness of a customer. This allows you to assign a credit level you extend to a customer.

Generic models (such as the *FICO score* and other scores provided by the credit bureaus) make use of data reported by lenders to the credit bureaus. A score is calculated to predict the likelihood of a customer defaulting on a new account.

In Oracle Credit Management, you document your enterprise's credit policies via user-defined credit checklists. Using various checklists, you manage the credit analysis process by defining the required and optional data points that are included in the credit review.

The folder when submitted is processed in the order of the configuration shown as follows. The process based on parameters and data points will review and match the risk position for a specific customer or a group of customers.

- Scoring model
- Checklist
- Assigning data points to collect customer balance data from Oracle Receivables is a major task (or open orders) and can also include additional external bank and trade references
- You can also request any other specific activity in Receivables
- Dun & Bradstreet data is optional (and must be purchased separately if needed), otherwise the system uses your historical data for the review
- Additional data points including external sources that are custom built
- Credit review/analysis
- Credit recommendations
- Implement credit recommendations

The following screenshot shows an example of one such scoring model:

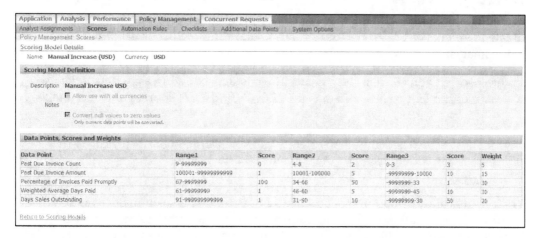

These scoring models help identify an open balance for invoice amounts and based on the score (and probably the weight) you can get a result for a possible credit score. This score can then be used to provide appropriate credit to the customer.

The next step creates a checklist that allows you to link the scoring model you created in the previous step and match it to a credit classification.

A checklist is based upon a combination of a credit review type and a credit classification. You *must* define a checklist for each combination of a review type and credit classification.

The default credit review types available within Credit Management are as follows:

- Credit checking
- Credit review
- Periodic credit review
- Credit application

The credit classifications (risks) are as follows:

- Low
- Moderate
- High

The checklist also allows you to specify the sources of data that you are going to use for the credit review for the client (or group of clients) that have the same credit classification.

Data points

A credit data point is a single piece of credit information, such as the number of late payments or DSO days (days sales outstanding), which is used during credit analysis.

In the checklist you can also assign specific outside trade sources of data to be used in your credit review; one of them is the Dun & Bradstreet source for credit analysis.

The Dun & Bradstreet data source is an additionally priced source and is not part of the E-Business Suite.

You can also add data points that relate to funds that have been made available to the customer, bank information, trade references, and other related financial information. None of this information is required; you choose as part of your configuration for each checklist what is required and what is optional.

If there is a required data element that is not available when running the credit analysis, then the system provides a warning, but completes the review and gives you a recommendation.

The only case where the review does not complete due to lack of data is when you choose to include a Global Access Data Product (D&B) and choose the **All Data Required** checkbox. The credit review will also fail if you have custom API calls using PL/SQL that do not return an appropriate single value.

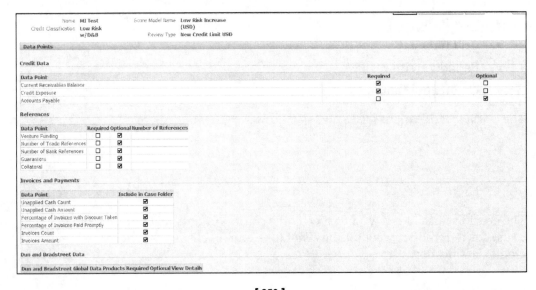

The previous screenshot shows the data sets that Oracle Credit Management allows you to summarize and maintain in tables that are accessed during the credit review process. These tables collect data from your Receivables data and need to be updated appropriately on a regular basis.

Automation

For any scoring model, you can define a set of automation rules to guide the implementation of credit recommendations without user intervention.

 Credit recommendations can be automatically configured to update the customers' credit classification and credit limit without intervention by a user.

Automation rules let a credit review proceed uninterrupted through the workflow, during which a credit recommendation is automatically implemented based on the score that the scoring model calculates.

To accomplish this automatic implementation of credit recommendations, you associate credit score ranges with recommendations when defining automation rules.

When you define automation rules, you can also indicate approval options for each decision.

Credit Management lets you decide if you want to skip the required approval on a credit decision. You can use Oracle Workflow or Approval Management Engine (AME) for these approvals and they are seamlessly integrated into your work environment.

You can define a set of automation rules for any of your scoring models, provided that:

- A checklist and scoring model are defined and assigned to a credit review type and credit classification combination
- Automation rules do not yet exist for the combination

All the previous processes assume that there has been a business event that has triggered the credit review process.

How would you do this for a new customer for whom you are requesting a Credit Check/Review for the first time, or a prospect?

The following are a list of tasks to manage this:

1. Query the customer on the **New Application** screen.

2. Choose to view accounts and choose the specific one for a given Operating Unit.

3. Click **Create Credit Application**.

4. Provide information about the type of review and the type of customer classification.

5. Provide the type of review you are looking for this customer — Trade Credit for most customers with Order transactions.

6. Provide other financial and related information as shown in the left panel — bank, trade, funding, and so on.

7. Provide amount and currency for the review since there is no transaction amount that is specified.

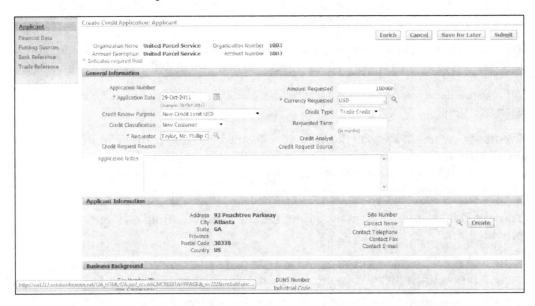

You can also choose to *enrich* the data, which is another way to get data from Dun & Bradstreet (D&B). When you choose to acquire data from D&B it is priced separately and purchased depending on the specific relationship your organization has with D&B.

The **enrich** button actually gives you up to the moment information from D&B so that you can get more current information for your review, other than your historical data from within your system.

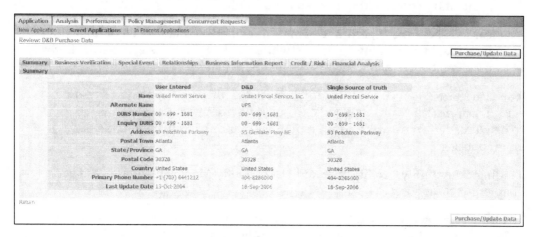

The information that you would most generally use in your scoring pattern would be the range of the credit rating that D&B assigns to a customer. This is a universally approved and defined credit rating source. Many businesses use this rating for making business decisions on managing their credit risk.

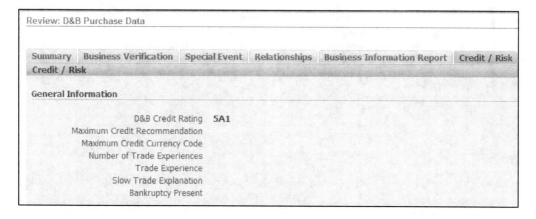

Summary

In this chapter, you learned how to manage your cash flow by configuring the Credit Management functions within the E-Business Suite.

You learned about the generic and standard methods to manage credit that you extend to your customer, using the erstwhile credit check rules and credit checks at transactional points within the system to help manage credit exposure.

You also learned how to manage credit reviews with an automated and more scientific approach, with credit policies and data from various external sources to help broaden your basis for the credit review and the implementation of these credit policies.

Trading Community Architecture and Data Quality Management are used in this chapter for clarity only.

In the next chapter, you will be introduced to another one of the new E-Business Suite products. This new product is called E-Business Tax.

We will give an overview of how this product works, what it can do, and how we can manage tax calculation and take advantage of the functionality in using an integrated product for your tax needs.

 The Credit Management product is best used (as per various discussion forums) with other products from Oracle—Oracle Deduction Management and Oracle Trade Management. This chapter only provides an overview of the capability of the Oracle Credit Management product.

13

E-Business Tax (EBTax)

The E-Business Tax (EBTax) module has been introduced in Release 12 to manage all the tax requirements, content, calculation, rules engine, and reporting from a centralized repository fully integrated with all other E-Business Suite business flows.

E-Business Tax is based on a global system architecture. It is configurable and scalable for adding and maintaining country-specific tax content. With E-Business Tax, you can model your tax requirements according to the needs of local and international tax requirements.

This includes:

- Simple and complex country-specific tax legislation
- Cross-border transactions
- Local compliance requirements for recording and reporting
- Continual changes to tax legislation, such as new taxes, local law changes, special tax rates, and special exceptions for products and customers

This ensures a uniform tax setup across applications, with a centrally managed system of automated tax services and control over manual intervention and update.

Overview

E-Business Tax includes the configurations that help you manage the engine to allow tax calculation as well as exemptions, exceptions, jurisdictions, including internal and external reporting.

The content of configurations can be listed as follows:

- Basic tax configuration
- Tax Jurisdictions

- Party tax profiles
- Fiscal classifications
- Exemptions and exceptions
- Country default controls

A brief explanation for each task is as follows:

- **Basic tax configuration**: The basic tax configuration includes the regime-to-rate flow for each **Tax Regime**. These involve defining a regime, tax, a tax status (standard or exempt), and rates—both for charging tax and recovery rates.
- **Tax Jurisdictions**: A Tax Jurisdiction is the geographic area where a tax is levied by a specific tax authority.
- **Party tax profiles**: You define profiles for the parties involved in tax transactions that are set up through a legal entity and Trading Community Architecture. Party tax profiles contain all of the tax information for each party, including tax registrations and party fiscal classifications.

  These parties can be you as well as the party you transact with, namely, customers and suppliers.

- **Fiscal classifications**: A fiscal classification is the way that a tax authority classifies each part of a transaction that includes parties and party sites, and products among other aspects. Fiscal classifications assist in configuring tax rules. The classifications provide one or more qualifications to identify when and how taxes should be calculated.
- **Exemptions and exceptions**: Tax exemptions let you define a party/party site or product as partially or fully exempt from tax. Tax exceptions let you define a special rate for specific products.
- **Country default controls**: This subcomponent lets you specify certain defaults countrywise. These defaults are used during transaction entry.

One of the important differences from previous releases is the use of legal entity. The legal entity is important when configuring E-Business Tax for your environment.

It defines the country where you have a statutory and legal requirement to collect taxes for your business and report on the collections to the relevant agencies/government bodies. The legal entity that you perform your business in, your legal entity, is referred to in many cases as the **First Party Legal Entity**. Once you define a legal entity you can identify the branches: divisions of your legal entity that may be independently called legal establishments. The relationship in many cases is one-to-one.

There are three specific data elements that impact the E-Business Tax. They are as follows:

- Transactions (what you do, sell/purchase)
- What you trade in (products)
- Who you trade, do business with, customers and suppliers

Based on these broad set of data elements that go into the decision of how E-Business Tax works it becomes a simple task to manage the configuration. These categorize elements and criteria that drives your E-Business Tax implementation rules for managing your tax commitments. The engine and the legal entity allow coverage for businesses in any given geographic area.

Geographic areas are identified within the Trading Community Architecture (TCA) and are linked to your third-party address to become an element in your tax derivation structure.

The first data element is transactions and these are seeded for the two most important business flows in E-Business Suite:

- Purchase (Procure to Pay)
- Sale (Order to Cash)

You can create subcategories of these based on what you procure and where you procure from.

The second data element, what you trade in, products (or items in E-Business Suite), helps you manage how taxes affect the products sold. These products (or items) can be categorized by Item Categories (briefly described in an earlier chapter), or you can create additional categories to apply to the products within E-Business Suite.

 The Item Categories defined in Inventory may be used from within E-Business Tax to drive any specific rules needed for tax calculation purposes.

The third data element encompasses the trading partners that you do business with, customers and suppliers, for each of the flows Order to Cash and Procure to Pay.

Trading partners (part of the TCA), can also contain specific data elements that drive if they are taxable or not (exemptions). Additionally, their address (geography) can drive whether they be charged taxes partially or fully for specific products or product categories. These driving factors are inherent in rules that you can create within E-Business Tax to manage your statutory tax commitments.

Configuration

Each country can have one or more systems of taxation. Each system deals with the taxation of specific aspects of a business transaction. For example, a sales tax system deals with the rules and regulations concerning how a sale should be taxed. Similarly, a Value Added Tax (VAT) taxation system deals with how the value addition in a manufacturing and/or sales lifecycle needs to be taxed.

- A Tax Regime can be defined as a single system of taxation.

- A Tax Regime is implemented by one or more distinct charges. Each such specific charge is called **Tax**.

- A Tax Regime may include one tax or several different taxes.

- The imposition of a tax is limited by a geographical boundary. The incidence of any tax on a specific geographical area is called a tax jurisdiction.

- Jurisdictions are maintained in the Trading Community Architecture and are directly linked to addresses in your legal entities that are party to your taxable transactions.

For the E-Business Tax engine to function properly one of the data elements is the location (address) of your trading partners. The framework to identify this location is built into the TCA geography hierarchy. An example of this would be State, County, City, Zip hierarchy in the U.S. This is shown in the following screenshot:

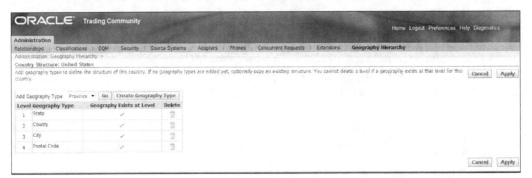

You need to maintain these for cases where taxes are levied at a level lower than the country level, for example, state or provincial taxes.

This needs to be performed before you can continue with the rest of the configuration including defining legal entities (including the first party, yourself), Tax Regimes, Tax Jurisdictions, Tax Rates, and Rules.

You create a geographic hierarchy for a country that has taxes at a level lower than the country; U.S., Canada, India are prime examples.

For each country that has a tax jurisdiction requirement below the country level you need to ensure this framework is in place. The TCA geography hierarchy provides a single reference point for all E-Business Suite products.

Using the TCA you can maintain the country structures below the country level as well as address validation for your jurisdiction levels so that accurate addresses are managed in your addresses throughout the system.

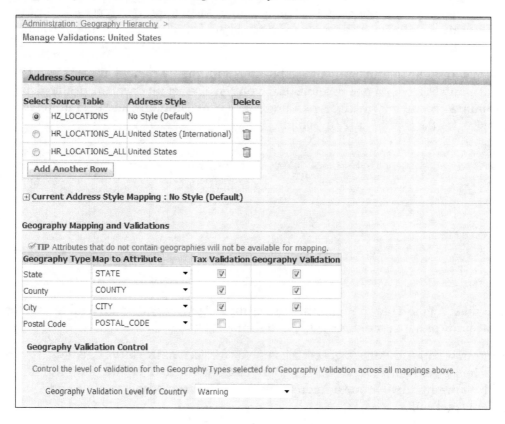

 The tax validation and the geography validation should not be checked for the **Postal Code** field. This ensures that problems with using a five digit or a 5+4 digit zip code are avoided.

Oracle E-Business Tax is not delivered with any predefined geographic hierarchies, though there is functionality and the capability to define the specific hierarchies as needed.

In the previous screenshot there are multiple source tables listed. The one that is to be used to validate is the HZ tables. HZ tables are ones that store information for TCA data elements. The other tables listed are HR tables and are not relevant to the current business processes covered in this book.

Legal entity

Creating your legal entity (First Party Legal Entity) is an important part of the setup and is used in your E-Business Tax configuration as an important lynch-pin for the identification and relevance for tax processes, namely, relevance, calculation, and reporting.

When you set up a legal entity or establishment (normally created as part of your legal entity as a one-to-one relationship), you can also set up party tax profile details, including general information, rounding rule, tax registrations, and defaulting controls for the country and/or regime.

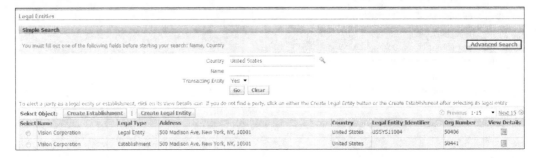

You must set the **Transacting Entity** to **Yes** for a legal entity if you intend to use this legal entity as a registered tax entity and a First Party Legal Entity.

You can set up additional legal establishments for each office, service center, warehouse, and any other location within the company that requires a registration with a tax authority for one or more taxes. Your legal establishments are under the parent legal entity.

 If you want to use multiple establishments additional configuration is necessary.

A legal entity always has a country assigned and the Tax Regime is assigned a level (normally country).

Self-assessment (use tax)

You can define a first party to self-assess the taxes calculated on the payables invoices it receives. A self-assessed tax is a tax calculated and remitted for a transaction, where tax was not levied by the supplier but is considered due, and therefore must be paid by the purchaser. Self-assessment is also known as *reverse charge* or *use tax* in certain Tax Regimes.

The self-assessment indicator is configured when defining the legal entity details.

Tax profiles

Party tax profiles contain the information that relates to a party's transaction tax activities, and identifies the legal entity to the tax authorities.

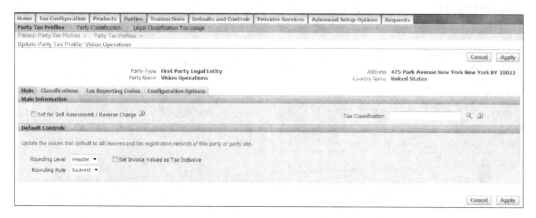

Tax profiles must be defined for all parties involved in tax transactions, including:

- All legal entities, legal establishments, and operating units in your organization that have a transaction tax requirement
- Your customers and suppliers and their locations
- Tax authorities that administer tax rules and regulations

Tax registrations are part of a tax profile and contain information related to a party's transactional tax obligations.

Tax registrations form part of the tax profile of a first-party legal establishment (you), a third party and/or a third-party site (customers, suppliers).

A tax exemption for a customer or a customer and product combination, identifies a discount or replacement percentage that reduces (normally) the applicable tax.

The configuration options identify the Tax Regimes associated with a first party and the configuration owner and service provider settings associated with each Tax Regime. Service providers and their usage is explained later in this chapter.

The configuration options are part of the tax profile of configuration owners, that is, first party legal entities and operating units owning tax content. These identify the characteristics of, and default values for, the transactions associated with a party.

The party fiscal classifications optionally assigned to a party are used as determining factors in tax rules. The tax reporting codes optionally assigned to parties capture tax information from transactions for both internal and tax authority reporting requirements.

Operating unit

Operating units organize your company data according to your internal accounting, financial monitoring, and reporting requirements. Legal entities let you more accurately model your external relationships to legal authorities.

Set up a tax profile for each operating unit. The operating unit tax profile can either use the tax configuration of the legal entity it belongs to, for transactions involving the legal entity and Tax Regime, or can act as a configuration owner for the applicable Tax Regime.

 Release 11*i* tax data in Oracle Payables, Oracle Receivables, and other applications migrate to E-Business Tax as operating units containing their own tax content.

In Release 12 the relationships between first party legal entities and the relevant tax authorities normally control the setup of the transaction taxes required by your business.

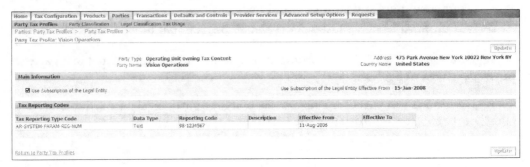

Once you choose to use the legal entity content for an operating unit for the party profile created you cannot revert.

TCA classifications

TCA classifications are used to classify third parties for tax purposes. You can define TCA class categories and class codes specifically for use in tax determination.

Configure and define class categories and class codes for use with rules and assign to third-party tax profiles. Third party legal entities are your customers and suppliers, your trading partners with whom you transact business, which may be taxable.

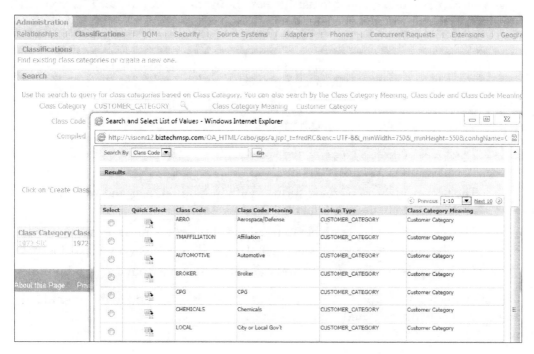

You must set up and maintain TCA classifications before you can perform these tax-related setups:

- Party fiscal classifications let you classify the customer/customer site or supplier/supplier site according to categories you define for tax-related purposes
- Use party tax profiles to assign party fiscal classifications to third-party tax profiles to be used in tax determination for invoices associated with the party

You can also use inventory categories in determining taxation relevance and rules. These have been briefly described in the *Chapter 4*, Inventory.

Managing migrated data

If upgrading from 11*i*, there is a challenge in understanding the changed perspective of the data model for tax in Release 12 E-Business Tax.

As part of the upgrade process the tax content that you had configured in Oracle Payables and Oracle Receivables is converted into singular tax content for an operating unit. This ensures that you can continue to transact and use the tax calculation functionality without loss of functionality.

Once you have decided on how to use the new E-Business Tax functionality you can transition to the new model at a later date.

 Once you transition and make the jump to the new model in an upgraded instance you cannot revert.

In prior releases the following conditions existed:

- Tax codes and rates were owned specifically by each product, Oracle Payables and Oracle Receivables
- The tax calculations were performed with individual rates and were not always stored at the most detailed level
- This separation of data ownership did not support seamless reporting needs and the tax amounts were recalculated every time a transaction was queried
- Reports were module specific and did not gather data from a single repository

The following is an excerpt of some important information related to the upgrade process and how the migrated data is transposed.

Release 11*i* tax codes and tax groups migrate to E-Business Tax as tax classification codes.

Payables and Purchasing tax codes migrate as tax classification codes under ZX_INPUT_CLASSIFICATIONS.

Receivables and Projects tax codes migrate as tax classification codes under ZX_OUTPUT_CLASSIFICATIONS.

You can set up additional tax classification codes for use with a migrated tax data model or as an additional determining factor in tax determination.

Tax content service providers

Oracle E-Business Tax does not come with any tax codes or rates, just like in previous versions.

You must have a connection between a geographic jurisdiction and a tax jurisdiction. This is needed so that the global repository has the capability to work with any specific geographic hierarchy needed for tax calculation in a central place. In previous releases service providers such as Vertex and Taxware provided tax rates and related location based tax information.

Service providers provide these geographic hierarchies for the U.S. and also supply the rates for each of the levels with periodic updates. They also provide tax content for other countries.

You should consider working with a service provider to procure the current geographic hierarchies and rates for each level if you choose to use one of the process flows for tax calculation and regular updates.

This is the easiest way to help jump start your configuration for your E-Business Tax requirements for the U.S.

There are other methods for building tax content. These are available for a few other countries from Oracle. (Refer to Metalink Note ID 463001.1 on E-Business Seed Data for details) This method provides only a one-time load for geography and tax jurisdiction information.

Using E-Business Tax

Once you have configured E-Business Tax for use in your environment, you have set the stage for beginning to use it in transactions.

In most cases you start with the Order to Cash process and manage calculation of taxes that you will charge your customers.

As mentioned before you can also use E-Business Tax to manage your self-assessed taxes (called use tax in the U.S.), and calculate tax on Procure to Pay transactions.

The tax rates are the same content that you receive from a service provider that would populate the jurisdiction and the tax rates for each jurisdiction as appropriate.

Third-party tax profiles

Create third-party tax profiles to manage your third parties' tax obligations to relevant tax authorities. These profiles allow you to specify third-party classification to the customers or suppliers to be used in tax determining factors and creating rules.

These classifications are not required but are a higher level classification that can be used for rules and determining factors.

You can still use the party name or party site name to build rules for specific third-party tax calculation criteria.

You may optionally set up tax registrations for your customers and suppliers, as necessary, to support specific tax regulations or reporting requirements.

Tax exemptions

A tax exemption is a discount/surcharge or replacement percentage from the base tax rate that reduces the applicable tax on a Receivables transaction.

 Tax exemptions apply only to specific transactions of a legal entity or operating unit; you cannot use the Global Configuration Owner to share tax exemption records.

A tax exemption usually applies to a specific customer or to a combination of a customer and specific product. A tax exemption record identifies the nature of the exemption, the configuration owner and Tax Regime, and where applicable, the related tax, tax status, tax rate, and tax jurisdiction.

Exemptions are applicable only at the party site level for Ship To. Bill To exemptions are applicable only when the exemption is defined at that party level.

These allow for the use of exemptions that you create and are allowed at various levels from Tax Regime through to the tax at the lowest level. This is true in countries where there are multi-level tax obligations, such as in the U.S.

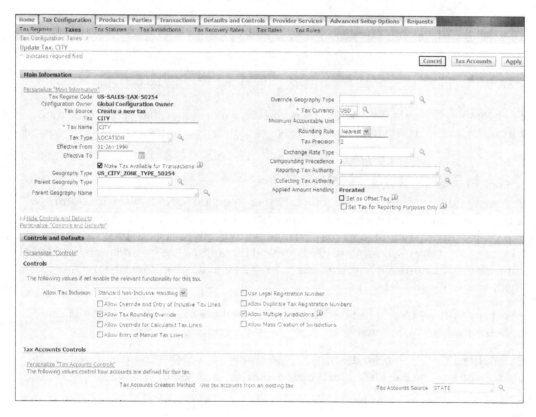

You may elect to inherit the tax exemption from the parent of the lowest level with a source level that is higher. As an example you can inherit the tax exemption source for a city tax from the county. The inheritance is based on your geographic hierarchy you created, State, City, County, Zip in TCA and the jurisdiction that has been created based on this for this address combination.

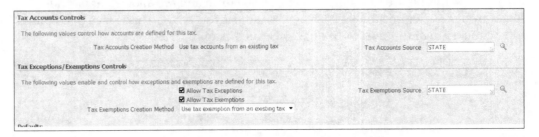

For example, this data is provided from the service provider that you choose to use for the tax rates, jurisdiction, and address validation data in the U.S.

Tax Rates and Rules

As mentioned in an earlier part of this chapter there are various ways to capture information about the latest rates for your tax calculations. In the U.S., where there is a probability that these rates may change periodically, a service provider (such as Vertex or Taxware) will provide geographical hierarchy, Tax Jurisdictions, and Rates for each jurisdiction on a regular basis as long as you have a licensed agreement with them to provide the data.

In other countries Oracle can be configured to load the initial rates for you at the country level, and you must keep these up-to-date as and when they change.

Exemptions that have been described in an earlier part of this chapter allow you to change the tax rate calculated for a transaction for a customer or customer site.

In many cases there are complex rules based on a customer type, location of Bill To/Ship To, and item/item category that can lead to a reduced tax rate for the combination of customer/customer site and item/item category.

The capability of creating dynamic rules in E-Business Tax allows you to create complex derivation to arrive at appropriate tax rates. These can be for transactions in specific jurisdictions or based on products sold.

The following is a short list of some of the rule types available when creating a rule:

- Determine place of supply

- Determine recovery rate

- Determine tax applicability

- Determine tax rate

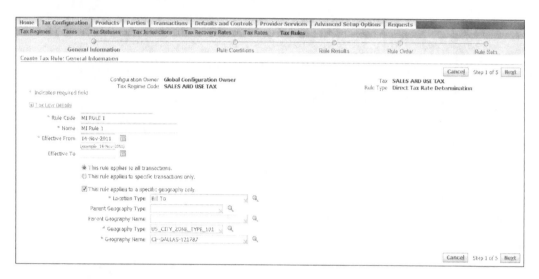

Summary

We reviewed the basics of E-Business Tax and the various new functions that have been introduced. We also covered briefly the capability of using data elements in rules to create a configurable product to meet your enterprise tax obligations.

This chapter has given you a high-level idea of how the product works and there is much more information in the documentation that should be reviewed and understood before a complex implementation can be successful.

The next chapter covers Oracle Workflow. It was an embedded product when it was initially released and then morphed into a product that was partly on the server and partly on your desktop. Workflow allows users to target specific business flows, accounting representations, and approvals for transactions to be customized to meet business rules.

The functionality for accounting representation creation is being progressively moved to SLA with the latest release. But workflow is still being used to progress transactions in various business flows to the next level and should be in use for a while.

14
Oracle Workflow

Oracle Workflow delivers a complete workflow management system that supports business process based integration with approvals for transactions. In some cases, workflow also enables generation of account code combinations as part of specific processes. Its technology enables modeling, automation, and routing information according to user-defined business rules. Oracle Workflow automates and streamlines transaction processes both within and beyond your enterprise; supporting traditional applications based workflow as well as E-business Suite integration workflow.

Business processes today involve getting many types of information to multiple people for approval according to rules that are constantly changing. Oracle Workflow can route supporting information to each decision maker in a transaction process, including people both inside and outside your enterprise.

Oracle Workflow lets you define and continuously improve your transaction processes using a drag-and-drop process designer. This is enabled by an add-on product called Oracle Workflow Builder that is installed on a desktop and lets you model sophisticated transaction processes. You can also decide which path to take based on the result of a stored procedure; you can use the power of Java and of PL/SQL, the language of the Oracle Database, to express any business rule that affects a workflow process.

Oracle Workflow extends the reach of business process automation throughout the enterprise and beyond and lets people receive notifications of items awaiting their attention via e-mail, and act based on the e-mail responses.

 Though Oracle Workflow is still used extensively in E-Business Suite, Oracle recommends that users migrate to Oracle BPEL (Business Process Execution Language) Process Manager. You can find the reference from the *Metalink Note - Oracle Workflow Cartridge 2.6.X [ID 391546.1]*.

Oracle Workflow lets you set up subscriptions to business events which can launch workflows or enable messages to be propagated from one system to another when business events occur.

Major features and definitions

Oracle Workflow comes with a basic set of overview components that will be discussed and listed in the subsequent sections. The following are the major components that make the product usable and flexible to be a business event handler that can integrate and help process transactions based on specified business rules.

Oracle Workflow Builder

Oracle Workflow Builder is a graphical tool that lets you create, view, or modify a transaction process (workflow processes) with simple drag-and-drop operations. The tool allows you to create and modify all workflow objects, including activities, item types, and messages. You can operate Oracle Workflow Builder from a desktop PC or from a disconnected laptop PC.

Workflow engine

The workflow engine embedded in the Oracle Database implements process definitions at runtime. The Workflow engine monitors workflow states and coordinates the routing of activities for a process. Changes in workflow state, such as the completion of a workflow activity, are signaled to the engine via a PL/SQL API or a Java API.

 This embedded engine is not available for Oracle Database versions 11*g* onwards; the Oracle Workflow product has reached end-of-life.

Business event system

The business event system is an application service that uses the **Oracle Advanced Queuing (AQ)** infrastructure to communicate business events within and between systems. The business event system consists of the Event Manager, which lets you define and register subscriptions to significant events, and event activities, which let you model business events within workflow processes.

Workflow definitions loader

The definitions loader is a utility program that allows users to move workflow definitions between database instances. You can use it to move workflow definitions from a development to a production instance. The definitions loader is integrated into Oracle Workflow Builder, allowing you to open and save workflow definitions in both the database and locally on a PC.

Complete programmatic extensibility

Oracle Workflow lets you include your own PL/SQL procedures or external functions as activities in your workflows. Without modifying your application code, you can have your own program run whenever the Workflow engine detects that your program's prerequisites are satisfied.

Electronic notifications and mail integration

Oracle Workflow lets you include users in your workflows to handle activities that cannot be automated, such as approvals for transactions. The workflow notification system processes e-mail responses from users in a workflow process and takes appropriate actions, such as approve, reject, and so on.

Electronic mail (e-mail) users can receive notifications of outstanding work items and can respond to those notifications using their e-mail application of choice.

As an example if a user enters a requisition that requires his manager's approval, an e-mail will be sent by the workflow process and can process the manager's response.

Monitoring and administration

Workflow administrators and users can view the progress of a work item in a workflow process by connecting to the workflow monitor using a standard web browser that supports Java. The workflow monitor displays an annotated view of the process diagram for a particular instance of a workflow process, so that users can get a graphical depiction of their work item status.

There are multiple setup configuration steps that need to be performed before you can start using Oracle Workflow. Luckily, there are very few that are required to use it as a standard tool. This is assuming that you intend to use default settings as they are and your enterprise does not require any specific changes/modifications.

If this is the case then you can start using the workflow system without a lengthy configuration. These are required and are listed as follows:

- **Setting global user preferences**: This task is performed by a Database Administrator who also performs other related tasks required to have Oracle Workflow operational. Setting up Workflow Directory Services is configured at the time of installation and is not a support analyst or user driven task.

- **Scheduling Workflow Background Processes to run periodically**: This is normally configured by your system administrator and he has the task of also monitoring if there are any issues with the process on a regular basis. This enables all the processes to run smoothly and all subscriptions to be processed in sequence and when they should be.

- **Set up Business event system**: This is only required if you want to configure your system to integrate with external systems. All business events configuration for E-Business Suite products is already preseeded.

Workflow usage

As mentioned previously the workflow system is built to manage process events and tasks as predefined process flows upon installation of E-Business Suite.

The components, as mentioned earlier in this chapter, features, and definitions all work together to allow users to view, manage, modify, and track processes as they occur. The user can review notifications online using a web page or via e-mail and respond to the notifications, if action is required.

Processes and functions

An event that is transacted by a workflow process uses functions. These are shown in image in the left-hand panel. You can add additional functions or processes if they are not available. In many cases, functions are added to provide logic that is not available within E-Business Suite that addresses your specific business requirements.

There are specific processes that Oracle Workflow has seeded or delivered as a default when you install Oracle E-Business Suite.

A sample of these workflow processes are listed for reference:

- AP Invoice Approval
- Requisition (Approval)
- FA Account Generator

- PO Accrual Account Generator
- Order Fulfillment
- Responsibility Access

As you can see in the previous short list there are processes that cover varied areas of processing within the E-Business Suite. Some cover account generation (creating code combinations) based on rules that are inherent (PO Accrual Account Generator) or some that you can configure (FA Account Generator), others cover approval processes (Requisition Approval), and others cover simple process steps (Responsibility Access).

The following is a simple Oracle Order Management line process flow that is not related to any approval or account (code combination) process.

This workflow is the crucial engine that allows you as a user to enter an order, book it, schedule a demand, plan (if needed), pick, and ship (fulfill) it to the final customer.

There could be an approval process if needed interspersed within this process flow but that is not how the default workflow functions. Workflows that process transactions do not normally have approval logic. However, there are order header level and line level flows that contain approval functions.

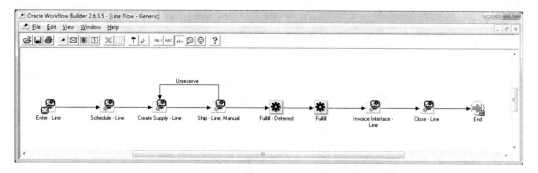

Beginning with the introduction of Subledger Accounting (SLA) in Release 12, Oracle is moving towards all account code generation to the subledger accounting product. This change benefits users by allowing them access to make changes in a forms-based environment and not having to resort to using the Workflow Builder tool or using the workflow product to generate accounting entries.

In either case it assumes an in-depth understanding of how the account generation inherently works and what data components you have to use to drive logic to create the code combination that you need.

The following are a few workflow account generators that can be easily transitioned to SLA user-defined rules:

- FA Account Generator (FAFLEXWF)
- OM: Generate Cost of Goods Sold Account (OECOGS)
- Project Web Employees Account Generator (PAAPWEBX)
- PO Requisition Account Generator (POWFRQAG)
- PO Account Generator (POWFPOAG)

> The names in the parentheses for the previous list are the internal names within the system. The reason I show these here is that in multiple places these are displayed on Metalink notes and other documentation.

These are just a few examples. There are more and all account generation workflows should be reviewed prior to use.

Even though this is a book focused towards a functional audience, I would like to highlight some technical aspects that are important in identifying the processes in the workflow.

Two important technical notations in a workflow process are briefly described as follows:

- **Item Type** can be defined as a grouping of items of a particular category that share the same set of item attributes. Item Type is also used as a high-level grouping for a process. As an example in the previous screenshot the Item Type is **Order Line Generic**.
- **Item Key** is a string that uniquely identifies an instance of an event. Together, the Item Type, Item Key, and event data fully communicate what occurred in an event.

Approval workflows

Approvals of documents require a workflow process as well as additional setups that help build the approval hierarchy. The most common usage is purchase requisition and purchase order approval.

These two transactions are an initiation of a contract between the organization and a supplier. These are deemed to need approval for pricing and/or total amount.

As indicated in *Chapter 5, Purchasing* there is a task of configuring your approval groups and approval hierarchies before a requisition (or purchase order) can be entered, approved, and transacted.

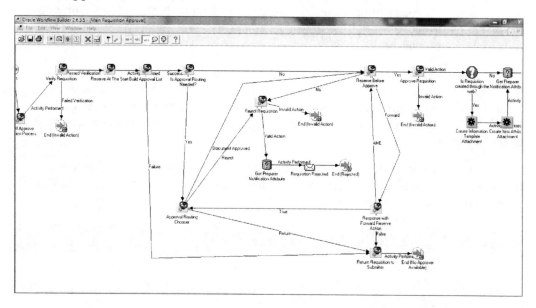

The approval groups assist in managing account and amount-based routing for approval. The hierarchy depends on the option you choose, supervisor or position. You can choose to make changes to the workflow to insert additional approvals, if needed. This change can be based on specific data elements that are in the transaction, item, price, and so on.

Some workflows come with a detailed flow. Other seeded workflows are a template to allow you to create your own workflow process.

Notifications

Oracle Workflow sends notifications to a user, group of users, or an external entity when the workflow engine executes a notification activity. The notification activity may designate the role as being responsible for performing an action or may simply relay process-related information.

To deliver a notification successfully to a role, there are additional configuration steps that are needed. These would be performed at the time of installation (or later) by your administrator. In case notifications are delivered via e-mail there are other related configurations in E-Business Suite and in your system environment that may be needed.

You can view a notification using any one of the three interfaces depending on your role's notification preference setting in the Oracle Workflow directory service. You can receive an e-mail for each individual notification, receive a single e-mail summarizing all your notifications, or query the Workflow Notifications web page. If you choose to receive e-mail, you can also choose the format in which you want to receive the e-mail messages.

Each notification message can include context-sensitive information about the process and directions on how to respond to the notification, if a response is required. The message can also include pointers to Web URLs and references to Oracle E-Business Suite forms that allow you to get additional information related to the notification.

As mentioned previously there are multiple ways to review these notifications; however, as e-mail delivery mechanisms, formats, and choices differ, the E-Business Suite web page option is used here for clarity.

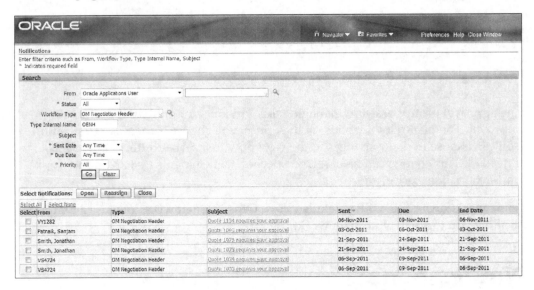

The previous screenshot is from the general ledger responsibility.

Other E-Business Suite products also allow you to access transactions notifications. This is true of iProcurement (as with other Self Service Applications).

The following is a screenshot from the iProcurement responsibility:

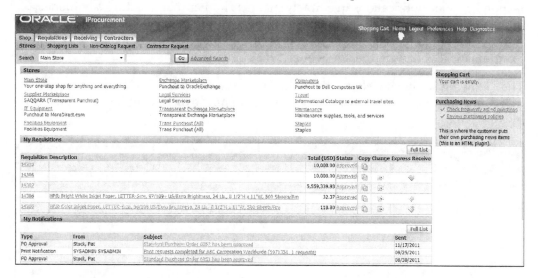

In this case you see the notification including your requisitions that you may have entered and their status. The home page for iProcurement has multiple panels of information and notifications are one of them; there are only a few that are shown.

You can choose to go to another tab that has all the notifications that are waiting for your review and response. You could also choose to click the **Full List** button just above your notifications and this launches a screen that shows all your open notifications.

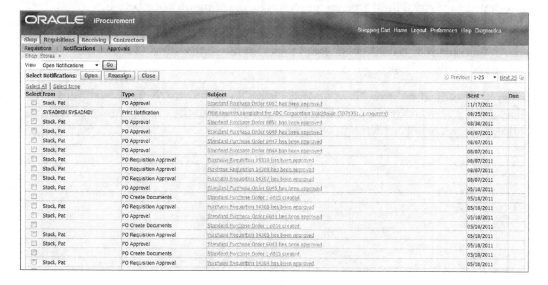

In some cases, such as if you are away on vacation, you will not be able to view or respond to your notifications in a timely manner. Rather than creating a bottleneck in the workflow process, you can take advantage of vacation rules, also known as routing rules or automatic notification processing rules, to direct Oracle Workflow to automatically manage the notifications for you.

The following screenshot shows the screen where you would create such a rule, for delegating or transferring a workflow process for approval or action to someone else in your team:

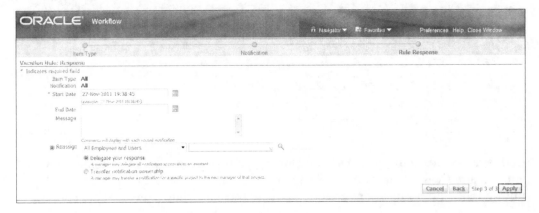

There is a subtle difference between delegate and transfer.

Delegation is assigning your responsibility to someone else in your team to respond to requests and act on notifications on your behalf. When you delegate you also assign your approval limits for the person who is acting on your behalf.

Transferring the notification means transferring a specific notification to someone else in your team or outside your team to act on the notification as though the transferee owns the notification.

When the notification is received and you have the authority (or approval limit) to approve a transaction you see a notification similar to the one in shown in the following screenshot, which you may act upon:

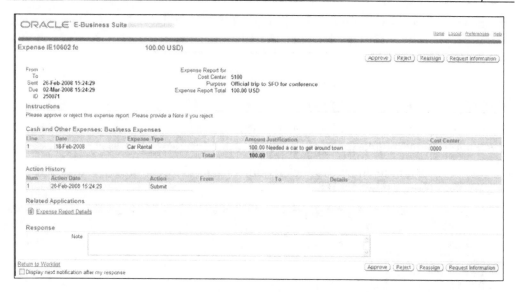

The previous screenshot shows an approval notification for an expense report (in iExpense). The content may differ based on the transaction that requires approval, but the buttons for the actions and the functionality are similar across the system.

The notification viewer can also show the process from the transaction. On the transaction form, a user can choose to view the workflow status. The user will see a screen similar to the following screenshot that shows the whole flow and the position where the current activity is waiting for the next action/activity:

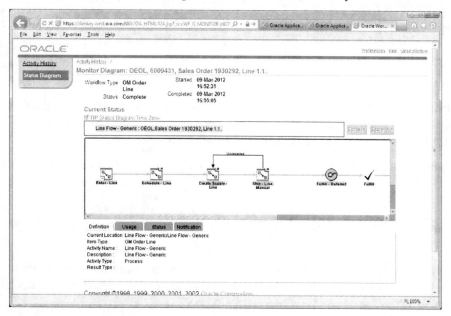

The previous screenshot shows the item name (OEOL) and the process steps that the flow is progressing through. The green line identifies the position in the flow. In this case it has progressed beyond the **Fulfill** task.

Workflow Builder

The following is a process flow screenshot as it appears in the Workflow Builder, which allows you to make changes to the existing workflow processes.

The following example illustrates the creation of accrual accounting on a procurement transaction:

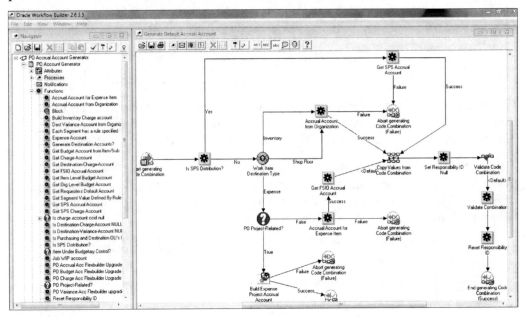

This transaction process workflow is delivered as part of the initial installation of E-Business Suite. You can change this as needed based on your business requirements. The changes are made using the workflow builder tool.

The previous screenshot shows a set of functions and process blocks that are routed based on data within the transaction.

On the left hand panel a list of functions are available for use within this process. You may add customized functions to manage the routing or behavior of the process task as needed.

The ability to add functions allows you to extend the application to suit your business needs with non-invasive extensions that are preserved when any updates are provided by Oracle.

If you intend to use a process flow to integrate and work with events from external systems other than E-Business Suite, you must create a new business event. This is followed by subscribing to that event. Subscriptions allow the system to invoke code that is based on the event having a specific outcome.

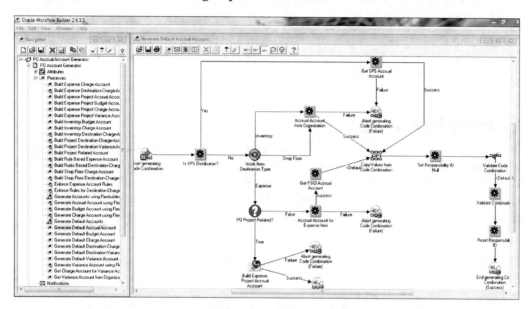

You can add processes and functions for use in your own workflows if you need to define these from the ground up.

If you are intending to use one of the existing business events, the only task you need to perform is to modify the workflow to process the transaction (or other task) according to the business rules in your organization.

There are several options to perform this task. They are as follows:

- Use the Oracle provided Workflow as is, with no modifications.

  One of the common cases where the seeded workflow is used is for approval of purchase requisitions.

- Customize or extend the workflow to suit your needs. This task will be impacted by any updates that Oracle provides relating to this process.

  Multiple clients will modify the workflow that creates the account combinations for accrual and few accounts created in assets. This is dependent on your business needs.

- Build a workflow from scratch which can use existing processes blocks and functions.

  The most common case is when you want to integrate your order processing with external vendors or get specific tasks performed before proceeding to fulfill the order.

It is recommended that if you want to use a specific event but change the way the transaction is processed, you may want to create a copy of the workflow provided by Oracle and make the necessary changes.

Business events

The business event system and manager within the Oracle Workflow product has not been widely used and most users are sufficiently subsisting with using the Workflow process modeller and process activity tasks. This is due to the fact that all business events that are used locally (within Oracle E-Business Suite) are already in place and the Business Events System is configured to effectively use this for the E-Business products.

This brief paragraph gives you an overview of what can be accomplished with the Business event system.

The Event Manager contains a registry of business events, systems, named communication agents, and subscriptions indicating that an event is significant to a particular transaction process. Events can be raised locally or received from an external system. The local system uses Oracle Advanced Queuing to manage these events and act upon them.

Business events are represented within workflow processes by events. By including event activities in a workflow process, you can model complex processing or routing logic.

The uses include:

- **System integration messaging hubs**: Oracle Workflow with the Business event system can serve as a messaging hub for complex system integration scenarios. The Event Manager can be used to hard-wire routing between systems based on the event and originator.
- **Distributed applications messaging**: Applications can supply generate and receive event message handlers for their business entities.

- **Message-based system integration**: You can set up subscriptions which cause messages to be sent from one system to another when business events occur, using the Event Manager to implement point-to-point messaging integration.

- **Business event-based workflow processes**: You can develop sophisticated workflow processes that include advanced routing or processing; including approvals, based on the content of business events.

- **Non-invasive customization of packaged applications**: Analysts can register interesting business events for their Internet or intranet applications. Users of those applications can register subscriptions to those events to trigger custom code or workflow processes.

An example of a seeded E-Business Suite business event that is used frequently is the Order Line Workflow. This event builds the steps an order line must go through from order booking to invoicing. The business event booking the order triggers the workflow to be initiated.

Summary

In this chapter, we discussed the various components that make up the workflow product in E-Business Suite. The product enables process tasks, approval mechanisms, and notifications in such a way that assists you in appropriately managing your transaction processes with relevant business rules and routings.

Workflow can also be a used instead of alerts, but it is not completely a replacement for the old Oracle Alerts product. This is one case where there may be a need to review and add a business event if needed.

In the next chapter, we will learn more about Approval Management Engine (AME), which is an improvement to creating approval hierarchies on the fly. This is slowly replacing the current approval hierarchy mechanism in Oracle Purchasing for requisitions.

In keeping with the focus of this book I have mainly stayed within the realm of the functional side of the Oracle Workflow product. This chapter does not purport to do justice to the technical capability of Oracle Workflow.

There is a large body of knowledge available and can easily be accessed in various publications and on the Internet. A couple of sources I would like to mention here are:

- *OAUG Workflow SIG*
- *The ABCs of Oracle Workflow for E-Business Suite Release 11i and Release 12*, by Karen Brownfield

15
Approval Management Engine (AME)

Approval Management Engine (AME) is a product that was introduced in E-Business Suite 11*i*. This was on the persistent request of many users to provide a more flexible rules engine to manage approvals of transactions in the E-Business Suite software.

Prior to the introduction of this product approval was only possible by creating an approval hierarchy, job-supervisor relationship or positional. These hierarchies were driven by Oracle HRMS with data in HR organizations. This led many organizations to make extensions and modifications (customizations) to enable their approval rules to be implemented.

Prior to the introduction of AME, approvals were predominantly managed using standard approval hierarchies (based on HR data) and were built for procurement transactions. Approval of other transactions was not supported till the introduction of Oracle Workflow.

The approval hierarchies have been entrenched with most users in the positional or job-supervisor hierarchy, and these are still in use. AME provides an opportunity where you can dynamically build hierarchies dependent on the transactional data elements.

The current framework, approval hierarchies built with the older functionality (positional or job-supervisor), workflow, notifications, and process flows are still used. AME adds to this equation, it allows for creation of dynamic and flexible approval hierarchies based on transaction data.

The Oracle Workflow product is still used to progress your transaction through the steps that it needs to be routed through. With AME you can use the transaction data to create a hierarchy for approval, rather than using the predefined hierarchy. Oracle Workflow is still used to notify users about approvals, rejections, or just FYI notifications.

You can describe the functionality of AME as follows:

- Transaction is entered (requiring approval).
- AME creates a hierarchy for approval based on the transaction entered.

  As an example based on a specific data within the transaction, say a value for the department, you may want a specific person to also approve the transaction or if the transaction is related to a project, then you would like to have the Project Manager also approve the transaction. You can also use the positional or job-supervisory hierarchy.

- Use Workflow to progress and route the transaction for approval.
- Notify users/approvers when their action is needed.
- Update the transaction once the transaction is approved.

The Approval Management Engine consists of the following components:

- Transaction type
- Attribute
- Rules
- Condition
- Action

These components function together to provide a robust and effective mechanism that enables you to implement your business rules for approval of multiple transactions.

Initially only procurement transactions (purchase requisitions and purchase orders) had the functionality to run through approvals. Starting in Release 11, Oracle introduced the workflow product that supported approval functionality for additional transactions.

All of these were disparate hierarchies and had to be defined in each of these modules separately. This was not efficient. With the introduction of AME (initially in 11*i*), the capability now exists to use a single approval hierarchy function and manage all these transactions.

Transaction types

There are multiple transactions that can be managed with the Approvals Management Engine. The following list shows a partial list for reference:

- AP invoice
- AP expense report (iExpense only)
- GL journals
- Receivable credit memo
- Advanced Global Intercompany System (AGIS)

For a complete list of transactions that support AME please refer to the AME Implementation Guide (Part No. E13516-04).

> Purchase orders do not and cannot use the AME functionality for approvals. Purchase requisitions do use the AME functionality.

You can also create new transaction types that use AME for approvals but these are considered as customizations.

In the following screenshot the attribute screen of the expense report AME approval transaction is shown for reference:

Name	Order Number	Parallelization	Sub-List Mode
Header	1	Serial	Serial
Line Item	2	Serial	Serial
Cost Center	3	Serial	Serial
project	4	Serial	Serial
award	5	Serial	Serial

Transaction Type: OIE Expense Reports

Transaction Type **OIE Expense Reports**
Application **Payables**
Transaction Type Key **APEXP**
AME Internal-ID **-223**

Attribute	Static Usage	Value/Query
ALLOW_DELETING_RULE_GENERATED_APPROVERS	Static	false
ALLOW_REQUESTOR_APPROVAL	Static	false
AT_LEAST_ONE_RULE_MUST_APPLY	Static	false
EFFECTIVE_RULE_DATE	Static	
EVALUATE_PRIORITIES_PER_ITEM	Static	false
REJECTION_RESPONSE	Static	Stop all processing
REPEAT_SUBSTITUTIONS	Static	false
USE_RESTRICTIVE_ITEM_EVALUATION	Static	false
USE_WORKFLOW	Static	true
WORKFLOW_ITEM_KEY	Dynamic	select report_header_id from ap_expense_report_headers_all where report_header_id = :transactionId

Item classes

Item classes are important components in AME as they uniquely identify a set attribute of a transaction, such as the line item cost, or line item cost centre. They can then be used in a rule to drive your business process for approvals using transaction values.

Item classes specify the data element that is part of a rule in building a hierarchy. These can be added to a transaction as needed to manage your business requirements.

An Item class can have multiple items within it to be used in the approval hierarchy building process. An Item can be used to identify a specific line or an identifying factor for that data element.

Attributes

Attributes are variables in a transaction with a single value. These can be used in a rule to manage how AME builds an approval hierarchy for the transaction or transaction line.

The transaction header has a specific item class and has attributes that identify the transaction. As an example, for a purchase order the header can contain the following attributes that identify the PO in a rule:

- PO number
- Supplier
- PO amount

In a similar manner there are other attributes that you can use on the lines of a transaction to be used in rules more specifically.

Attributes are generally shared across all transactions that are used (or will be used) in AME. As an example, an attribute called TRANSACTION_AMOUNT can be used across all transactions used in AME. It will have the same properties regardless of which transaction that it is used for.

Shared attributes are a big benefit of AME because they allow you to be consistent in your rule definitions across business processes.

There are two major ways to use an attribute:

- Static
- Dynamic

A static attribute is used with a given value. It is used at runtime with that value which will not change.

It is reasonable to assign a static type of an attribute to mandatory attributes so that they are always assigned and have a value. This ensures that as part of the rule being evaluated the attributes that are required will always be available.

Dynamic attributes are normally used in non-mandatory attributes. These identify specific data from the transaction that are used to create the rule and used as a component in building the hierarchy.

> This does not mean that a dynamic attribute cannot be used for mandatory attributes; it is only recommended that you use static ones. This ensures there is always a value for a mandatory attribute.

This is efficient because you can now use this value to drive your approval rules and even your approval hierarchy if needed. Based on this dynamic attribute and its value the generalized approval rules are now more flexible and can be changed depending on the transactions that need to be approved.

Approval rules

Approval rules are constructed using conditions and actions. An approval rule has the task of replicating your business requirement in a rule form using item classes, item attributes, conditions, and resultant actions to generate an approval (or rejection). This will also update the transaction with an action response.

The action could be to update the transaction as approved!

In procurement prior to the introduction of AME, the approval groups and approval assignments that you created were static and worked on the basis of the following simple rules:

- Accounting Flexfield value
- Transaction amount

These two were framed against the hierarchy (positional or job-supervisor) that HRMS maintains to approve your transaction against multiple levels until a position or level had the appropriate authority.

The workflow engine is used to progress the transaction to the next level. The notification functionality notifies approvers (in the hierarchy) about a transaction requiring their action.

All this changes with AME because any of these attributes used in the previous example as the attribute of the Accounting Flexfield value and the transaction amount can be used to change the hierarchy that approves the transaction.

This allows the introduction of an additional level (or multiple levels) of authority to a transaction based on what it is used for (account) and how much it costs (transaction amount).

You can also have subitems (line level attributes) to take the rules to a more granular level for specific transactions.

Conditions

Conditions are used to build a rule and expand your business logic within an approval activity. You use conditions to evaluate your transactions and decide on the routing to manage for approving the transactions.

When conditions are evaluated, tasks can be assigned based on the evaluated results.

Once the conditions are met within your rule, you choose to act upon the results based on the actions that you create. One action might be approving the transaction. Another could be to reject it.

There are two types of conditions:

- Regular
- List modifiers

Regular conditions are pure expressions of a value that is matched against a transaction attribute. As an example:

- PO Amount > 500?
- PO for a specific supplier?
- PO an expense PO?

In this case the conditions are ordinary and can be evaluated simply for a yes or no situation. Then you could have exceptions to these conditions, and exceptions can only be used in exception rules, which are an override of the rule.

As an example:

- PO for a specific Supplier? But is also an expense PO
- PO Amount > 500? But is also for a specific Item/Item Category

These flexibilities make the rules engine very conducive in creating complex business scenarios into rules so that these can appropriately manage approvals as you want them.

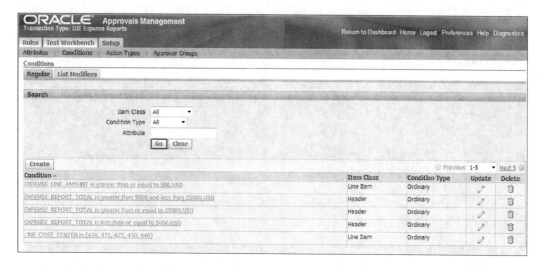

The other type of condition is list creation. This is where based on an attribute value you need to perform a certain action to include additional people in the approval chain.

The following figure shows an example of each of these types of conditions for a better understanding:

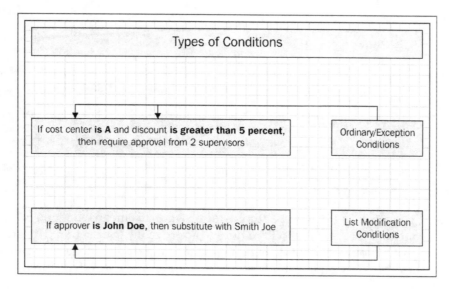

Conditions such as attributes are shared across any transaction process that uses the attributes that the condition references. This allows you to generate conditions and rules that can be used across all such transactions where the attributes are similar. This ensures that there is a commonality in the approval rules across the enterprise.

Actions

The previous sections discussed the specifics of how you build a rule, use an existing attribute, evaluate conditions and then perform an action. This action is the result of a condition having been satisfied in your rule and progresses the approval process to the next step.

The action can be either to modify the approval process, or set the approval process to have a number of levels of approval.

One of the actions that you have within AME states that you need approval up to two (2) levels.

An HR hierarchy exists that can be used; and you have a supervisor for the initiator of the transaction, and the supervisor's supervisor. In this case you already have a chain of authority. Using this existing hierarchy AME progresses (using workflow) the transaction for a maximum of four levels of approval.

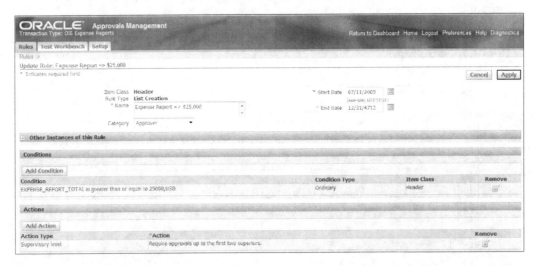

The other action type is a chain of authority approval. This means that you can create a group of approvers that will require to approve the transaction. The group is defined as part of your AME implementation and configured to include certain sets of users. These can be used in conjunction with your existing HRMS hierarchy.

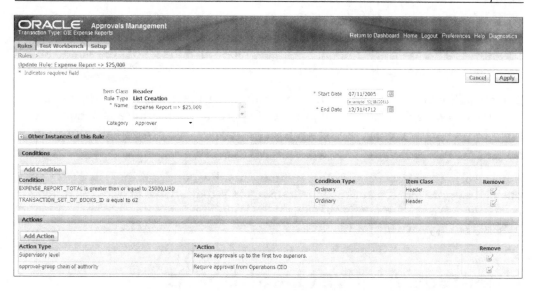

The previous screenshot displays multiple conditions. This example shows you how conditions may be joined creating a complex rule with multiple actions. This capability enables you to use the AME engine for managing additional approvers based on the transactional values.

This functionality provides users with a long awaited requirement to use an approval manager/engine that is truly user friendly and mitigates the need for continuous assistance from technical resources.

This truly puts the reins in the hands of the business user who is the direct user and provider of these rules.

Action types

Action types allow you to modify the way approvals are managed. The different elements of action types that allow this functionality are as follows:

- Order number
- Ordering mode
- Voting method

Order number defines how the notifications are sent to the approvers for their action. This identifies the sequence in which the notification for action is sent to each approver.

Ordering mode defines how it is sent—either serially—one after the other, or in parallel. If you choose to send in serial mode then each notification is sent after the previous one has been acted upon. In parallel mode all notifications are sent to all approvers simultaneously.

The capability to choose a voting method is an interesting component. The serial voting method depicts the normal process of approval notification and action, one after the other. The parallel option allows a consensus, which means all approvers have to approve and only then is the transaction approved.

You can also choose one of the other options, **First Responder Wins**. Then any one of the approvers can approve the transaction if they are the first to act on the notification. Another option is available that allows anyone in the chain of command to be able to approve the transaction.

Business Analyst Dashboard

The portal for a business user is called the Business Analysts Dashboard and is a launching pad for creating rules, conditions, actions, and test plans. One of the more important and unique functionalities that has been introduced is the capability to perform a test on a rule you have created and see the result of what would happen if a transaction was run through the engine.

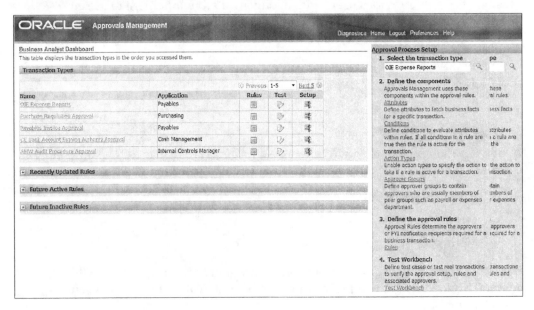

The previous screenshot is the Business Analyst Dashboard that allows you to review and prepare rules for specific transactions.

The panel on the left-hand side shows the transactions that are supported by AME to manage approvals.

 The AME engine has seeded transaction types, attributes, and rules. Additional configuration is needed for enabling specific products to use AME.

As an example in iProcurement, requisitions are by default set to use AME for approval. You need to change this to use the standard approval if you do not want to use AME.

On the right-hand panel the following options are available to a user:

- **Attributes**
- **Conditions**
- **Actions**
- **Action Types**
- **Approver Groups**

The previous data elements are defined for a specific transaction. You choose the transaction that you want to work with and then make a choice on the right-hand panel.

Capability also exists to utilize real transaction data to run through the engine and verify/review the results of the rule and the actions using the dashboard and test framework.

Once you have reviewed the seeded ones or created new components you may choose the test workbench to test how your rule would work with sample data. You can create test transactions on AME's test workbench, or real transactions in the integrating application. You can store the simulated and the real transaction test cases for future reference.

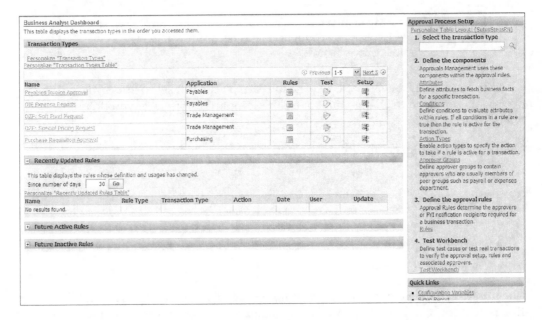

The test workbench displays a list of previously defined test cases. You can copy a test case, and have many variations on a standard transaction. This enables you to exhaustively test your approval setup. When defining or updating a test case, you can supply values for the attributes of interest. For the test case, it is possible to define header values and if appropriate create detail lines in order to mimic an invoice for example.

The test workbench enables you to check for item level, approver level, and transaction level productions. For reviewing and testing, you can see the various stages of the approver list.

Summary

We discussed how Oracle Approval Management Engine allows flexible use of conditions and rules to manage all your approval needs within the Oracle E-Business Suite.

Index

A

AAD 74
account defaulting 112
Account Derivation Rules. *See* ADR
Account Generator 206
accounting
  about 167, 168, 210, 236
  AP/AR Netting feature 236, 237
accounting actions 189, 190
Accounting Application Definition. *See*
  AAD
Accounting Date 80
Accounting Flexfield (AFF)
  about 16
  segment qualifiers 19, 20
Accounting Methods Builder. *See* AMB
accounting policy management, SLA
  about 71
  accurate accounting 72
  comprehensive accounting 71
  SLA processes, configuration options for
    72, 73
accounting reports 77
accounting sequence 80
Accounting Setup Manager. *See* ASM
account inquiry 45, 46, 79
account rules, consolidation 55
Accounts Payable 125
accruals 123, 124
accurate accounting, accounting policy
  management 72
actions 288, 294, 295
action types
  about 295, 296
  elements 295, 296

action types, elements
  about 295
  ordering mode 296
  order number 295
  voting method 296
Add to Asset option 155, 156
Adjusted Current Earnings (ACE) 164
adjustments only option, secondary ledger
  36
adjustment transaction 224
administrative security 26
ADR 74
Advanced Global Intercompany System. *See*
  AGIS
Advanced Shipment Notices (ASN)
  functionality 119, 203
AGIS
  about 57, 289
  benefits 57
  security, defining 58
aliases 21
AMB 73
AME approvals engine 106
amount type option 62
AP/AR Netting feature
  about 144-146, 236
  configurations 237
AP expense report 289
AP invoice 289
application object library (AOL) 13
application security
  about 24
  administrative security 26
  core security 25, 26
approval group 106

Approval Management Engine (AME)
about 131, 287
components 288
functions 288
**Approval Management Engine (AME),
        components**
about 288
action 288, 294, 295
action types 295, 296
attribute 288, 290
condition 288, 292, 293
item classes 290
rules 288, 291
transaction type 288, 289
approval rules 291
approvals
about 105, 136, 220, 221
managing 131
workflow notifications 107, 108
**Approvals Management Engine (AME) 105,
        107**
approval workflows 276, 277
approve button 42, 43
AP Trial Balance report 76
ASM
about 33, 34, 75
adjustments only option 36, 37
balance option 36, 37
E-Business Suite 36
journal option 36, 37
ledger, configuring 36
ledger, defining 36
ledger, tasks 35
legal addresses 34
legal entity address, defining 34
legal entity, defining 34
legal entity, need for 35
reporting ledger 37
reporting ledger, maintaining 37
subledger option 36, 37
Assemble to Order (ATO) 207
Asset Books
about 151
types 151
Asset Books, types
Budget 151
Corporate 151, 163, 164

Tax 151, 163, 164
asset categories 152
asset impairments 160
asset key flexfield 149
assets
about 147
transferring 159
assets, types
intangible 147
tangible 147
attributes
about 288, 290
types 290
attributes, types
about 290
dynamic 291
static 291
authorization 189
autocopy batch button 41, 42
autocopy button 43
AutoInvoice 219, 220, 232
automatic debit memo 132
automatic receipts 229-231
automation rules 251-253
Auto-Reconciliation feature 174

B

Back to Back order process
about 202
steps 203
BAI2 174
balance control option 60
balance option, secondary ledger 36
balances 47
balancing segment 19
bank account balances
managing 176
bank accounts 171
bank balance
managing 187, 188
bank balance management 187, 188
Bank Reconciliation
about 170, 173, 187
bank transaction codes 174
open interface 174
bank setups 170, 171

bank transaction codes 174
basic tax configuration 256
benefits, Bill Presentment Architecture
       (BPA) 236
Bill Presentment Architecture (BPA)
   about 236
   benefits 236
Bills Receivable functionality 226
BI Publisher 76, 236
Blanket Purchase Agreements (BPA) 116
Blanket Releases 116
BPEL 271
Budget Book 151
budgeting
   about 50
   values maintaining, rollup groups used 50
   values maintaining, summary accounts
       used 50
Business Analysts Dashboard 296-298
business event system
   about 272, 284
   benefits 284, 285
business event system, benefits
   business event-based workflow processes
       285
   distributed applications messaging 284
   message-based system integration 285
   non-invasive customization of packaged
       applications 285
   system integration messaging hubs 284
Business Group 84
business process flows, Oracle E-Business
       Suite
   Order to Cash (O2C) 10
   Procure to Pay (P2P) 10
buyer 113

C

calendars 151
capital budgeting 166
Capital Cost Allowance (CCA) 166
Capital-in-Process. See CIP
Capital Purchases 108
cash flows 178
cash forecasting 170, 174, 175
cash forecast specifications 174

cash inflow 174
cash levelling 177
cash management
   about 169, 170
   bank setups 171
   configuration 170
   integrating, with payables 172, 173
   integrating, with payroll 173
   integrating, with receivables 172
   integrating, with treasury 173
cash management integration 172
cash outflow 175
cash positioning 176
cash transactions
   about 177
   transfers 177
category 89
category flexfield 149
change currency button 42
change period button 42
change sign on variance option 61
change sign option 61
chargebacks
   about 232
   managing 232
Chart of Accounts feature 10
check funds button 42
checklist 248, 249
CIP 148-160
CIP assets 160
CIP Clearing Account 153
columns, FSG
   amount type option 62
   control value option 62
   currency option 62
   offset option 62
Column Total. See CT option
commitment transactions 224
comprehensive accounting, accounting
       policy management 71
conditions
   about 288, 292
   types 292
conditions, types
   about 292
   list creation 293
   regular 292

configuration
  for order capture functionality 206
configuration, for order capture functional-
    ity
  account generator 206
  credit checking rules 206
  order types 206
  pick and ship rules 206
  process constraints 206
  system parameters 206
  workflow 206
configuration options, E-Business Tax 215
configuration options, iReceivables 214
configurations, E-Business Tax
  basic tax configuration 256
  country default controls 256
  fiscal classification 256
  legal entity 260
  operating units 262
  party tax profiles 256, 261, 262
  self-assessment 261
  tax exemptions 256
  tax jurisdiction 256
  TCA classifications 263
configuration steps, Oracle Assets
  about 148
  Asset Books 151
  calendars 151
  flexfields 149
  system controls 150
Configure to Order (CTO) 207
configuring
  Oracle Payments 138, 139
  Payables 127
  flexfields 17, 18
consolidation
  about 53
  account rules 55
  across multiple ledgers 54, 55
  segment rules 55
  within E-Business suite 54
content sets, FSG
  CT (Column Total) option 62
  N (No Override) option 62
  PE Report Expand 62
  PT Report Total 63
  RB (Row Both) option 62

RE (Row Expand) option 62
RT (Row Total) option 62
Context Field 14
Contract Purchase Agreements 117
control accounts, SLA controls 71
controls, SLA
  about 69
  control account 71
  online accounting 69, 70
  preview accounting 70
  streamlined accounting 71
control value option 62
conversion 52
core requisitions 110, 111
Core Security 25, 26
Corporate Book 151, 163, 164
Cost Manager 96
Cost of Goods Sold (COGS) 209, 210
country default controls 256
create accounting 31
credit balances 198
credit card payment 231
credit checking 244
credit checking rules 206
credit check rules
  about 241-243
  pre-calculated exposure 243
credit checks 244, 245
credit data point 250, 251
Credit Management
  about 239, 246
  automation rules 251-253
  checklist 248, 249
  credit checking 244, 245
  credit check rules 241-243
  customer data, managing 247
  data points 250, 251
  payment terms 240, 241
  scoring models 248, 249
  workflow process 246, 247
credit memos 223, 289
credit recommendations 251
Cross-validation rules. See CV rules
CT option 62
currency option 62
currency rates manager 53
customer addresses (sites) 198

customer data
  managing 247
customer profiles 196, 197
customers
  about 196
  creating 196
  managing, in Oracle Receivables 221
  profiles 196, 197
CV rules 21

D

data access sets
  about 39
  and ledger sets 38
data elements, E-Business Tax
  trade 257
  trading partners 257
  transactions 257
Data Quality Management (DQM) 248
data security 25
Date Placed in Service (DPIS) 160, 163
deal 182
debit memo 221-223
debit memo reversals 229
delegated administration 26
dependent value set 17
depreciation 164, 165
Descriptive Flexfields (DFF)
  about 14, 77, 217
  using, with Accounting Flexfield segment
      qualifiers 20
  versus Key Flexfields (KFF) 14
Direct Procurement 108
discounts
  about 233
  earned discounts 233
  partial payments discounts 234
  tiered discounts 234
  unearned discounts 233
display option 60
display row option 60
display zero option 60
document printing 235, 236
draft accounting. *See* preview accounting,
    SLA controls

drop-ship orders
  about 203
  steps 203
Dun & Bradstreet (D&B) 240
dynamic attributes 291

E

earned discounts 233
EBiz Suite R12 8
EBTax. *See* E-Business Tax
E-Business Suite
  budgeting 50
  consolidation 54
  intercompany transactions 56
  legal entity 34
  mass allocations journals 44
  multi-currency 51
  sequences 80
  sources 75
  supporting references 76
E-Business Suite 11i 287
E-Business Tax
  about 214, 255
  configuration 258, 260
  configuration options 215
  data elements 257
  migrated data, managing 264
  overview 255-257
  tax content service providers 265
  tax exemptions 266, 268
  tax rates 268
  tax rules 268
  third-party tax profiles 266
  using 266
EDIFACT 174
EDI transactions 204
Electronic Funds Transfer (EFT) 126
enterprise 147
Enterprise Resource Planning. *See* ERP
equity
  about 186
  need for 186
ERP
  about 8
  and Oracle E-Business Suite (EBS) 8, 9

exchange rates, types
corporate 51
spot 52
user 51
expense category accounts 111, 112
expense report 128, 131
Express Receipt functionality 119

F

factor option 60
FCC 166
features, Oracle Workflow
administration 273, 274
complete programmatic extensibility 273
electronic notifications 273
mail integration 273
monitoring 273, 274
FERC 166
FICO score 248
financial reporting
about 59
columns 62
content sets 62
report manager 63
row definition 60, 61
row order 63
Financial Statement Generator. *See* FSG
Financial Statement Generator reports. *See* FSG reports
Finished Goods (FGI) 97
First Party Legal Entity 256
fiscal classification 256
fixed assets 148
flexfields
about 149
additional information 19
aliases 21
configuring 17, 18
CV rules 21
dynamic inserts, allowing 20
fundamentals 14
security rules 21
types 149, 150
flexfield structure 17
flexfields, types
about 149

asset key 149
category 149
location 150
foreign exchange deals 184
format option 60
FSG 47, 59
FSG reports 33
Fulfilment Sets functionality 210
Funds Capture functionality 138
future dated transactions 156

G

GAAP rules 18, 164
General Ledger. *See* GL
generic models 248
GL
about 7, 11, 12, 31, 67
transactions 32
GL Date. *See* Accounting Date
GL_INTERFACE 80
GL journals 289
Global Blanket Agreements 116
Globalization Flexfields 16
Government Reporting Legal Entity (GRE) 21
group depreciation feature 166

H

hedging 187
Help link 30
hold management 135
HR tables 260
Hybrid 207
HZ tables 260

I

iExpense
about 129, 130
approvals, managing 131
independent type value sets 17
Indirect Procurement 108
inquiry, ledger sets 39
intangible assets
about 147
copyrights 147

goodwill 147
patents 147
trademarks 147
inter-company funding 184-186
intercompany transactions
about 57
managing, ways 56
inventory 83
inventory management
about 83
transaction configuration 94, 95
transaction processing 97-100
transactions 94
inventory organizations 86, 87
Investment Tax Credits (ITC) 164
invoice 131, 221-223
invoice data 133
Invoice Summary Level functionality 126
invoicing
about 131
approvals 136
automatic debit memo 132
expense report 131
hold management 135
Pay on Receipt functionality 132
procurement card transactions 135
iProcurement 109
iReceivables
about 214
configuration options 214
iSupplier Portal 105
item attributes 91-94
item categories 89, 90
item classes 290
Item Flexfield 89
Item Orderability 206
items
about 89, 194, 195
status controls 90, 91

J

Java API 272
JED 74
JLD 74
JLT 74

journal entries
about 40, 184
account inquiry 45, 46
approve button 42, 43
autocopy batch button 41, 42
autocopy button 43
category 41
change currency button 42
change period button 42
check funds button 42
description 41
elimination, journal transaction 43
journals button 41
line drilldown button 42
mass allocation, journal transaction 43
mass allocations journals 44
monetary journal 41
new batch button 43
new journal button 43
non-monetary transactions, characteristics 41
period 41
post button 41-43
posting 45
recurring, journal transaction 43
reserve funds button 42
reverse batch button 41-43
review batch button 43
review journal button 43
single/manual, journal transaction 43
T_Accounts button 42
tax batch button 41-43
view results button 42
Journal Entry Actions
accounting entries, managing 189, 190
Journal Entry Actions screen 184
Journal Entry Description. See JED
Journal Line Definition. See JLD
Journal Line Type. See JLT
journal option, secondary ledger 36
journals button 41

K

Key Flexfields (KFF)
about 14

examples 16
versus Descriptive Flexfields 14

L

ledger sets
about 39
and data access sets 38
tasks 39
ledger sets, tasks
inquiry 39
open and close periods 39
reporting 39
translation and revaluation 39
legal addresses 34
Legal Entity 10, 34, 85, 260
level of detail option 60
limits 182
line drilldown button 42
line number option 60
list creation condition 293
List of Values (LoV) 15
location flexfield
about 150
examples 150
lockbox processing 233

M

mass additions
about 153, 154
Add to Asset option 155, 156
future dated transactions 156
Merge button 154
post mass additions 156, 157
Split option 155
Mass Additions Create program 153
Mass Additions Prepare 153
mass addition transactions
statuses 157
mass addition transactions, statuses
about 157
COST ADJUSTMENT 157
DELETE 157
NEW 157

ON-HOLD 157
POST 157
mass allocations journals
A * B / C, formula 44 44
mass transactions
about 162
tasks 162
material transaction manager 96
Material Transactions 96
Merge button 154
migrated data
managing 264
miscellaneous receipts 227, 229
**modules, Multiple Organization Access
    Control (MOAC)**
Oracle Cash Management 22
Oracle Order Management 22
Oracle Payables 22
Oracle Purchasing 22
Oracle Receivables 22
Oracle Release Management 22
Oracle Shipping Execution 22
money market deals
about 184
inter-company funding 184-186
Move Transaction 96
MRC 32
multi-currency
about 51
conversion 52
currency rates manager 53
exchange rates 51
revaluation 52
translation 52
multiple ledgers, consolidation 54, 55
**Multiple Organization Access Control
    (MOAC)**
about 22, 24, 85
modules 22
multiple procurement activities
about 108
direct procurement 108
indirect procurement 108
Multiple Reporting Currencies. *See* **MRC**

N

navigation
    within Oracle E-Business Suite, with focus
        on Release 12 26-30
Navigator link 30
new batch button 43
new journal button 43
non-monetary transactions, journal entries
    characteristics 41
No Override. *See* N option
N option 62
notes receivable 231
notifications, Oracle Workflow 277-282

O

OAUG 28
offset option 62
online accounting, SLA controls 69, 70
open and close periods, ledger sets 39
open balances listing 76
open interface 174
operating unit (OU) 22, 24, 85, 262
Oracle Advanced Collections
    about 234
    benefits 234
    configuration steps 235
Oracle Advanced Queuing (AQ) 272
Oracle Approvals Management Engine
        (AME) 9
Oracle Assets
    accounting 167, 168
    configuration steps 148
    depreciation 164, 165
    other transactions 162
    transactions 153
Oracle Cash Management 12
Oracle Cost Management 101
Oracle E-Business Suite
    about 7
    and ERP 8, 9
    business process flows 10
    integration and process flows 10
    organizations 84-88

processes 10
system entities 21
Oracle E-Business Tax 9
Oracle ERP Application 7
Oracle Financial products 8
Oracle Financials applications 9
Oracle Financials suite
    products, for integration 9
Oracle General Ledger. *See* GL
Oracle HRMS 287
Oracle Inventory 11, 12
Oracle Order Management 11
Oracle Payables 170
Oracle Payables/iExpenses 12
Oracle Payments
    about 137, 138
    configuring 138, 139
Oracle Projects 213
Oracle Purchasing/iProcurement 12
Oracle Receivables
    about 213
    configuration options 217
    customers, managing 221
    transactions 221, 222
Oracle Receivables, configuration options
    about 217
    approvals 220, 221
    AutoInvoice 219, 220
    Descriptive flexfields (DFF's) 217
    remit to address 218
    system options 217
Oracle Receivables/iReceivables 11
Oracle Receivables, transaction
    adjustment transaction 224
    Bills Receivable functionality 226
    commitment transactions 224
    credit memos 223
    debit memo 222, 223
    invoice 222, 223
    revenue management 225
Oracle Treasury
    about 181
    activities, managing with configuration op-
        tions 181-183

Oracle User Management 24
Oracle Web ADI. *See* Web ADI
Oracle Workflow
  about 9, 271
  approvals 276, 277
  components 272
  features 273
  functions 274-276
  notifications 277-282
  overview 271
  processes 274-276
  uses 274
Oracle Workflow Builder 271, 272
order actions 207, 208
order capture 200-202
order entry 200-202
order form booking, to invoicing
  steps 209
Order Import 204
Order Management
  about 193, 213
  overview 193, 194
Order to Cash (O2C)
  about 8, 10, 11
  Oracle Cash Management 12
  Oracle General Ledger 11
  Oracle Inventory 11
  Oracle Order Management 11
  Oracle Receivables/iReceivables 11
organizations
  about 21, 84-88
  fundamentals 21-24

P

parent values 47
partial payments discounts 234
party tax profiles 256
Payables
  configuring 127
  expense report, creating 128
  specific supplier considerations 125-127
  transactions 128, 129
Payables integration
  with cash management 172, 173
Payables module 125

payment batches 142-144
Payment Process Profiles 139, 140
payment terms 240, 241
payment transactions 141
Pay on Receipt functionality 132
Payroll integration
  with cash management 173
people, as assets 147
percent of row option 61
PE Report Expand 62
Periodic Mass Copy program 164
pick and ship rules 206
picking 208
Pick to Order (PTO) Item (Kit) 207
Pick to Order (PTO) Model 207
Planned Purchase Orders 117
PL/SQL API 272
post button 41-43
posting 45
post mass additions 156
Post QuickCash 233
PPE 148
pre-calculated credit exposure data
  building 243
Pre-Calculated Exposure 243
prepayment functionality 232
preview accounting, SLA controls 70
price lists 199
primary ledger 32
procurement
  about 103
  processes 103
procurement card transactions 135
Procure to Pay (P2P)
  about 8, 10, 12
  Oracle Cash Management 12
  Oracle General Ledger 12
  Oracle Inventory 12
  Oracle Payables/iExpenses 12
  Oracle Purchasing/iProcurement 12
profile options, SLA
  about 80
  disable journal import 80
  Initial Date for Historical Upgrade profile
    option 80

property, plant, and equipment. *See* PPE
PT Report Total 63
punchouts 110
purchase order (PO)
   about 113
   types 116, 117
purchase order (PO), types
   Blanket Purchase Agreements (BPA) 116
   Blanket Releases 116
   Contract Purchase Agreements 117
   Global Blanket Agreements 116
   Planned Purchase Orders 117
   Scheduled Releases 117
   Standard Purchase Orders 116
purchase order transactions 116-118
purchase requisitions 289
purchasing agent. *See* buyer
purchasing options
   configuring 114, 115

Q

quick and manual payments
   processing 144
QuickCash 233

R

Raw Materials (RAW) 97
RBAC 26
RB option 62
receipt classes 227
receipt reversals
   about 228
   debit memo reversals 229
   standard reversals 228
Receipt Routing 120
receipts 227
receipt transactions
   importing 233
Receivables integration
   with cash management 172
receiving function 119
receiving options
   configuring 120
receiving transactions 121, 122

refunds 144
regular conditions 292
remit-to address
   creating 218
RE option 62
replacement account. *See* streamlined accounting, SLA controls
reporting currencies
   versus translation 38
reporting ledger
   about 38
   maintaining 37
reporting, ledger sets 39
reporting sequence
   about 80
   accounting sequence 80
report manager, FSG 63
Request for Quotation (RFQ)
   about 112
   creating 112, 113
requisitions
   about 108
   creating 110, 111
   expense category accounts 111, 112
   iProcurement 109, 110
reserve funds button 42
Resource Cost Transactions 96
responsibility 27
retirement transaction 161
Return Material Authorization (RMA) 95, 122, 205
Return to Supplier (RTS) functionality 132
revaluation 52
Revenue Management 225
reverse batch button 41, 43
review batch button 43
review journal button 43
RMA Receipt Routing 120
Role Based Access Control. *See* RBAC
rollup groups
   about 48, 49
   used, for maintaining budget values 50
Row Both. *See* RB option
row definition, FSG
   about 60
   balance control option 60

change sign on variance option 61
change sign option 61
display option 60
display row option 60
display zero option 60
factor option 60
format option 60
level of detail option 60
line number option 60
percent of row option 61
row name option 61
Row Expand. *See* **RE option**
row name option 61
row order, FSG 63
Row Total. *See* **RT option**
RT option 62
rules 288

S

sales agreement 204
salespersons 199
Scheduled Releases 117
scoring model
  about 248
  example 249
secondary ledger 32, 33
security rules 21
segment 17
segment qualifiers, Accounting Flexfield
    (AFF)
  about 19
  balancing segment 19
  cost center segment 19
  intercompany segment 19
  management segment 19
  natural account segment 19
  secondary tracking segment 19
segment rules, consolidation 55
  about 55
  Assign Value 55
  Copy Value From 55
  Use Rollup Rules from 55
self-assessed tax 261
sequences
  accounting sequence 80
  reporting sequence 80

Service Contracts 213
settlement
  about 188
  transaction validation 188, 189
shared entites
  about 13
  with corresponding product owner 13
shipping
  steps 208
shipping execution
  about 208
  setting up 208
Ship Sets functionality 210
shopping lists 110
short tax years 159
sites 198
SLA
  about 67
  accounting policy management 68
  advantages 68, 69
  controls 68
  example 68
  other functions 69
  profile options 80
SLA controls. *See* **controls, SLA**
SLAM 73 74
SLA, other functions
  accounting reports 77
  account inquiry 79
  configuration 75
  open balances listing 76
  reporting sequence 80
  subledger journal entries 78
  supporting references 76
sources 74
Split option 155
standard invoices 133, 134
Standard Purchase Orders 116
standard receipts 227
standard reversals 228
static attribute 291
stock 83
stores 110
streamlined accounting, SLA controls 71
Subledger Accounting. *See* **SLA**
subledger accounting layer 31

Subledger Accounting Method. *See* SLAM
subledger journal entries 78
subledger option, secondary ledger 36
summary accounts
  about 48
  used, for maintaining budget values 50
supplier management
  about 103-105
  functionality 105
supporting references 76
Swan user interface 26
SWIFT940 174
system controls 150

T

table value sets 17
T_Accounts button 42
tangible assets
  about 147, 148
  cash and cash equivalents 147
  inventory 147
  prepaid expenses 147
  receivables 147
  short-term investments 147
tax 258
tax batch button 41, 43
Tax Books 151, 163, 164
tax content service providers 265
tax exemption 256, 266, 268
tax jurisdiction 256-258
tax profiles 261, 262
tax rates 268
tax regime 258
tax rules 268
Taxware 265
TCA classifications 263
templates 181
third-party tax profiles 266
tiered discounts 234
tolerances
  about 183
  managing 183
Track as Asset flag 153
Trading Community Architecture (TCA)
    104, 195, 196, 216, 247, 257

trading partners 257
transaction configuration 94, 95
transaction managers 96
transaction objects 73
transaction processing 97-100
transactions
  about 94, 128, 184, 221, 222
  foreign exchange deals 184
  money market deals 184
  types 95
transactions, Oracle Assets
  about 153
  asset impairments 160
  CIP 159, 160
  manual entry 157, 158
  mass additions 153, 154
  mass transactions 162
  retirements 161
transaction sources 95
transaction types 95, 288, 289
transaction validation 188, 189
transfers 177
translatable dependent value set 17
translatable independent value set 17
translation
  about 52
  versus reporting currencies 38
translation and revaluation, ledger sets 39
treasury 181
Treasury integration
  with cash management 173

U

unearned discounts 233
User Management (UMX) 170
use tax 266

V

Value Added Tax (VAT) 258
value set 17
Vertex 265
view results button 42

W

Web ADI
  about 64
  Excel 2003, settings 64
  Excel 2007, settings 64
  internet explorer, settings 65
workflow 108, 206
workflow administrators 273

Workflow Builder
  about 282
  overview 282, 283
workflow definitions loader 273
workflow engine 272
workflow notifications 107, 108
workflow process, Credit Management 246, 247
write-off receipts 234
Writing Down Allowance (WDA) 166

Thank you for buying
Oracle E-Business Suite Financials R12:
A Functionality Guide

About Packt Publishing

Packt, pronounced 'packed', published its first book "Mastering phpMyAdmin for Effective MySQL Management" in April 2004 and subsequently continued to specialize in publishing highly focused books on specific technologies and solutions.

Our books and publications share the experiences of your fellow IT professionals in adapting and customizing today's systems, applications, and frameworks. Our solution based books give you the knowledge and power to customize the software and technologies you're using to get the job done. Packt books are more specific and less general than the IT books you have seen in the past. Our unique business model allows us to bring you more focused information, giving you more of what you need to know, and less of what you don't.

Packt is a modern, yet unique publishing company, which focuses on producing quality, cutting-edge books for communities of developers, administrators, and newbies alike. For more information, please visit our website: www.packtpub.com.

About Packt Enterprise

In 2010, Packt launched two new brands, Packt Enterprise and Packt Open Source, in order to continue its focus on specialization. This book is part of the Packt Enterprise brand, home to books published on enterprise software – software created by major vendors, including (but not limited to) IBM, Microsoft and Oracle, often for use in other corporations. Its titles will offer information relevant to a range of users of this software, including administrators, developers, architects, and end users.

Writing for Packt

We welcome all inquiries from people who are interested in authoring. Book proposals should be sent to author@packtpub.com. If your book idea is still at an early stage and you would like to discuss it first before writing a formal book proposal, contact us; one of our commissioning editors will get in touch with you.

We're not just looking for published authors; if you have strong technical skills but no writing experience, our experienced editors can help you develop a writing career, or simply get some additional reward for your expertise.

Oracle E-Business Suite 12 Financials Cookbook

ISBN: 978-1-84968-310-4   Paperback: 384 pages

Take the hard work out of your daily interaction with E-Business Suite financials by using the 50+ recipes from this cookbook

1. Delivers practical solutions that can be easily applied in functional EBS environments

2. A step-by-step tour through the EBS R12 Financials core modules in this book and eBook

3. Demonstrates the functional integration points between the EBS R12 Financial modules

Oracle E-Business Suite R12 Supply Chain Management

ISBN: 978-1-84968-064-6   Paperback: 292 pages

Drive your supply chain processes with Oracle E-Business R12 Supply Chain Management to achieve measurable business gains

1. Put supply chain management principles to practice with Oracle EBS SCM

2. Develop insight into the process and business flow of supply chain management

3. Set up all of the Oracle EBS SCM modules to automate your supply chain processes

Please check **www.PacktPub.com** for information on our titles

Oracle PeopleSoft Enterprise Financial Management 9.1 Implementation

Oracle PeopleSoft Enterprise Financial Management 9.1 Implementation

ISBN: 978-1-84968-146-9   Paperback: 412 pages

An exhaustive resource for PeopleSoft Financial application practitioners to understand core concepts, configuration, and business process

1. A single concise book and eBook reference to guide you from PeopleSoft foundation concepts through to crucial configuration activities required for a successful implementation

2. Real-life implementation scenarios to demonstrate practical implementations of PeopleSoft features along with theoretical concepts

Oracle Enterprise Manager Grid Control 11gR1: Business Service Management

Oracle Enterprise Manager Grid Control 11g R1: Business Service Management

ISBN: 978-1-84968-216-9   Paperback: 360 pages

Ahands-on guide to modeling and managing business services using Oracle Enterprise Manager 11gR1

1. Govern Business Service Management using Oracle Enterprise Manager 11gR1

2. Discover the evolution of enterprise IT infrastructure and the modeling paradigms to manage it

3. Use and apply various techniques in modeling complex data centers using Oracle Enterprise Manager

Please check **www.PacktPub.com** for information on our titles

CPSIA information can be obtained at www.ICGtesting.com
Printed in the USA
LVOW09s0950050715

445010LV00010B/333/P